# The Story
## of
# Architecture
### OF THE 20TH CENTURY

With contributions from Wolfgang Hoffmann and Philipp Meuser

Drawings: Meuser Architects, Berlin

© 1999 Könemann Verlagsgesellschaft mbH
Bonner Strasse 126, D-50968 Cologne

Managing Editor: Peter Delius
Editing and layout: Ulrike Sommer

⋯

Reproductions: Omniascanners, Milan

Original title: Geschichte der Architektur des 20. Jahrhunderts

© 1999 for the English edition:
Könemann Verlagsgesellschaft mbH
Bonner Strasse 126, D-50968 Cologne

Translation from German: Susan Bennett in association with Goodfellow & Egan, Cambridge
Editor of the English-language edition: Philippa Youngman in association with Goodfellow & Egan, Cambridge
Typesetting: Goodfellow & Egan, Cambridge
Project Management: Jackie Dobbyne for Goodfellow & Egan, Cambridge
Production: Ursula Schümer

Printing and Binding: Sing Cheong Printing Co. Ltd., Hong Kong

Printed in Hong Kong, China

ISBN 3-8290-2045-7

10 9 8 7 6 5 4 3 2 1

**Jürgen Tietz**

# The Story
# of
# Architecture
## OF THE 20TH CENTURY

**KÖNEMANN**

# Contents

1890

**ARCHITECTURE AT THE TURN OF THE CENTURY**
The Roots in the 18th and 19th Centuries  6
Art Nouveau  10
Adolf Loos  15
Frank Lloyd Wright  16

1910

**THE FIRST MODERNS**
Modernization and Industrialization  18
Neoclassicism  22
Peter Behrens  23
Expressionism  24
Cubism  28
Futurism  29

1920

**THE INTERNATIONAL STYLE**
Architecture after the First World War  30
De Stijl  31
The Bauhaus  33
Constructivism  34
Rationalism versus Neoclassicism  36
New Building in Germany  37
Town Planning in the 20th Century  40

1920

**AMERICAN ARCHITECTURE**
Land Speculation and Architectural Engineering  42
Europe meets USA  44
Art Deco  46

1930

**ARCHITECTURE AND POWER**
The Rule of Force  50

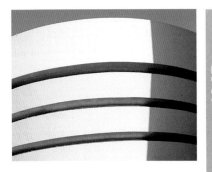

## THE GLOBALIZATION OF MODERN ARCHITECTURE

Visions of a City Architecture 56
The Bauhaus Tradition in the USA 58
Mies van der Rohe 59
Reactions 62
Architecture as Sculpture 62
Le Corbusier 63
The New City 64
Town Planning in the 20th Century 66

1945

## VISION AND REALITY

Socialism versus Capitalism 68
Brutalism 69
Expression in Concrete 70
Louis I. Kahn 71
Alvar Aalto 72
Approaches to History 76
The Glass Office 77

1960

## HIGH-TECH AND POSTMODERN

High-Tech Architecture 78
De-Architecture 82
Postmodernism 82
Kenzo Tange 83

1970

## CROSSING BOUNDARIES

Culture as Experience and Consumerism 88
Deconstruction 91
The Rationalist Tradition in Italy 94
James Stirling 96
The School of Tessin 97
Japan 98

1980

1990

## LOOKING INTO THE FUTURE

Contemporary but Eternal 100
Architecture in the Virtual Age 101
The Aesthetic of Simplicity 105
Sculpture and Architecture 108
Architecture in the 21st Century 110

Dictionary of Terms 112
Index of Names 116
Picture Credits 120

## Stocktaking and impulses

# Architecture at the turn of the century

### 1890–1910

## THE ROOTS IN THE 18TH AND 19TH CENTURIES

### The world around us

Our everyday life is conditioned to a significant degree by the architecture that surrounds us each day – at home, in the workplace, out shopping. Even during our leisure time, at the pool or in the football stadium or at the museum, architecture creates the necessary architectural environment for our activity. Without architecture, human society would be impossible.

Our cities present a colorful, multilayered world. Buildings from many centuries mingle with contemporary architecture to form a living organism. Towering next to Gothic cathedrals are high-rise buildings made of steel and glass, or with reflecting granite façades. Exciting museum buildings, almost like sculptures large enough to walk in, coexist with soberly functional factories or dreary administration buildings.

Architecture at the end of the 20th century is as multifaceted as life itself. We experience cities as bewildering assemblages of a variety of functions, to which architecture, in all its widely differing manifestations, lends the necessary framework.

### New worlds …

The swift development of architectural technique and form in this century has roots that go as far back as the 18th century. The Enlightenment, which enhanced the significance and the social status of every citizen, was accompanied by a fundamental change in political culture. Centuries-old monarchies gave way to democratic constitutions whose stock of ideas spread outwards in ever-increasing circles. It was these thoughts that were enshrined in a comprehensive and enduring form in the American Declaration of Independence (1776), and found direct political expression in the French Revolution (1789).

Following the start given by the 18th century, it was almost inevitable that the 19th should be an era of revolutionary changes affecting every area of life. The industrial revolution, which spread from England to the whole of Europe and North America, created a new type of worker: the wage-laborer or proletarian, who earned a hard living in the ever more numerous factories. A symbol of the increasing mechanization of the world was the steam engine, invented by Watt in 1785, whose proliferation into newly built machine shops and iron foundries engendered an appropriate type of building.

A second, no less meaningful symbol of the new age was the railway. In 1830, Crown Street Station was built in Liverpool, the first station intended for passengers, who could now travel comfortably by rail between

**1833**: First law against child labor in England.

**1837**: Victoria crowned queen of England.

**1842**: China cedes Hong Kong to England, and opens its ports to west European forces.

**1848**: Karl Marx publishes his *Communist Manifesto*

**1861**: Abraham Lincoln becomes US president and abolishes slavery.

**1869**: The Suez Canal is opened, shortening the sea route to India.

**1871**: Founding of the German Empire after the end of the Franco-Prussian war.

**1876**: Alexander Graham Bell patents his "membrane speaking telephone." International Centennial Exhibition held in Philadelphia.

**1886**: The Statue of Liberty erected in New York, a present from the French Republic commemorating the anniversary of the Declaration of Independence.

**1889**: Paris hosts an international exhibition, the Exposition Universelle. Completion of the Eiffel Tower.

**1895**: Wilhelm Conrad Röntgen discovers X-rays. Sigmund Freud lays the foundations of psychoanalysis. First film shows given by Max Skladanowsky in Berlin and the Lumière brothers in Paris.

**1899**: First peace conference held in The Hague to discuss the peaceful settlement of international conflicts; passing of the Convention relating to the Laws and Customs of Warfare on Land. The United Fruit Company sets up the first monopoly trade in bananas in Central America.

**1900**: Exposition Universelle and Olympic Games held in Paris.

**1900-01**: Boxer rising in China, put down by an expeditionary force of the European powers.

**1901**: Theodore Roosevelt becomes US president. Thomas Mann's novel *Buddenbrooks* published. Picasso's "Blue Period" begins, with scenes from Parisian life, and the lives of circus people. Pavlov begins his experiments in animal psychology.

**1903**: Margarete Steiff presents the first toy teddy bear at the Leipzig Fair.

**1904**: First performance of Puccini's *Madame Butterfly*. Death of Anton Chekov.

**Max Skladanowsky with his bioscope (projecting equipment) in 1895**

**1905**: Erich Heckel, Ernst Ludwig, and Karl Schmidt-Rottluff found the Expressionist art movement "Die Brücke."

**1906**: San Francisco destroyed by earthquake and fire.

**1907**: Maria Montessori opens her first "Children's House." Sun Yat-sen announces his program for a Chinese democratic republic with social legislation.

**1908**: Matisse coins the word "Cubism" for a painting by Georges Braque.

**1909**: First permanent wave in London. Ford specializes in the mass production of the Model T: around 19,000 are sold in this year alone.

**1910**: Japan annexes Korea. The 13th Dalai Lama, fleeing from the Chinese, takes temporary refuge in India. Robert Delaunay completes his painting *The Eiffel Tower*. Feininger begins to make his mark with his characteristic Cubist/Expressionist style.

Liverpool and Manchester. A whole network of railway lines spread over Europe, and made it possible for both people and goods to be transported over immense distances very much faster than by coach. This in turn had consequences for architecture, for, in order to cross valleys and mountains, tunnels and massive bridges made of either stone or *iron* were required – real masterpieces of *civil engineering*. Within a short time railway stations were springing up, palatial buildings of ever greater size and splendor, which, because of the amount of space they took up, were generally placed on the edge of town.

### ... new buildings ...

It was not only technical progress that found expression in the architecture of the 19th century, but also new democratic forms of government. Thus, prestigious parliament buildings sprang up, such as the Houses of Parliament in London, designed by Charles Barry (1839–52), the German Reichstag in Berlin by Paul Wallot (1884–94), Imre Steindl's Budapest parliament (1885–1902), and town halls that served as centers of state government and administration, while at the same time gave emphatic expression to

the newly developed self-confidence of the bourgeoisie. This self-confidence was also reflected in numerous other architectural models that arose at almost exactly the same time, such as the museum – for example Klenze's Sculpture Gallery in Munich, Germany (1816–34) or Smirke's British Museum in London (1823–47). These "temples of the muses," open to all, took the place of the aristocratic private collections: a concrete proof of the will of the middle classes to educate themselves.

While this was going on, metropolises such as Paris, London, and Brussels saw the birth of the first great department stores and arcades – roofed-in shopping streets – which became synonymous with the burgeoning commercial world of the 19th century.

### ... familiar forms

The requirements that architecture was being called upon to fulfill were changing fundamentally in the 19th century, and totally new tasks for the builder were constantly arising. Yet a great deal of architecture at this time was marked above all by the need to create an imposing effect – a need which the rising bourgeoisie inherited from the aristocracy as

**Joseph Paxton, *Crystal Palace*, London** 1851, moved to Sydenham 1855, destroyed by fire 1936

A pure space carved out of the atmosphere – that was the impression created by the Crystal Palace, erected by the gardener and architect Joseph Paxton for the Great Exhibition of 1851, the first international exhibition to be held in London. Its basic module was the largest sheet of glass that it was then possible to produce. All the component parts of the exhibition building were standardized and prefabricated industrially. It was thus possible to erect the great hall – 750,000 square feet (70,000 square meters) – in less than five months, and then remount it in Sydenham.

Bare of all the ornamentation then in fashion, the *iron*, glass, and wood construction of the Crystal Palace is stripped of all sense of solidity. As the first high point of the new field of *architectural engineering*, it inspired a great deal of emulation. At the beginning of the 20th century it was celebrated as a breakthrough into modernity.

they replaced them in the function of running the state. As early as 1828 the German architect Heinrich Hübsch asked "In what style should we build?," putting into words the general uncertainty of the 19th century as to what architectonic *style* was appropriate to the requirements of the day.

The search for an appropriate and universally valid style of building is one of the most characteristic features of architecture in the 19th and early 20th centuries. One of its foundations was intensive scientific research into architectural history – an enterprise that had already begun in the 18th century. For example, the results of lengthy research trips to Athens, Rome or Sicily to visit what was left of the monuments of antiquity were published as large-format collections of engravings, which made them available for the first time to numerous architects throughout Europe.

Besides the archaeological study of antiquity, the new disciplines of history and fine art also focused on the *Romanesque*, the *Gothic*, the *Renaissance*, and the *Baroque*. An important impetus for this engagement with the most varied facets of history was the search for the national roots of states, as well as of building styles. The century of nationalism had begun. For instance, the *neo-Gothic* style flourished with especial vigor in Prussia in the first half of the 19th century, because it was assumed that the Gothic had German roots – until research uncovered the fact that the Gothic style had arisen in medieval France.

Not only did the people of the 1800s begin a scientific study of the architectural relics of previous eras, they handled the buildings themselves with new respect. Efforts were made to preserve them (conservation) or, if they were already severely damaged, to rebuild them (restoration). The era of the conservation of historic monuments had begun.

As research penetrated ever deeper into the contexts and developments of architectural history, contemporary architects suddenly had at their disposal a whole spectrum of building styles that they could use in their own work. Heinrich Hübsch answered his own question about what style he should build in by opting for a *round-arched* style borrowed from the Romanesque. But the 19th century offered many additional answers to Hübsch's question. Whereas the 1800s brought forth a Europe-wide flowering of *classicism*, with buildings that looked back to ancient Greece, Gottfried Semper also established the neo-Renaissance as a suitable style for large buildings with his Dresden Opera, which was built between 1838 and 1841. (It was reconstructed between 1871 and 1878. The present opera house was built in 1985.) A different trend, destined to sweep all before it, the *neo-Baroque*, was initiated by Charles Garnier with his new Paris Opera (1861–75). This growing tendency to look to history as a source of inspiration, which reached its apogee in the second half of the 19th century, is generically termed *historicism*, whatever epoch or style individual architects took as their reference.

For a long period in the 20th century it was usual to look down somewhat on the architecture produced by historicism, for supposedly not having any creative force of its own. So it came about that in the wake of the *Neues Bauen* (new building) movement of the 1920s, people simply threw away the façades of houses dating from those formative years. Cities that had already been markedly depleted by the wars of the 20th century thus suffered further losses that were not possible to repair.

## The aspect of the town

With the change in architecture, the aspect of towns changed. The small town that could be taken in at a glance, which was still the general rule in 1800, had been replaced at the end of the 19th century by the Moloch big city. The medieval walls had long crumbled, and the city boundary was extending ever further into the countryside. But, most significantly, the factories and industrial installations were surrounded by the dwellings of millions of workers and their families, who, in the hope of work and better living conditions, had turned their backs on their homes in the country.

Speculation in land favored erection of the notorious and ever increasing tenements, with their numerous stone back yards, into which neither light nor healthy air could penetrate. Crushed together into the smallest possible spaces, whole sections of the population became increasingly enfeebled and ill, whereas the more affluent members of the bourgeoisie cultivated the lifestyle of the nobility, that which they had previously disparaged.

**Gustave Eiffel, *Eiffel Tower,* Paris 1889**

The Eiffel Tower, erected by Gustave Eiffel and Maurice Koechlin in 1889 for the Exposition Universelle, came to symbolize the highest point of both *architectural engineering,* and the Parisian skyline. Eiffel, engineer and entrepreneur, concentrated all the experience that he had gained in the construction of innumerable bridges and railway stations into it. For 40 years the tower, besides being almost free of any practical utility, was also the tallest construction in the world. Its then unimaginable height of 1000 feet (300 meters) was achieved by means of a framework of prefabricated iron girders riveted together, offering maximum stability with minimal weight. The dispersal of forces is visible from its shape. Only the four arches linking the legs were added later for decorative effect. They did not stop the Parisians finding it hard to live with, describing it as "naked architecture" and seriously debating whether to pull it down. But by 1900 the Eiffel Tower had already become the symbol of Paris, and was discussed as a work of art.

Toward the end of the 19th century these living conditions gradually began to change. Light and air were permitted to enter the homes of the less privileged members of the population. Raymond Unwin and Barry Parker built Letchworth (in Hertfordshire, England), the first garden city, between 1898 and 1914, and in 1893 Alfred Messel built the blocks of flats for rent in the Sickingenstrasse in Berlin, thus laying the foundation for the housing reform movement that reached its height in the ambitious housing developments of the first half of the 20th century.

## Glass, iron, concrete – new building materials create new possibilities

Alongside the familiar building materials that had been in use for millennia – wood, stone, and brick – in the 19th century new materials such as iron, zinc, steel, and glass increasingly found their way into architecture. As they were not always used in a visible way, it could quite easily happen that a building that looked historicist on the outside had modern encroachments on the inside: a daring roof-construction in iron perhaps, or a glass skylight.

As early as the mid-19th century a single-material building was created: the Crystal Palace in London. This glass palace, erected for the first of the international exhibitions, the Great Exhibition of 1851, was free of all traditional styles. Paxton created a monumental structure that consisted purely of a supporting iron frame with walls made not of stone but of sheets of glass. Today, in an age marked by glassy high-rise buildings, it is difficult to imagine how revolutionary the people of that time felt this novel construction to be, when all that was around it was stone.

The erection of this iron and glass exhibition building was the first step in a development that was to lead to a systematic reduction of architecture to its functional components. Most of the buildings inspired by historicism were still marked by a taste for luxuriant and ostentatious decoration, which was applied regardless of their function – whether as factories, or administrative buildings, or simply dwellings. In opposition to this the demand arose that every architectural undertaking should be carried out in the most functional way, avoiding all superfluous decoration. This thinking is summed up in one pregnant phrase, attributed to the American architect Louis Sullivan: "Form follows function." It was to become one of the guiding principles of modern architecture in the 20th century.

Paxton's glass palace also demonstrated that innovation in 19th-century architecture could be found, not least, in the masterpieces of the civil engineer. Another modern icon, the Eiffel Tower, was also built by engineers: Gustave Eiffel and Maurice Koechlin. The construction of the tower at the edge of central Paris on the old Champ de Mars, as part of the Exposition Universelle of 1889, met with considerable opposition at the time. Eiffel judged that only a framework of iron girders would do for building a tower 1000 feet (300 meters) high; a more solid construction would offer too large a surface area to the wind, and would be bound to collapse.

Glass, iron, and steel changed the face of architecture, but it took a mixture of sand, gravel, and cement to revolutionize it. Only when concrete came along was it possible to produce the architecture that has set its stamp on our cities, both positively and negatively, right up to the present day. Concrete, being relatively light and not requiring plaster, opened up an extraordinarily rich spectrum of forms that was unattainable with traditional materials like stone, which was heavier, or wood, which was more fragile.

Although the new material had been developed in the 1890s, the French building entrepreneur Auguste Perret was the first to use it to very striking effect in 1902, for a residential building: the apartment block at 25 rue Franklin in Paris. The startlingly simple core of the building is a grid of *reinforced concrete*, reinforced, that is, with an iron skeleton to give it stability. The *façades* between the concrete load-bearing elements could thus be filled with patterned *ceramic tiles* in Art Nouveau style. The banks considered Perret's plan of constructing a residential building out of concrete such a risky undertaking that they refused to give him credit.

## The Arts and Crafts movement

Although the breakthrough into modern architecture had already begun in the middle of the 19th century, the swiftly growing metropolises were largely dominated right till the end of the century by stone colossi, all displaying the same unfeelingly reproduced "Gothic" or

**Auguste Perret, *House in the rue Franklin,* Paris, 1902–03**

A completely open ground floor, and above it projections and recesses and differing ground-plans: 25 rue Franklin, by Auguste Perret, was the first demonstration in a multi-story building of the potential of a new material, reinforced concrete. With this technique, only the skeleton of piers and beams is set firm; the wall areas can be filled in as desired. Accordingly, the façades had large areas of glass and were richly decorated with floral tiles.

**Victor Horta, *Hôtel Tassel,*** Brussels, 1893

The year 1893, in which Victor Horta built a house for Paul-Emile Tassel, can be considered as the beginning of Art Nouveau. Its greatest novelty lay in the fact that the architect had no longer drawn his forms from the established canons of architectural history, but from a precise study of nature. Horta's floral shapes were more than a decoration added on to a building, they were stylistic elements that turned the house into a consistently designed organic whole. The basic design was no longer the sum of clearly separated rooms and corridors, but a single interconnecting space. All of the ornamented interior, from the sweeping ironwork to the beautifully crafted mosaics, supports the dynamic of this architect's first pure Art Nouveau building.

"classic" ornamentation. The real picture of the city and its inhabitants was one of grim clusters of tenements with five or more courtyards behind, erected at breakneck speed. At the end of the century, therefore, people were as disappointed with the inability of this architecture to cope with social problems as they were with its didactic academicism.

General disaffection with the traditional architectural forms of the 19th century was the starting point for the search for a new means of expression, a new *style.* In a period of growing industrialization, boundless faith in progress, and ever-increasing urbanization, the Arts and Crafts movement arose in England. As early as the mid-19th century, its adherents began campaigning for a return to the craft tradition of the Middle Ages.

It was the object of the Arts and Crafts movement, under the leadership of the artist-craftsman William Morris, the architect Philip Webb, and the influential writer, art, and

architecture critic John Ruskin, to fill people's everyday lives with quality products made in the art and craft tradition, so that mass-produced industrial goods did not gain the upper hand and destroy the aesthetics of objects. William Morris, who was much influenced by the symbolist painting of the Pre-Raphaelite artist Dante Gabriel Rossetti, opened up his own business in 1861, making products ranging from furniture and glassware to fabrics and wallpapers, which he decorated with repeating patterns of stylized flowers. Although Morris, the most prominent figure in the Arts and Crafts movement, was not himself an architect, his work had an astonishing influence over architecture right into the 20th century.

## ART NOUVEAU

### Vegetal forms spread across Europe
Since history plainly did not offer any style that could adequately express the new era, people turned to the models provided by nature in their search for a new way. From the middle of the 19th century, painters, especially in France, had been going out into the countryside and putting up their easels in the midst of nature, instead of working shut up in a studio as they had done before. This intense involvement with nature led to new themes in painting and to new types of representation. People began to translate the crooked lines of a tree or the involuted petals of a bud into a new formal language of *ornamentation*, generally rather two-dimensional in appearance, which broke entirely with the repertoire of forms in use before this. In architecture too, these *vegetal* forms drawn from the natural world joined with the new building materials of glass and iron to create a new formal language, and as the new materials were placed unadorned next to traditional ones like brick, *freestone,* and marble, the way was opened not only to a new style but also to a previously unknown material aestheticism.

In Germany, the movement was called Jugendstil – a programmatic-sounding name, somewhat out of keeping with its floral inspiration and its idealistic evocation of renewal, awakening, and youthful freshness, which it derived from the art magazine *Die Jugend* (Youth). This had been published since 1896 in Munich, which had become a center of the new art movement through the activities of Richard Riemerschmid, Bruno Paul, and August Endell, three architects.

Like *classicism* in the 1800s, Art Nouveau captured the whole of Europe at the beginning of the century. But, in contrast to classicism, which permitted only a slight deviation from the canons of traditional architectural form, it developed as many different names as regional variants: the French "Art Nouveau" was "Jugendstil" in Germany, "Modern Style" in England, "Stile Liberty" in Italy, "Modernismo" in Spain. Luxurious and playful in the work of Victor Horta in Brussels, fantastic in Antoni Gaudí's Barcelona, emotional in Raimondo D'Aronco's Constantinople and Turin, cubic and severe in the work of Josef Hoffmann in Vienna and Charles Rennie Mackintosh in Glasgow, there were as many national variants as there were names. What united all of Art Nouveau's facets, however, was their unconditionally innovative character compared with the *historicism* of the outgoing century.

## Brussels and Paris

The year 1893, in which the Belgian architect Victor Horta designed a house for Emile Tassel, a professor of geometry, at 6 rue Paul-Emile Janson in Brussels, was also the year in which Art Nouveau architecture was born. From the curving door handle to the vegetal sweep of the banisters, the slender iron pillars and the coiling patterns of the mosaic floor, Horta created a delicate and total work of Art Nouveau with a unified underlying design.

Between 1896 and 1899 Horta realized a completely different building project: the Maison du Peuple for the Belgian Socialist Party, which was to become the model for numerous 20th-century buildings with a similar purpose. In this "house for the people," Horta united technical innovation and new-style decoration in exemplary form. The spacious assembly hall on the top floor was roofed by a bold ironwork construction, which was not only without supports, but was also elegantly curved. The whole building was dominated by glass and iron. Despite its importance for architectural history, it was ruthlessly pulled down in 1969.

A Frenchman, Hector Guimard, was as extravagantly decorative as Horta in his design for the entrances to the underground stations

in Paris. Visitors to the Exposition Universelle were able to admire these in 1900, whereas the Métro itself only came into operation the following year. The entrances were constructed of *moulded iron* in a wide spectrum of playful floral shapes. Guimard differentiated between the various types of Métro entrances, according to whether they were either roofed-in or open.

But the limitations of Art Nouveau itself were already visible at the 1900 Exposition. Next to Guimard's playful but nonetheless crisp ornamentation, tendencies to rococo-like excess appeared. By way of example, one might quote the striking formal language of the Italian Raimondo d'Aronco, whose pavilion at the Turin arts and crafts fair of 1902 was almost theatrical in its *mise en scène* of architectural forms and sculptures.

A review of Art Nouveau in France would be incomplete without a look at the most important craft of this period: the works of art

**Hector Guimard, *Entrance to a Métro station,* Paris 1900**

Hector Guimard's entrances to the Parisian Métro are some of the most impressive examples of French Art Nouveau. With a lavish profusion of forms, they conduct the dynamic of the city traffic under the earth into a new world. The plant-like cast-iron shapes of the leek-green street lamps, railings and glass roofs growing out of the pavement reconcile the world of technology, as it increasingly took over areas of everyday life, with that of nature – admittedly in appearance only. For in truth these floral pavilions had nothing to do with the Métro, either symbolically or functionally. They involuntarily laid bare not only the novelty of the transport system but also a basic problem of Art Nouveau. More than any preceding style, it quickly degenerated into overblown decoration – and it was soon to swamp all Europe.

**Antoni Gaudí i Cornet, *Casa Batlló*,**
Barcelona 1904–06

Balconies like masks, a roof in the form of a dinosaur's back, a layout without right-angles – the block of luxury flats Casa Batlló demonstrates to the full the imagination and the technical mastery of a totally unique artist, the Catalonian architect Antoni Gaudí. The above view, taken from the street, shows one of the typical cylindrical side towers of the house, the façade of which has a changing pattern of *natural stone* and colorful *small ceramic tiles*. Unlike the products of other representatives of Modernismo or Art Nouveau, Gaudí's organic, close-to-nature forms are not *ornamentation* that has been added on; they pervade the whole building, determine its construction: architecture becomes sculpture.

in glass created by the school of Nancy and its chief representative Emile Gallé. He created costly objects, glasses like jewels, covered with stylized floral patterns or shaped in vegetal forms. Their effect is enhanced by their delicate coloring, sometimes gleaming with a matt sheen, sometimes brilliantly sparkling. This has made them into highly prized collectors' pieces. The only work that approaches the art of Gallé is that of the American Louis Comfort Tiffany.

## Gaudí and Modernismo in Spain

The work of the Catalan Antoni Gaudí is unique in architectural history. Gaudí, almost all of whose buildings are in Barcelona, was the most important representative of Modernismo, the Spanish variant of Art Nouveau. Ignoring functionality, Gaudí developed an opulent formal language that included *Gothic* and *Moorish* elements as well as creations of his own. Fragments of glass and bits of pottery were assembled by Gaudí into lively *mosaics* that animate the façades of his houses and the undulating benches in the Güell Park, named after his most important patron, Eusebi Güell.

The height of Gaudí's success in his lifetime were the two residential buildings, the Casa Batlló and the Casa Milà. Instead of a conventional façade, Gaudí gave the Casa Batlló one that went in and out, and was sometimes gently bowed, with an iridescent surface additionally enlivened by small round *ceramic* plates. The ground floor takes its character from pillars like elephants' feet; the weird window-openings on the first floor look like the gaping mouths of prehistoric beasts. Bizarrely formed mask-like balconies enliven the already richly alive façades. Rounded forms predominate in the interior as they do in the exterior, with windows and doors of a species all their own, created by Gaudí's fertile imagination. The house is crowned by a roof reminiscent of a dinosaur's spine, and the chimneys arising out of the loft behind a *fascia*, shaped like the crest of a wave look like a congregation of unearthly giants.

Gaudí's abstract architectural fantasies awaken a crowd of associations in the mind that can never, however, really be pinned down, so that in spite of all the imagination that has been displayed, the beholder is still left somewhat perplexed.

The Sagrada Familia cathedral in Barcelona, started a hundred years ago, is still awaiting completion. It is hardly surprising that Gaudí occupies the position of a much-admired bird of paradise in the history of architecture, but is without a successor. Not only would the wild extravagance to which Gaudí's houses bear witness represent a budgetary factor that any architect would underestimate at his peril, but his sheer unquenchable creativity would by no means be easy to emulate.

## The Jugendstil in Germany

The work of the Belgian Henry van de Velde demonstrates, perhaps more clearly than any other, that the Jugendstil, like the Arts and Crafts movement, is much more than an architectonic fashion. His vision of an art that was youthful amounted to a liberation from all traditional constraints and conventions, not only in architecture, but in all areas of life. Each everyday object was recognized as a craft product that could be shaped with artistry, and must be subjected to a specific design process. So van de Velde's œuvre encompasses not only costly bookbindings, new styles of lettering, and stylish furniture with curving lines, but designs for women's dresses representing, as he put it in the title of a book, "women's apparel raised to the level of art."

After his first artistic sojourns in Brussels – in the neighborhood of which, in Uccle, he created a house for himself, the Bloemenwerf house – and in Paris, van de Velde went on to create his most important work in Germany. Between 1901 and 1902 he created the interior decor for the Folkwang Museum, which was erected by the industrialist Karl Ernst Osthaus in Essen. Van de Velde's friend and mentor Harry Graf Kessler, whose diaries are still considered to be some of the most impressive sources of turn-of-the-century cultural history, brought him to Weimar to the court of the Grand Duke, Wilhelm Ernst. There, from 1907 to 1914, he designed, and then directed, the school of applied art, out of which came Walter Gropius's Bauhaus after the First World War.

Another Weimar nobleman, Ernst Ludwig von Hessen, commissioned Jugendstil additions to his residence. In 1899 he invited a number of artists to Darmstadt, including Joseph Maria Olbrich from Vienna. The artists' colony that grew up at the Mathildenhöhe in the following years, under the patronage of Ernst Ludwig, achieved great importance as a center of the German Jugendstil, especially through the realization of architectural projects, which went on right until Olbrich's untimely death in 1908.

Olbrich's best-known building in Darmstadt, apart from the Ernst-Ludwig-Haus, which served as a workshop for the artists in the colony, was the Wedding Tower. The red brick tower is crowned by five arched elements like fingers, covered in blue ceramic tiles.

The Mathildenhöhe is dominated by the late work of Olbrich, but it was here that another artist, Peter Behrens (see page 23) took his first steps as an architect, after previously distinguishing himself as a painter and craftsman. He was later to become one of the most influential personalities of European architectural history.

## Cube instead of curve: Glasgow and Vienna

Just as Horta's work in Brussels and Gaudí's buildings in Barcelona stamped their image on those cities, so the work of Charles Rennie Mackintosh became the trademark of the Scottish metropolis of Glasgow. His key work, the school of art, provoking violent controversy among his contemporaries, was not plant-like, but heavily *stereometric* in its basic design. Smooth, almost menacing façades of natural stone are opened up by large windows.

In 1900 Mackintosh was invited to present his work in Vienna. His furniture designs, with their largely cubic forms, gave the impetus to the founding by Josef Hoffmann of the Vienna workshops in 1903, and they were to remain a center of applied art production until they were closed down in 1933. Mackintosh's work was displayed in Vienna in the Secession exhibition building, which Joseph Maria Obrich had built just before he moved to Darmstadt.

In 1897 a highly varied collection of artists, from the painter Gustav Klimt and the sculptor Max Klinger to the architect Josef Hoffmann, had withdrawn from the traditional Vienna art world and its exhibitions of academic art, and

**Joseph Maria Olbrich, *Wedding Tower*,** Darmstadt-Mathildenhöhe, 1908

Grand Duke Ernst Ludwig von Hessen was one of the few German aristocrats who promoted political reform together with reform in visual art. He called seven artists to Darmstadt and put Mathildenhöhe at their disposition, to create a "document of German art of enduring worth." When their studios were opened to the public in 1901, it was the first art exhibition of that kind. Joseph-Maria Olbrich, a pupil of Otto Wagner, designed a "five-fingered" wedding tower for the second anniversary of the grand duke's marriage, completing one of the most important ensembles of Modernist work.

**Henry van der Velde, *Karl Ernst Osthaus Museum*,** Brunnenhalle, Hagen, 1901–02

The interior of the Folkwang-Museum, whose basic structure was built by C. Gerard, belongs to the most important early works in Germany of the Belgian van de Velde. He was contracted by the banker's son Karl Ernst Osthaus, a major patron of the arts. Van de Velde had established himself as a leading exponent of the Jugendstil with the *vegetal* formal language that is to be seen in this impressive museum, but it is particularly noticeable for its economic use of materials. Stone, wood, glass, and metal work together to define their own new aesthetic: an aesthetic that has its counterpart in the great works of engineering of that time. The impact of the materials on the senses is underlined by the flowing, yet flattened shapes created by van de Velde, as can be seen in the top-lighted pillars in the fountain court (*Fountain with Boys* by Georges Minne 1901).

### Charles Rennie Mackintosh, *Glasgow School of Art,* 1896–1909

Viewed in passing, the Glasgow School of Art, created by the Scottish architect Charles Rennie Mackintosh, appears a radically sober, rational building. Outside it is angular, cubic; its block-like enclosed quality is further emphasized by the use of *natural stone*, and a row of large north-light windows indicating the studios that lie behind. Inside, it has a flexible layout that predates Mies Van der Rohe by many years with its use of moveable partition walls. But the rough-hewn clarity of the whole is overlaid by delicate, fluid details, which are not applied to the building as decor, but which humanize and animate it: the arches over the entrance, the filigree alcoves, the sweeping stair-rail, and the interior details in wood and metal, all bear witness to Mackintosh's penetrating graphic imagination.

In the harmony between these two principles of form lies the strength of Mackintosh's architecture, and it was this that made him a model for the Vienna *Secession* and the moderns.

founded the Vienna Secession, which dominated the art scene at the turn of the century in the Austro-Hungarian capital. The newly founded association of artists was to become the model for other secessions, such as those in Munich and Berlin.

But it was not only the unusual Secession building, with its crowning cupola of iron laurel leaves, that was different from the general architectonic picture of the city: the Secession exhibitions themselves presented an extremely different image to the familiar traditions of exhibiting. Instead of walls so full that it was impossible to see anything

adequately, with pictures hanging several rows deep, the exhibitions favored selection and presentation, which gave each work of art an appropriate space within which to develop its effect.

The architecture of the Vienna Jugendstil, with its severe tectonic language, was clearly different from either the work of Horta with its leaning toward *vegetal* models, or the overflowing fantasy of Gaudí. This gave it a particularly important role as a link to the predominantly functionalist development of modern architecture. Although Otto Wagner did cover the façades of his so-called "Majolika House" at 40 Linke Wienzeile Strasse with luxuriantly floral decoration, the formal language of his buildings in general is cubic, and much more restful.

An example of this is the large cashiers' hall of the Vienna post office savings bank, laid out on a severe rectilinear grid, and overarched by a gently curving glass skin through which light floods into the room. An additional stroke of artistry on Wagner's part was to light the rooms under the hall through ceiling areas made of glass blocks.

A very similar paring-down of form can be seen in the work of another Viennese architect, Josef Hoffman, whose key work is the Palais Stoclet in Brussels. This house, built for the banker Adolphe Stoclet, is characterized by its interpenetrating cubic blocks, and its economical use of decoration on the *façade*: elements that look forward to modern architecture after the First World War, when the

### Otto Wagner, Austrian Post Office Savings Bank, Vienna 1904–06

The interior of this trapezoid building, especially the large cashiers' hall, is of an elegant economy. Free of any decoration, it derives its charm from the reduction of its elements to the simplest form: the extremely narrow steel supports in the arched glass roof, and the columns that, for structural efficiency, grow narrower toward the base. The construction of the roof, which Wagner derived from the principle of the suspension bridge, is given particular emphasis by the fact that the pillars plainly do not support the roof, but run right through it. The post office savings bank underpins Otto Wagner's *Theses on modern architecture*, which he had propounded in 1896 in the book of the same name. In it he argued for a modern style appropriate to the time bringing together architecture and engineering in a new, practical, total artwork. "Anything impractical cannot be beautiful."

# ADOLF LOOS

Adolf Loos belongs to the architect-writers among the moderns, who were able to translate their theories into designs. Whereas Adolf Loos, who was hard of hearing, couched his thoughts in flowery parables and imaginative essays, when formulating ideas about design he favored unadorned architecture and archaic forms. His texts constantly reflect a search for a "pure architecture" freed from the influence of other disciplines. Architecture, according to Loos, was not art in three dimensions, but the organisation of space. As a *functionalist* he campaigned for a rejection of decorative elements, for instance *stucco* in interiors, demanding that his fellow architects concentrate on the technical aspects of a building's use. A combination of dandy, artist, architect, and art critic, lifelong friend of the writer Karl Kraus, Adolf Loos was one of the most brilliant and multitalented personalities of 20th-century architecture.

He was born in Brünn, in Moravia, and started out, oddly enough, as a member of the Vienna Secession – a group who, in the tradition of the English Arts and Crafts movement, believed in the merging of crafts and architecture. He was a member of the so-called "Coffee house trio," the other two members being Joseph Maria Olbrich and Josef Hoffman, who were enthusiastic proponents of the Jugendstil. But in 1898, Loos broke away from the circle on

*Adolf Loos, circa 1930*

matters of principle, and later became one of its most vehement critics.

From then on he promoted the thesis that lack of ornament was a sign of spiritual strength, and that "the evolution of culture implies the removal of ornament from objects of use." By this dissociation from art, Loos sought to strengthen the authenticity both of art and architecture. He saw this separation as the precondition for cultural modernity, even going so far in his work as journalist and writer to leave his texts in lower case, in order to break away from the ornamental capitals used in printing at the time.

While he was studying in Dresden, Loos spent three years (1895–98) in the United States, where he visited the World's Fair and became acquainted with the *Chicago School* (see page 42). There he studied the theories of Louis Sullivan, who had suggested as early as 1885 in his essay "Ornament in Architecture" that decorative elements in architecture should be abandoned, for a few years at least, since they unnecessarily disrupted the organic relationship between function, form, material, and expression.

Loos developed this proposal further by decrying ornament as socially and economically wasteful. All that the builder was actually paid for was the house itself. Ornamentation was regarded as on a level with "wasted labor and spoiled materials."

What the architectural consequences of this attitude were, Loos himself revealed in his design for the building on the Michaelerplatz (built in 1909–11 and reconstructed 1981), which finally brought about his breakthrough into architecture. Commissioned by the tailoring firm Goldman and Salatsch, he erected a spare, plastered building, whose only decorative feature – dictated by the materials – was the *natural stone* of the

*The building incorporating residential floors and a shop for the tailoring firm Goldman & Salatsch on the Michaelerplatz in Vienna, 1909–11*

ground floor. The building was both a dwelling and a shop, and is remarkable for the sensitivity with which Loos incorporated elements from the neighboring buildings (such as the portal of the Michaelerkirche), and for the fact that the owner gave town planning considerations precedence over economic by placing the building in a commanding position with one wall facing the square, rather than opting for maximal use of the site in the traditional way by building it on the corner. Loos is famous both for his open fight against decorative building but also for his idea of "spatial planning," though in fact this was not formulated by him, but was a response to his works. The essence of spatial planning is to work out the dimensions for individual rooms in a building by their functional and display roles. Loos took his idea of having rooms of different heights from England, where the gallery-construction of the medieval hall had found its way into country houses. Always a provocateur, he maintained that an architect should not do sketches, design façades or do cross-sections. Much more important was to "design space." The result of this was that Loos designed buildings that were sets of boxes within boxes, joined by staircases, as in the Moller building

(Vienna, 1928) or the Müller house (Prague, 1930). The latter is the most worked-out translation into practice of spatial planning by Loos himself. The living room, dining room, library, and ladies' drawing-room were all on different levels, together composing a coherent open organisation of space. Every room is in expensive materials – marble, mahogany, lemon-wood – which underline Loos's starting point: that the artifice of ornament should be replaced by the effect of noble materials.

Among the best-known works of Loos, which relates to his experience in the USA, is the Kärnter Bar in Vienna (1908) which incorporates the American idea of the bar where you stand to drink. Four highly polished marble columns support a sharply projecting canopy roof portraying a stylized banner of the Stars and Stripes. The lettering is so artistically executed in brightly colored broken glass, that it almost makes a nonsense of Loos's edict about the forcible separation of architecture and art. Loos had laid down that only a small part of architecture belonged to the realm of art – tombs and monuments, neither of which had any architectural sense or function, except perhaps of a symbolic nature.

However, the most convincing interpretation of Loos's theories came not from their originator but from the philosopher and architect Ludwig Wittgenstein who, in 1926–29, together with Loos's pupil Paul Engelmann, erected a building made up of unadorned cubes fitted within one another, which looked just as if it had been carried out by the "master" himself.

*Unadorned: the flat symmetrical garden side of the houses (completed 1910) for Lilly and Hugo Steiner in Vienna, which exemplify Loos's battle against decorative architecture*

# FRANK LLOYD WRIGHT

To be the "greatest architect in America," that was the wish of Frank Lloyd Wright's mother for him when he was born in 1869. When he died, 90 years later, he had indeed given a direction to the architecture of his country.

*Frank Lloyd Wright, 1957*

Wright left behind well over 400 buildings and projects, many of the rank of icons, which can barely be subsumed under any academic category since so many styles and stylistic variants are expressed within them. He was forerunner, protagonist, contemporary, and executor of the greatest overarching line of development of 20th-century architecture: Modernism.

At first sight it appears that it is only Wright's own will to design everything that unites his work. The foundations for the perfectionist urge, which caused him to work personally through every stage of a project from the long-distance view to the details of the furniture, and to give his personal stamp to even such rebarbative projects as the Romeo and Juliet windmills (1896), were laid when he worked in Louis Sullivan's studio (1887–93). While everyone was drowning their buildings with *historicist* decoration, and long before the Modernists had made a criterion of the thesis (attributed to Sullivan) "form follows function," Sullivan himself was carrying it out in practice, developing the design of a building to work in unison with its construction, and the construction to work in unison with the material.

Wright did not, however, enjoy the benefit of having been to a specialist college, which would have given him a theoretical grounding in architecture. Because of a lack of money he was only able to take a draftsmanship course at the third-class state university of Wisconsin, which he dropped in order to work for Sullivan. In 1894 he set up his own studio in Chicago. In 1906 he traveled to Japan, where the art made a deep impression upon him. In Europe, which he visited in 1910, he exhibited in Berlin, and the

*Perfect symbiosis with the waterfall: the Kaufmann house, named "Falling Water"*

description of his work published by the publisher Wasmuth ensured his importance in Europe as a stimulator of innovation. But he did not personally engage much with the concepts of his sternly rationalistic colleagues Gropius, Le Corbusier, and Mies van der Rohe. Although he did take note of almost all of the themes of Modernism, it was not in an abstract, theoretical way, but practically, in his designs. An example of this is the "machine." Whereas his European colleagues translated the way it worked into making buildings, for Wright it was an instrument for creating art. So it was that he created the Charles Ennis house out of industrially produced prefabricated concrete blocks in 1924, thoroughly in the spirit of Modernism. But Wright used the technology in an Arts and Crafts way and decorated the façades in Mayan style, whereas Modernism rejected such things, in the spirit of Adolf Loos's dictum "Ornament is criminal."

The real theme that the self-taught Wright developed himself, and spent his life propagating with missionary zeal, was that of organic architecture: "A building is only organic when the exterior and the interior exist in unison, and when both are in harmony with the character and nature of its purpose, its reason for existence, its location, and the time of its creation."

His first step in this direction was the "Prairie House," the layout of which was of a revolutionary freedom for that time, with the whole living area assembled around a hearth. Under wide projecting roofs, set on a massive base, the house opens on to the landscape through an expanse of windows that occupy all sides. With their dominating horizontals the buildings "make it credible," as Vincent Scully has said, "that the Americans had been living on their continent for ever." From 1910 dozens of buildings of this type were produced.

Later on the buildings became more individual, adapted to the particular requirements of the project and terrain. The Kaufmann house of 1936 is simply named "Falling Water," due to its perfect symbiosis with the waterfall over which it is constructed. Other buildings, such as the Marin County Civic Center of 1957, are enthroned like fantastic apparitions on a hill. But the basic motifs developed in the prairie houses remain the same.

Wright took up his own position in the landscape. Born in a little town in Wisconsin, the son of a preacher, he spent his whole life far from the centers of civilization. In 1911 he moved back to Spring Green, Wisconsin. In the valley of his forefathers he built Taliesin (first completed 1914, renovated following a fire 1925). In Taliesin

architecture became a model for life. The property was dwelling, studio, and farming enterprise all together. In 1938, the very deliberately named Taliesin West was created in Scottsville Arizona. In the depths of the prairies, under the steep wooden frame of the drawing hall, Taliesin College students and their egocentric father-figure came together in almost spiritual communion.

Anyone who lives that way must have a hostile attitude to the town. Wright wrote of Chicago: "It was so cold, so black, and so damp! The dreadful bluish-white sheen of the arc lamps dominated everything. I shivered." Consequently Wright built mainly in the open landscape. His few constructions in a city context all turn away from the city and create their own rich inner worlds. The Larkin building in Buffalo, New York (1905), is a brick fortress on the outside, but its large interior, lit solely from above, is a revolutionary design for a commercial headquarters. This same effect is achieved by the factory buildings for the Johnson Wax Company in Racine, Wisconsin (1936–39). An internal road places the entrance within the complex. Under a forest of mushroom-like pillars there is one of the most impressive single-room interiors ever seen. In the Guggenheim Museum in New York (see illustration on page 63), a lift sucks the visitor up from Fifth Avenue into the heights. A spiral ramp

*Under a forest of mushroom-shaped supports, the large central office space of the Johnson Wax Company in Racine, Wisconsin (USA)*

leads him down through an interior space so breathtaking that he forgets both city and art.

Wright designed an anti-urban countermodel to set against metropolises such as New York. In "Usonia" everyone would live as he did in Taliesin. Unlike the European garden city, Usonia does not start with the community, but with the freedom of the individual, upon which American societies are based. So Wright demanded for each family a minimum of one hectare of land and stressed the right of each person to have his own car. Finally in 1935 he developed a plan intended to bring about the harmony of individuals with each other and the landscape: Broadacre City (see pages 40–41).

This vision came to life simply as a faceless suburb. The architect did not become, as he had dreamed, the savior of modern American culture. In his "Testament" Wright acknowledged with resignation: "The United States is the only civilization to go from barbarism to degeneracy with no culture in between."

influence of movements such as De Stijl in the Netherlands (see page 31) or the Bauhaus in Germany (see page 33) was dominant.

Despite its innovative aspects, the Palais Stoclet is clearly the last extravagant flowering of the Jugendstil. Extravagant in its use of materials too, the whole façade of the house is clothed in sheets of marble, set in borders of bronze. In the interior Gustav Klimt's mosaics melt into the decor, which Hoffmann carried out in cooperation with the Vienna workshop, to form a single, unique work of art.

## Elemental architecture

The idea of reducing forms to their appropriate and necessary shape was the guiding principle of the Dutch architect Hendrik Petrus Berlage, who both as an architect and as a theoretician was one of the most important forerunners of the modern architecture of the first half of the 20th century. His work not only exerted a direct influence on subsequent Dutch architecture of the De Stijl movement, but also on German architects such as Peter Behrens or Ludwig Mies van der Rohe.

When designing the Amsterdam stock exchange, Behrens moved away from the formal repertoire of historicism in favor of an architecture based upon fundamental *tectonic* needs, which used materials in the most appropriate way.

When Adolph Loos turned away from the Jugendstil, pronounced ornamentation to be a criminal offense, then produced the extremely pared-down Steiner house and the Michaelerplatz building, the first phase of 20th-century architecture was drawing to its close.

American architecture at the end of the 19th century had virtually nothing to do with the developments taking place in Europe. It was only with the work of Frank Lloyd Wright, with his free designs ranging widely into the surrounding countryside which revolutionized the architecture of the single-family house, that American architecture gained a direct influence over European practitioners.

**Josef Hoffmann, *Palais Stoclet,*** Brussels, 1904–11

Whereas the general external appearance of Josef Hoffmann's Palais Stoclet is one of *rationalist* aesthetic severity, the detail is rich and recherché almost to the point of decadence. This duality makes the work a prime example of the transition in architecture from the 19th to the 20th century.

Reform and Expressionism
# The First Moderns
1910–1920

## MODERNIZATION AND INDUSTRIALIZATION

### The age of imperialism ends in the First World War

Retrospectively, the European march toward the First World War has an ineluctable logic to it. At the beginning of the century the great powers – England, France, Austro-Hungary, and Germany – were making ever more threatening imperialist gestures at each other. At the same time the balance of power, which had been so laboriously established at the end of the 19th century, was beginning to shift again. The nationalist strains were sounding ever louder, and the arms race drove an ever deeper wedge of mistrust and ill-will between the European nations. In both politics and economics, it was national self-interest, driven by an unhealthy spirit of competition, which dictated the actions of the power-holders.

The murder in Sarajevo on 28 June 1914 of the Archduke Franz Ferdinand, the heir to the throne of Austro-Hungary, accelerated this process in spite of intensive secret diplomacy, and resulted a few weeks later in the outbreak of the First World War.

But the euphoric war fever of the first few weeks and months was destined to be short-lived. Years of disputing the same positions in the trenches at Verdun or on the Somme quickly brought home to English, French, and Germans alike that this war was a daily succession of horrors. The First World War brought the end of the "long 19th century." The era that had begun with the French Revolution of 1789 finally submerged in the bloody fever of a world war.

### The German Werkbund

At the beginning of the 19th century the gap in economic development between Great Britain and Germany had been still wider. Intensive efforts were made on the Continent to challenge the British Empire's long and undisputed supremacy, and to compete with it in terms of *industrialization*. But Germany had a great way to go before it could make its industries and their products competitive on the world market.

While William Morris and his Arts and Crafts movement (see page 10) strove to renew art through a romantic harking back to the lost craft traditions of the Middle Ages, the forces for reform in prewar Germany went a different route toward reaching their goals. By using industrialization and mechanization, their aim was to turn out well-designed, high-quality products, as well as to achieve a new style in architecture. The combined economic and artistic strivings of industrialists, artists, and craftspeople came together in 1907 in the "Deutsche Werkbund" (German artwork union). The enlightened goal of the Werkbund was to achieve a better quality of design in objects for everyday use, and in ordinary life in general.

**1911**: Revolution in China under the leadership of Sun Yat-sen; the governors of several provinces join the revolution, and the Manchu Dynasty (established 1644) relinquishes power. IBM (International Business Machines Corp.) founded.

**1912**: The Italian film *Quo Vadis?* and the Russian film *War and Peace* shown in cinemas. 90% of all films shown in the world are of French origin. Sinking of the *Titanic*.

**1913**: The Indian poet and philosopher Rabindranath Tagore receives the Nobel Prize for Literature.

**1914**: The assassination of Archduke Franz Ferdinand of Austria in Sarajevo leads to the outbreak of the First World War (ends 1918). Henry Ford begins the assembly-line manufacture of the Model T. Mahatma Gandhi, who has been in South Africa since 1893, returns to India. Opening of the Panama Canal.

**1915**: Einstein begins developing his theory of relativity.

**1916**: Battle of Verdun. Ferdinand Sauerbruch constructs moveable false limbs. The German Expressionist painter of animals, Franz Marc, is killed in action. The Dada art movement comes into being in Zurich and Geneva (this ends around 1922).

**1917**: Nobel Peace Prize awarded to the International Committee of the Red Cross in Geneva. The October Revolution in Russia ends czarist rule. Lenin, Trotsky, and Stalin found the Soviet Union. George Grosz completes his collection of socially critical lithographs: *The face of the ruling class.*

**1918**: Otto Hahn and Lise Meitner discover the radioactive element protactinium. The Russian Kasimir Malevich paints his monochromatic *White square on a white ground*, the high point of Suprematism.

**1919**: Peace conference begins in Paris. Founding of the League of Nations. Signing of the Treaty of Versailles. The leading left-wing socialists Rosa Luxemburg and Karl Liebknecht murdered by far-right officers. The Weimar Republic declared. Commencement of Prohibition in the USA.

**1920**: Gandhi begins his non-violent campaign for Indian independence. Mary Wigman opens her dancing school in Dresden, launching "expressive dance." The English writer Hugh Lofting brings out the children's *Dr. Dolittle* books. The Expressionist film, *The Cabinet of Dr. Caligari,* is premiered.

**Production of the Model T Ford in Detroit. Photo dated 1913**

Sociopolitical and economic interests merged in the Werkbund to reform German craft. Among the founder members of the union were such important architects as Hermann Muthesius, whose writings in particular had great influence on residential building in Germany, and Peter Behrens (see page 23), who rose to become the house architect and designer of Emil Rathenau's Allgemeiner Elektricitäts-Gesellschaft, AEG.

The Werkbund had a great influence on modern architecture in Germany right up till 1933, and it was an architect from Munich, Theodor Fischer, who became its first president. Fischer, the creator of the Garnisonskirche in Ulm, was likewise an extremely influential teacher for many architects of the next generation. The Werkbund's program-setting exhibition, held in 1914 in Cologne only a few weeks before the outbreak of the First World War, offered an overview of the various architectural currents of the time. Henry van de Velde called for a more strongly individualized and more craft-oriented direction. He was a champion of the Jugendstil, and had built the Werkbundtheater for the exhibition. This somewhat retrospective position was successfully opposed by Hermann Muthesius, who demanded a thoroughgoing move to industrial production, even of products that were traditionally handcrafted, and in this he included architecture.

### Glass brings us the new age – industrial culture

The outstanding architectural event of the Werkbund exhibition in Cologne was the Glass Pavilion by Bruno Taut.

Set upon a curving *base*, the building was spanned by a *cupola* made of lozenge-shaped panes of glass. With its delicate many-colored brightness, the building was an example, inside as well as out, of the early Expressionism of German architecture with its *Gothic* derivation. Taut's glass architecture was inspired by the utopian verses of the poet Paul Scheerbart, whose aphoristic text also adorned the *façade* of his friend Taut's pavilion. "Glass brings us the new age, the culture of brick gives us only pain."

A year earlier, in 1913, Taut had produced another agenda-setting work, the monument to iron in the steel industry for the building exhibition in Leipzig, which served as a

model by means of its use of new forms and materials. Instead of *historicist ornamentation* or the floral decoration of the Jugendstil, the monument showed an exemplary respect for its materials. Even from the outside it was a clear demonstration of the principles of *building in iron*.

It was these same principles that gave its exceptional quality to a factory for making shoe-lasts, the Fagus Factory in Alfeld an der Leine, designed by Adolf Meyer and Walter Gropius (1911–13). It is rightly regarded as one of the founding buildings of 20th-century Modernist architecture. Scarcely anyone in Europe had until then designed so clear and functional an industrial building where every constructional element was on display without ornament: not even Peter Behrens, in whose office Gropius and Meyer had worked till 1910.

The model for these new factory buildings, with their functional, technical language of forms, were American silos and industrial buildings, whose persuasive functionality was now increasingly recognized to have an aesthetic dimension. The publication by Gropius of a collection of American "industrial architecture" in the Werkbund's yearbook for 1913 brought about a widespread appreciation of these exemplary buildings.

Also influential in Europe were the factory buildings with concrete skeletons that Albert Kahn and the engineer Ernest Ransome erected for the industrialist Henry Ford's thrusting new automobile works in Detroit.

**Bruno Taut, *Glass Pavilion,*** Werkbund exhibition in Cologne, 1914

19th-century engineers had used glass exclusively as a rational facing material. Now Bruno Taut showed off its many-sided potential in his pavilion for the German glass industry at the Cologne Werkbund exhibition. He was also making a point: in a time overshadowed by war, he made a construction in which everything had either mirrors or colored glass in it, from the roof to the steps, including a glass cascade with water bubbling down it, in a vision of a new, paradisiacal world. The building style, as well as the aphoristic texts by Paul Scheerbarts that decorated the exterior, elevated material to the status of a component in a new morality. Taut later developed this design into a whole series of fantastic sketches of crystalline "city crowns," none of which, however, were built.

**Walter Gropius and Adolf Meyer,**
*Fagus Factory,* general view (right) and detail of the stairwell (below), Alfeld, 1911–13

The Fagus factory was Gropius's first important building. The long workshop block of this shoe-last factory is of convincing, unadorned simplicity. In it, he discriminates between the load-bearing structure and the non-load-bearing façade, which is constructed as a curtain wall. The impression of lightness stems chiefly from the all-glass corners, whose vertical sheets of glass seem to hang from the jutting cornice above because the columns are recessed. There are no columns within, so that the stairways float freely in their glass towers. These elements, and also the fact that all the parts of the building (with the exception of the chimney) are given equal significance, made the Fagus factory into *the* stylistic model of modern architecture.

The name of Ford is still linked above almost any other with the sweeping success of the car in the 20th century. His revolutionary economic and social initiatives had to be matched by production buildings that were just as revolutionary. Ford's motor company had began producing cars in 1903. His recipe for success was signal in its modernity: only a few mass-produced parts were needed to assemble each car. The stringent rationality with which each task followed the next, the increased division of labor, and the resultant low production costs all contributed to making Henry Ford one of the most successful car manufacturers of his day. Comparatively high pay and low working hours increased his employees' motivation.

Kahn's buildings reflect this sternly economic point of view with its total renunciation of display, in that they are soberly cubic in form without any superfluous decoration. Being constructed of concrete, the buildings were relatively cheap to produce. The production sheds with their conveyor belts were rationally designed, laid out all on one level, and were notable for their bright interiors, full of natural light coming in through large windows set into the supporting concrete skeleton. The great art of Kahn's utilitarian buildings lies in their renunciation of everything traditionally considered artistic.

In Europe, on the other hand, architecture was not yet as clearly modern as Kahn's buildings or the early work of Gropius and Meyer. Modern and *historicist* elements were

still often mixed together. This situation is hardly to be wondered at when considering the centuries-old – in some cases thousand-year-old – regional building traditions in Europe. The synthesis of building traditions is exemplified in the early works of the Berliner Hans Poelzig, whose own idiosyncratically expressive architectural language increasingly takes center stage, as in the case of the chemical factory that he built between 1911 and 1912 in Lubau, near Posen. The brick building could be seen to be composed of geometrically stacked cubes, thus putting its industrial nature clearly on display. In Breslau in 1911 Poelzig designed an office building entirely of reinforced concrete, notable for its horizontal lines of windows and its rounded corners, both motifs that were to recur frequently in the 1920s in the work of other Modernist architects such as Erich Mendelsohn and Hans Scharoun.

### The triumph of concrete
New materials were proving themselves to an ever greater degree. Materials that at first were used only for industrial and utilitarian buildings gradually conquered the field of traditional building projects. It was above all the previously unheard-of possibilities of concrete that revolutionized architecture.

Suddenly it became possible, using the new materials, to roof an immense hall without needing to put in any additional support in the form of pillars, which would decrease the view within the space. The first example of this was

the Jahrhunderhalle (Centennial Hall) built by the city architect of Breslau, Max Berg. Although the *dome* of the Hall was three times bigger than the stone-built dome of St. Peter's in Rome, Berg's inspired creation with its reinforced concrete ribs weighed only half as much!

The more concrete, with its vast potential as a building material, entered architects' fields of vision, the more their approach to it changed. Gradually it was recognized as having an aesthetic value of its own in its unadorned form.

Whereas August Perret had covered the construction of the concrete supports in his apartment house in the rue Franklin in Paris with ceramic tiles, by 1905, when he built the garage at 51 rue de Ponthieu, he showed the reinforced concrete grid quite openly; it was simply painted to protect it from the weather. The wall spaces between the supports were completely filled with glass.

Cars were swiftly becoming popular in Paris at the beginning of the century, and making a building to park them in was an entirely new task for the architect. Perret's response was appropriately new, inside as well as out. Using the potential of concrete for *spanning* a large space, Perret was able to produce a relatively unobstructed covered area, which could be set up to service all the requirements of short- and long-term parking.

The movement in which Perret was instrumental, which aimed to reduce architecture to a functional supporting armor of concrete, reached its spiritual peak in his church,

Notre-Dame-du-Raincy, built near Paris in 1924. The vaulted roof of the nave, made out of unadorned concrete, rests on slim pillars, and the walls are so pierced with openings that daylight can stream into the church almost unhindered.

The Swiss architect Charles-Édouard Jeanneret – who under the name Le Corbusier was to become one of the most important Modernist architects, and who for a time had been employed in Auguste Perret's office – was keen to use *architecture in reinforced concrete*, which had been developed by Perret, for residential building. As early as 1915 he had developed the "Dom-ino-System" for re-building Flanders, which had been devastated by the battles of the First World War. This was a plan for mass-produced housing, whereby it should be possible to construct a concrete skeleton within a few weeks. The precondition for this was a far-reaching uniformity in the construction units, particularly the formwork for the concrete. The Dom-ino houses represent Le Corbusier's first attempt at thoroughgoing rationalization and total functionality. Although his plans remained an unrealized project, they were characteristic of the later development of his views on architecture and town planning.

## NEOCLASSICISM

### In search of a national style
Although a few modern buildings were being planned and realized in 1910, the rationalist

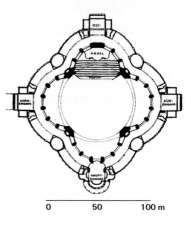

| 0 | 50 | 100 m |

**Auguste Perret,** *The Church of Notre-Dame-du-Raincy,* near Paris, 1924

The pioneer of *reinforced concrete* used it for a religious building drawing on the traditions of *antiquity* and the *Gothic* era. The concrete is visible everywhere, still rough from the formwork. Ornamentation is spare and dictated by the structure. The walls consist of ready-made concrete elements set with colored glass. They create a room out of light, in a way that is comparable to Gothic cathedrals. The church, with its three naves and barrel vaulting, belongs to the basic typology of a Romanesque basilica.

and functionalist trends in architecture were far from being the only ones in the prewar period. Far from it: a heterogeneous mix of the most varied *styles* prevailed in towns. Many buildings were indeed an *eclectic* jumble of historicist, Modernist, and Jugendstil forms.

At the beginning of the century the question of the *right* style suddenly dominated discussion again, a question that stemmed entirely from the 19th century, especially from *classicism* and the *neo-Renaissance*. The few really modern buildings that had so far been realized were in sharp contrast to the continuing tradition of grandiose *historicist* buildings, which employed an architectonic repertoire that had been handed down over the centuries. Yet the conservative shell of a *neo-Baroque* palace might have a steel skeleton or a concrete construction concealed under its luxuriant stucco decoration.

In the search for a national style that would also correspond to the nation's external self-image, *neo-Classicism* became, around 1910, the dominant doctrine, adding a further facet to the already rich spectrum of contemporary architecture.

Peter Behrens in particular, in his important buildings for AEG, including the Turbine Room in Berlin, tried to make a clear use of models from the history of architecture. The *rough-cast,* slightly curved corner *quoins* of his turbine room were very clearly reminiscent of ancient Egypt. Through this borrowing from history, the factory – a project quite without spirituality – managed to achieve a unique nobility that lifted it directly on to a plane with the temples of ancient Egypt

despite all the modernity in its functioning. In the St. Petersburg embassy of 1911, Behrens increased his classical borrowings. The result was an at that time unrivalled *Doric* monumentalism that made clear the conscious grandeur and power of those who had commissioned it.

But it was not only in Germany that neo-Classicism took root, and carried on right into the 1920s and 1930s. Edwin Lutyens used the style, which was generally understood to be the language of power at the time, to demonstrate the imperialist pretensions of Great Britain in the new buildings of New Delhi in India (1915–24).

Henry Bacon used the same monumental formal language in his Lincoln Memorial, which was designed in 1917 in Washington DC, feeling that he was under an obligation to reflect the classicist style of the old government buildings. The acceptance of this old architectural language for new buildings and national monuments deliberately placed them within the older tradition, with its connotations of upholding the state.

**Classicism and Modernism**

Heinrich Tessenow used an even more reduced language of form than Behrens or Lutyens. But even his Festspielhaus (festival hall) at Hellerau near Dresden was inspired by the classicist repertoire of forms. So the main façade had a monumental *pillared portico* as high as itself, supporting the tympanum of the steep pitched roof. The interior of the hall was constructed in such a way that it could be variously configured for different types of performance, and could be used for new artistic manifestations such as eurythmics, modern music, and free dance.

Likewise, Mies van der Rohe (see page 59), who had worked in Behrens' office, kept faith with a model of purified *classicism* in the early villas he built for well-heeled clients in Berlin and Potsdam.

Mies van der Rohe was very much involved, right through till his late work in the 1960s, with the architectural heritage of Karl Friedrich Schinkel, the most important Prussian architect of the 19th century. Mies realized better than anyone else how to transfer Schinkel's innovative use of materials – for example his early use of iron and zinc – and his strict articulation of space into his own work. Little

# PETER BEHRENS

When Peter Behrens built a house for himself in 1901 in the Mathildenhöhe artists' colony in Darmstadt, it created a sensation. A native of Hamburg, he was already a respected figure in Germany, having made his name as an exponent of the Jugendstil both as a painter and a craftsman. But in architecture he was a newcomer.

Perhaps it was through this versatility and openness to the various art forms that Behrens was destined to become one of the most influential all-round artists in Germany in the first half of the 20th century. Today he is best known as an architect, but he was also a book designer, a designer of typefaces, and craftsman, so that he has to be seen as one of the earliest "designers."

A milestone in Behrens's career, as well as in the history of German art, was his connection with Emil Rathenau's AEG (General Electricity Company), which was the biggest industrial concern in Germany around 1910. In 1907, industrialist and designer began a partnership that was at that time unique. Through his work for AEG, designing their products according to artistic criteria, Behrens provided a model for that cooperation between art, craft, and industrial production that was one of the goals of the *Deutscher Werkbund*, founded in the same year. He thus became one of the grandfathers of "industrial design" and "corporate identity." But it was not only his industrial products for AEG that brought him public notice. There was also his turbine factory (1909), designed for the company in Berlin, which even today, and despite its

building so interpenetrate each other that the flat roofs of the lower parts of the block serve as terraces for the dwellings above.

The Nazis, who were attracted by the neo-Classicist side of Behrens, also tried to get him to build for them. Just before his death he was going to build the new AEG headquarters on the north-south axis planned by Albert Speer for Berlin. But the project went no further than the models (1937–39), and it foundered with the Third Reich.

This monumental Doric style, through which Behrens became the leader of European *neo-Classicism*, is not simply to be found in prestige buildings like the German embassy in St. Petersburg (1911–12). He makes an even greater use of it in private houses, like the sparely beautiful Villa Wiegand in Berlin-Dahlem, with its

*The AEG company emblem evolved from an elaborate historicist style to a Jugendstil version and then to Behrens's functional form. Behrens also created a typeface for AEG.*

*Behrens as industrial designer: the AEG-Sparbogenlampe was devised specifically for interiors with limited hanging space*

monumental feel, remains one of the icons of modern architecture with its pared-down language of form. These were to become even more reduced in his AEG assembly shop (1912) in the Voltastrasse, the façade of which, with its clear lines and its total absence of decoration, gives it an almost revolutionary character, comparable with the early major works of Gropius and Kahn.

The outstanding feature of Behrens's buildings, apart from their functionality, is their imposing monumentality, for example in the turbine factory or in AEG's small motors factory of 1910. This quality is achieved through the buildings' sternly cubic volumes, but also through their *classical* formal language, mainly employing the *Doric* order.

unique pillared hall. Apart from his enthusiasm for the industrial production of artistically valid objects, this pared-down neo-Classicism was the main theme he handed on to his younger colleagues in his Berlin architectural practice. Many were to number among the most important architects of the succeeding generation: Le Corbusier, Ludwig Mies van der Rohe, and Walter Gropius among others.

It was one of Peter Behrens's attributes as an architect that he was very much in tune with the spirit of the times and was able to render the demands and desires of those who commissioned him in architectural forms appropriate to the times. His openness to new styles and forms of artistic expression is shown in the brick building for the headquarters of the Hoechst dyeworks company, the high, cathedral-like entrance hall which displays all the colors of the rainbow. Behrens, a neo-Classicist before the war, here joins the *Expressionist* movement, with a building inspired by the *Amsterdam School*.

Behrens was a part of the next evolution of architecture too, from Expressionism to *Neues Bauen*. It was not a surprising move: the most important representatives of Modernism in architecture had been his pupils and colleagues. As a founder-member and leading representative of the Deutscher Werkbund, he had contributed to the Stuttgart building complex, the Weissenhofsiedlung (see page 39), a stepped apartment block. Behrens had a masterly grasp of how to put the contemporary forms of Neues Bauen to personal use. The cubic volumes of the

*An Expressionist brick building: the entrance hall of the head office of the Hoechst dyeworks. (1920–24)*

by little, Mies van der Rohe succeeded in translating the classicist repertoire of forms employed by Schinkel, without any *historicist* motifs, into abstract modern architecture.

## EXPRESSIONISM

### The way to variety in color and form

A completely new direction in architecture began in around 1905. It occurred almost simultaneously with a completely new direction in painting: that taken by the Fauves, led by Henri Matisse and Maurice de Vlaminck in France, and the German Brücke group in Dresden including Erich Heckel, Karl Schmidt-Rottluff, Ludwig Kirchner, and Max Pechstein.

**Heinrich Tessenow, *Festival Hall,***
Hellerau near Dresden, 1910

The most ambitious housing project before the First World War was the garden city for the Hellerau workshops near Dresden. In the middle was the festival hall by Heinrich Tessenow, completed in 1910. The heart of this cultural center was a revolutionary flexible hall, with a single stage made up of mobile elements, dedicated to the promotion of social harmony through the art of movement. The exterior was equally high-minded, but more traditional in its formal language, for which Tessenow had abstracted elements of *classicist* architecture.

Glowing colors and strong brush strokes were among the revolutionary innovations of this emotional, boundlessly subjective painting, as was its radical reduction of forms to the verge of *abstraction*. The exponents of the new painting were open to influences of all kinds. For them, art could be creating sketch-like nudes with a few brush strokes in an open-air setting, or connecting to the so-called "primitive art" of Africa or Oceania: themes that had not till now been considered valid parts of artistic endeavor. Another creative involvement of these Expressionist painters was with the energetic forms of *Gothic* architecture, with its pointed arches and immense spirituality.

Just before the First World War architects also began to be interested in Expressionism. Thus, concurrently, with the functional formal language of for example Walter Gropius, there emerged another lively branch of Modernism, the mobile language of Expressionism.

Expressionism was expressed in architecture largely through the materials of *brick* and glass. Glass and Crystal Expressionism was a utopian architectural project that was initiated in 1914 by Bruno Taut's glass pavilion at the Werkbund exhibition. Expressionist architecture in brick held sway right into the 1920s, especially in the Nordic countries, which could look back on a continuous tradition that dated back to Gothic times. The red-brown through to bluish-violet coloring of the bricks, in addition to their differing surface textures, ensured that the façades were full of variety in both color and form. The individualized production of bricks made them particularly suitable for the frequently small-scale and extremely detailed Expressionist decoration.

### The Amsterdam School – new directions in the Netherlands

Early on a group of architects who named themselves the "Amsterdam School" formed in the Netherlands, whose imaginative and expressive designs quickly became famous.

The prelude to Expressionist art in brick in the Netherlands was at the same time its climax. This was the Schiffahrtshaus (shipping building) erected between 1912 and 1916 by Johann Melchior van der Mey, together with Michel de Klerk and Pieter Kramer. This striking office building derived its name from the Amsterdam shipping companies who commissioned it as the base for their representatives. Following their demand for a "not too sober building in brick," van der Mey designed a façade decorated with a multitude of *ornaments*, sculptures and *friezes* made up of small parts. The imagery, drawn from the realms of shipping, sea, and trade with inexhaustible imaginative flair, exerts such a direct spell over the beholder that he almost forgets that the playful brick surface of the shipping building is simply the icing on top of the load-bearing concrete structure underneath. Van der May was reproached by rationalist critics with the fact that the façade was a surface, but it is perfectly in keeping with the picturesque charm of the building. Even this early example of Expressionist architecture shows how very much its exponents saw their buildings also as sculptures, and ornamented them accordingly, or else treated them as complete entities whose role was that of *architecture parlante*.

With his housing complex at the Spaarndammerplatsoen, which was built in several stages between 1913 and 1920, Michel de Klerk made his most important contribution to residential building in Amsterdam at that time. It was a step in the direction of housing reform, albeit of a bourgeois type, which was only practicable in small countries like Holland. The complex may not be as lavishly ornamented as the shipping building, but it is remarkable for its combination of the most varied expressive motifs and types of window, from the semicircular to the trapezoid, so that there is no monotony in the façades, and de Klerk's individual signature is clearly recognizable.

Together with his friend and colleague Pieter Kramer, de Klerk began putting up the workers' housing development De Dageraad in 1918, for the cooperatively organized workers' organization of the same name in the south of Amsterdam. Extensive town-planning initiatives devised by Hendrik Petrus Berlage took place in the same area. At De Dageraad – once again using *brick* – de Klerk developed an extraordinarily rich spectrum of the most varied types of building that even for his contemporaries evoked a wide range of associations. There are cubic shapes, wave motifs, cylinders, quotations from ship-building, roofs that extend far down the side of the buildings, and sculptures in brick. De Dageraad was a short-lived but innovative showcase of dynamic building ideas, which nonetheless fitted together as a whole.

De Dageraad was an artistic statement, but it was also a social and political one; it was a rejection of the barrack-like tenements built under *historicism*. The dominant theme in this housing development for working-class families was light and air in a richly varied environment. The cooperative nature of the body that commissioned it was a further element in the social commitment of De Dageraad.

Although residential building in the 1920s – as carried out by De Stijl (see page 31) in Holland and also in places in Germany where a great deal of it was going on (such as Frankfurt and Berlin, see page 37) – differed markedly from the expensive Expressionist architectural language of Klerk and Kramer, the estate which they built at De Dageraad was a decisive step forward in the reform of working-class housing.

The architectonic spectrum of the 1920s is very broad. However, if you mentally transport yourself to that era, it becomes clear that the first transposition of Frank Lloyd Wright's clear cubic shapes in reinforced concrete to Europe was the Villa in Huis ter Heide, designed by Robert van't Hoff when the members of the Amsterdam School were developing their multiform Expressionistic architectural language.

### From the Einstein Tower to the Chile Building – Expressionism in Germany

Expressionism in architecture began in Germany with Bruno Taut's Glass House at the Werkbund Exhibition in Cologne in 1914. Its major creations did not arise until after the First World War.

Building activity almost ceased in Germany between 1914 and 1918. It seemed that architectonic endeavor had exhausted itself in laying out war cemeteries, or in producing

**Johann Melchior van der Mey, Michel de Klerk, and Pieter Kramer,** *Schiffahrtshaus,* Amsterdam, 1912–16

Three leading members of the Amsterdam School built the headquarters for a group of shipping companies. They faced the *reinforced concrete structure* with a variety of materials including tiles, concrete, and terracotta. The richly exotic, sculptural forms seek to establish a symbolic link with shipping and the distant worlds it opens up. The building is thus an early example of the sculptural inventiveness of Expressionism, and an *architecture parlante.*

**Robert van't Hoff, *Villa,* Huis ter Heide, 1916**

Van't Hoff's villa imports characteristic features from the work of the American architect Frank Lloyd Wright, who had become known in Europe though the publication of the famous Wasmuth edition of his works (1910–11) and an exhibition in Berlin. These included the strip windows, the skylights, and in particular the emphasis on the horizontal through the clear cubic form and gray-painted horizontal blocks of the reinforced concrete structure. The British architect had studied in the USA, where he had got to know Wright personally and helped compile an inventory of his works. This enabled him to incorporate in the villa a union of French *Cubism* with Wright's theses, even before the Dutch De Stijl group was formed in 1917, around the three artists Piet Mondrian, Theo van Doesburg, and Gerrit Thomas Rietveld.

**Erich Mendelsohn, *Einstein Tower,* Potsdam, 1920–24, sketch**

As he was preparing his first important commission, Erich Mendelsohn created with a few strokes of the pen, a key work of architectural drawing. The completed building became *the* icon of Expressionism. Its purpose is not rationally expressed in its structure, but symbolically in its form. With its heavy *plinth* and its upwards-striving tower, the building, which housed a powerful telescope, an underground laboratory, a workroom at ground-level, and sleeping accommodation, mediated between heaven and earth. The sculpture in concave and convex planes was intended originally to be cast in *reinforced concrete*, which would have made the ultimate use of the plasticity of the medium. But because of technological difficulties, the walls above the plinth were constructed in the conventional way and plastered.

visionary and Expressionist drawings and watercolors. To promote the circulation and discussion of such ideas, Bruno Taut set up the forum "Gläserne Kette" (glass chain), which lasted from 1919 to 1921.

He expressed his utopian concepts of a new society and an ideal architecture for the cities within it, in his legendary essays *Alpine Architektur* (1918) and *Stadtkrone* (City crown) (1919). However, he did not carry out these visions during his tenure as city architect for Magdeburg (1921–23) nor when he went to practise as an architect in Berlin. Instead, he engaged in a pragmatic, socially committed program of *working-class housing*, becoming the leading architect in this area in the 1920s.

One of the few people who was able to put his vision into practice was Erich Mendelsohn. Mendelsohn translated the organic language of forms, which he too first envisioned in drawings, into a real building: the Einstein Tower in Potsdam. Built as an observatory and astrophysical institute for the study of Albert Einstein's theory of relativity, this striking tower brought Mendelsohn immediate fame.

The design he drew for the building in 1920 with only a few strokes of the pen, but which displayed all the concentrated dynamism characteristic of him, has become an icon of modern architectural drawing.

The thought-through plasticity of the Einstein Tower and the organic interweaving of its forms are strongly reminiscent of the buildings of the Amsterdam school of architects, who on the completion of the tower very logically invited him to Amsterdam to study what they themselves had built.

But, surprisingly enough, behind the formally innovative exterior of the Potsdam tower there are traditionally built walls. This came about chiefly because of the difficulty at that time of making appropriate formwork for the curved façade that Mendelsohn had designed to be made in concrete.

Very much more *stereometric* in design when compared with the Einstein Tower was the hat factory (its site now inevitably largely built over) that Mendelsohn designed for Steinberg Hermann and Co. in Luckenwalde (1921–23). It also represented a transition to the rationalist offices and department stores that Mendelsohn created after 1925. The Luckenwalde hat factory united functional design and technical innovation (like the arrangement for dispersing the poisonous fumes emanating from the dyeing installation) with what was, for the 1920s, an unusually expressive form for an industrial building

Shortly after the First World War another Berlin architect, Hans Poelzig, designed a huge theater, holding 5,000 spectators, in the center of Berlin for the renowned theater director Max Reinhardt in 1919. It was pulled down in 1986. From the interior of its crowning *dome* hung elongated shapes, making it look like a cave of stalactites. Not long afterwards (1920–22) Poelzig carried out a very similar design for a theater in Salzburg, cave-like and intricate as the icing on a cake.

German Expressionist architecture reached another peak in the brick buildings of the Hamburg architect Fritz Höger, who was for a time on the committee of the Deutscher Werkbund. One of his main works is the Chilehaus in Hamburg, which he built for a shipping company in the form of a giant ocean liner. One of the building's best-known features is its southeast corner which is sharply pointed like the bow of a ship.

The building was constructed in dark red *clinker*. Höger's inspiration for the building was not only marine architecture but the *Gothic* cathedrals constructed in brick that are widespread in the northern part of Germany. These borrowings are also evident in the arcades within the building, some of which also narrow toward the end, and the accent on the vertical in the whole edifice, chiefly achieved by the architect's use of *external piers* to articulate the façade. In order to ventilate the gigantic complex adequately, and to supply sufficient light for all the rooms, Höger built it around three big inner courtyards.

The Chilehaus and the Amsterdam Schiff-fahrtshaus built ten years earlier are, for all their many differences, linked as buildings in the Expressionist style, by their function and their use of brick, and also in their manifold small-scale ornamentation.

## CUBISM

### Architectonic independence in Prague
In Prague around 1911 there was a group of intellectuals whose work was influenced by

the clear *stereometric* architecture of Otto Wagner, who was a representative of the Vienna Jugendstil. The other important model and influence for them was the work of Robert Delaunay, Georges Braque, and Pablo Picasso, with its radically deconstructed and then reassembled forms.

While he was in Paris, Delaunay had been through a stylistic phase in which the object represented was broken down into basic geometric forms – the cube, ball, and circle. Delaunay's Cubist pictures, such as that of the Eiffel Tower or the giant composition City of Paris, were dramatic in effect, full of the dynamism of the big city, and the Prague Cubist architects took them as the inspiration for the façades

**Fritz Höger, *Chilehaus*, Hamburg, 1921–24**

This office building was designed by Fritz Höger for a shipping company. Inside and out it evokes a giant liner. There are lines of identical office cells like cabins. The set-back strips and horizontal railings emphasize the prow-like point of the triangular building. The dark red clinker on the façade and the arching ribs within are also reminiscent of the tradition of north German Gothic construction in brick.

**Josef Gočár, *"The Black Madonna"***
**Department Store,** Prague 1911–12

Josef Gočár was one of the leading representatives of Cubism in architecture, and kept up a lively intellectual exchange with the writers and artists of his time. He originally designed the department store in the modern classicist mode. But after fundamental revision, the *reinforced concrete skeleton* acquired its distinctive cubic elements, in particular the front entrance, the dormer windows and the *capitals* on the columns of the façade. This design lays particular emphasis on the effect created by shadow, which stresses the three-dimensional quality of the building. The architect's design continues in the interior, including a Cubist café on the top floor, which, however, was quickly disfigured by alterations. To this day the harmonious insertion of this building – a provocative one for its day – in its historic neighborhood is exemplary. The mansard roof can be seen as a concession to the heritage conservation lobby.

**Josef Chochol, *Hodek Apartment***
**Block,** Prague, 1913–14

The architecture of Josef Chochol includes some of the most thorough-going translations of Cubist theories of surface and space. One typical example is the shape he gives to the windows of the ground floor of the Hodek building, which itself stands out in a point on a steeply sloping site. The building, housing several families, is totally in the spirit of the day, down to the last detail. Even the corner rooms are polygonal.

of their houses, which they decorated with rows of cubic or prismatic shapes. As with the contemporary *Expressionist* movement, the whole building was treated in sculptural terms, so that it conveyed something of the impression of being a sculpture capable of being lived in.

The Prague architects could also cite the example of late *Gothic* architecture, with its almost abstract vaulting, of which Prague has, even today, a great deal. For a long time the Cubist architecture of Prague was wrongly interpreted as a purely regional manifestation, but now it has been re-evaluated as a related but independent alternative to northern European Expressionism.

Josef Gočár's department store, *The Black Madonna*, which is one of the most important works of Prague Cubism, clearly demonstrates the differences between Expressionist and Cubist architecture. Instead of the intricate, figurative ornamentation that characterizes the buildings of the *Amsterdam School*, Gočár designed a lucid, clearly structured building. The crystalline shapes that break up the façade create a fascinating play of light and shade, giving the building a particular, almost living, charm.

A similar architectural language is employed in the five-story Hodek apartment block that was designed by Josef Chochol.

In spite of being modeled in cubes and prisms, the façade is actually subdivided according to a strict grid of both vertical and horizontal elements. The ground floor in particular is given a specific emphasis with its unusually shaped six-cornered windows. The diamond shapes above the windows are echoed in the jagged relief of the jutting-out cornice that tops the façade, thus giving the building, in spite of its dynamic feel, a harmonious conclusion.

## FUTURISM

### Italy breaks out into modernity

The problem of human perception and appropriation of the world was one of the central themes of art at the beginning of the century. Whereas the approach of the *Expressionists* would be to conjure up an extremely subjective view of the world on their canvases, the *Cubists* favored the dissection of everyday objects, such as a chair or a guitar, into their basic geometric structures. They would then put them back together in a way that was both surprising and disorienting for the viewer. The object that had originally seemed familiar to the eye became something else. At the same time the viewer was challenged into a new, critical perception of the original object – the real chair or the real guitar. The result of this was in any case a sharpened perception of reality.

The Italian Futurists' experimentation took a different turn from that of the Cubists: dissecting the phases of the movement and reassembling them on a single plane.

The artistic concept of Futurism, which was first developed in painting, poetry, and sculpture before it moved on to architecture, was to make visible phases of movement and the power of speed derived from them, a dynamism that they recognized as a defining characteristic of the future. Although the Italian Futurists were denied the realization of their architectonic and town-planning designs, their drawings, expressive of both a denial of the past and a belief in progress, place their visions among the important trends of modern art in the 20th century.

A leading exponent of Futurism was Antonio Sant'Elia, who, in his manifesto of July 1914 on futurist architecture, took a clear stand against all "solemn, theatrical, and decorative building." Instead, he wanted to "invent and build the futurist city. It must be like a great resounding shipyard and be swift, mobile, and dynamic in every part; the futurist house must be like a giant machine." Sant'Elia's sketches of a "Città Nuova," with its intersecting traffic planes for cars, railways, and aircraft, its electricity works and its glassy exterior lifts on residential buildings, reflect his conception of a really modern technological world. However, they remained only a vision. He published his revolutionary visions of architecture in Milan in 1914 ("Architecture means the ability to bring man and his environment freely and boldly into harmony with each other"). Tragically, two years later he was killed in the First World War, without having had the chance to realize them.

However, it was largely his futuristic architectural visions of stepped skyscrapers and monumental, emphatically vertical electricity works, which started the move away from 19th-century *historicism* and toward rationalist architecture in Italy. This made it possible after the war to link with contemporary movements and especially with the Russian avant-garde.

**Antonio Sant'Elia,** *Electricity Works,*
Architectural Vision 1914, Consuelo
Accetti collection, Milan

The technology and the entirely new potential of electricity was a leitmotif of the Futurists and their innovatory thinker Sant'Elia. They transposed the concentrated energy and dynamism of the electric current into their sketches for architecture imbued with the spirit of technology and into urban visions that broke radically with traditional forms and conceptions of the city. This spirit is precisely conveyed by this drawing by Sant'Elia in which the pressure lines hurtle rather than fall, the chimneys rear up from a low-angle perspective, and the electric cables flow powerfully out of the picture: a new aesthetic for modern architecture takes shape from industrial forms.

Modernity establishes
itself

# The International
# Style

1920–1930

## ARCHITECTURE AFTER
## THE WAR

### The war destroys the old world

Long before the First World War, movements
for political and cultural reform had gathered
strength in Europe and the United States. New
directions in art such as *Art Nouveau* and,
shortly afterwards, *Expressionism*, *Futurism*,
and *Cubism* broke with traditional art and
searched for new concepts and forms of
artistic expression in a world that was
progressing at lightening speed and was
marked by continuous technical innovation.
But it was only following the First World War
that the foundations of the traditional world
order finally crumbled. The centuries-old
hegemony of Europe was destabilized. Not
only did the Austro-Hungarian state with its
multiple races disappear from the map of
Europe, but the monarchies of Russia and
Germany were swept away by revolutions, and
while the United States stepped on to the
world stage for the first time, the British Empire,
which had previously spanned the world,
slowly began to break up.

The First World War was the defining
experience of a whole era. Modern weapons,
such as tanks and aircraft, had been brought
to a high degree of technical perfection and
were employed for the first time. Soldiers
no longer faced their opponents face to face,
but ' as the anonymous "enemy", hidden
behind gas masks and in the trenches. Already
existing social and economic problems
increased, and the economic uncertainty

of the postwar era brought to the fore the
demand for a solution to the misery of hunger,
unemployment, and homelessness.

### Programmes for dealing with social need

The generalized deprivation that had struck
whole areas of the population was a
challenge to artists and writers, as well as to
politicians. At this time, artistic and political
programs went hand in hand, from Moscow
to Amsterdam, with aims of changing the face
of the world and the ways of being that it
offered, both in society as well as in art. The
increasing political commitment of art
expressed itself in themes such as social
criticism – as seen in George Grosz's biting
pictures – or in fiery outcries against the
inhumanity of war as Henri Barbusse put
forward in his novel *Le Feu.*

In architecture too, there was a
thoroughgoing drive to develop functional
new ways of building and to use new building
materials: glass, concrete, and steel. The new,
more rational and economical building
methods were not just an expression of the
spirit of the times, with its repudiation of
*historicist* buildings covered in outdated
ornamentation. They also had a definite social
component, especially when applied to the
*housing developments* that were carried out
with a great deal of urgency to address the
problem of homelessness.

The period 1900–20 was a determining
one for the direction of modern art and
architecture. But from 1920 to 1930, following
the disaster of the First World War, an

1921: Washington agreement on
the banning of the use of poison
gas as an element of international
law. Discovery of insulin as a
treatment for diabetes. Arturo
Toscanini becomes director of the
Scala, Milan. Nobel Prize for Physics
awarded to Albert Einstein for the
discovery of the photon and his work
in theoretical physics. Charlie
Chaplin's film *The Kid* premiered in
America. Women start wearing their
hair bobbed.

1922: Following a fascist coup in
Italy, Mussolini is named prime
minister by the king. James Joyce
completes his novel *Ulysses.*

1923: Kemal Atatürk becomes
president of Turkey. Hitler putsch in
Munich.

1924: Death of Lenin. Submission of
the Dawes plan for the settlement of
German reparations. Première of
Gershwin's *Rhapsody in Blue.*

1925: Geneva Convention banning
chemical and bacterial warfare. The
"king of jazz," Louis Armstrong, sets
up his Combo Hot Five.

1926: Founding of the British
Commonwealth of Nations. First
performances of Fritz Lang's
*Metropolis* and Sergei Eisenstein's
*Battleship Potemkin.* First successful
television transmission in London.
Walt Disney's *Mickey Mouse*
cartoons first screened.

1927: After a murder trial in
Massachusetts (USA) arousing
international controversy, Sacco and
Vanzetti are executed. Charles
Lindbergh flies non-stop across the

Atlantic. Sven Hedin begins his
expedition into the interior of Asia.
Martin Heidegger's *Being and Time*
is published, initiating a secular
philosophy, existentialism. Proust
publishes the seventh and last
volume of his *Remembrance of
Things Past.* Josephine Baker, the
American-born French dancer and
singer, takes Paris by storm.

1928: Briand-Kellogg pact outlaws
war as a means of resolving
international differences. Chiang
Kai-shek unites China. Penicillin
discovered by an English
bacteriologist, Alexander Fleming.

1929: The Wall Street crash
precipitates a world economic crisis.

George Grosz, *The Pillars of
Society,* 1926

**Theo van Doesburg, Cornelius van Eesteren, *Study for an apartment block*, 1923**

The world of 19th-century art was more or less one where each object and phenomenon had individual identity. But however multiform the world may be, there is an abstract geometrical order underlying it. A right-angled grid dominates space. Every form can be represented by small right-angles, every shade of color through a combination of the primary colors: red, yellow, blue. This was the semi-philosophical analysis of the world that united the De Stijl movement, which began in 1917 and was composed of Dutch painters, architects, and craft-workers. The works of art that they produced were ultimately based upon combinations of single-color surfaces. It was the spokesman of the De Stijl group, the painter and theoretician Theo van Doesburg, who took the step from surface to space. His sketch for an apartment block, which reduces it to a complex of closed walls, penetrating each other at right-angles, does not form a homogenous building, but only parts of an endless space. Everything is open. There are no longer rooms, and the interior and the exterior are only marginally demarcated. Without the force of gravity the upstairs and the downstairs would not be clearly differentiated. The material of the walls remains unnaturally vague. It is a triumph of abstract space over the physical that up till that time had dominated architecture.

undreamed-of period of revolt and euphoria broke out. Now at last a new, more relevant, architecture, which was backed by social purpose, joined the cityscapes.

## DE STIJL

### Geometry and abstraction in the Netherlands

As early as the Expressionist architecture of the *Amsterdam School* (see pages 24–25), Dutch architects had been ahead of the field in architecture and, since the country had not become embroiled in the conflicts of the First World War, other avant-garde tendencies could develop there at a particularly early period compared with the rest of Europe.

Some architects thought that the intricate *ornamentation* and the use of *brick* in Expressionist architecture was too individualistic and saw them as a sign of conservatism. Influenced by the buildings of Frank Lloyd Wright, which had appeared in the Wasmuth editions of 1910 and 1911, and by the French *Cubists*, they had a vision of a different sort of architecture, one structured in plain cubes with interpenetrating planes such as was exemplified in Walter Gropius's Fagus factory.

The work of the Dutch painter Piet Mondrian was especially meaningful for the development of these architects. Mondrian's early work was composed of largely conventional neo-impressionist pictures, but as early as 1907 he began making the objects he was depicting ever more abstract, and gradually submitted them to a cubic structuring of forms. At the end of this development – around 1914 – he produced those famous, object-less pictures, in which the pictorial space was made into a harmonious structure by a framework of black lines. But this grid enclosed a number of squares and rectangles that were either left white, or were colored in. The colors he used were dominated by flatly painted primary colors – red, blue, or yellow – without any shaping or shadow. Mondrian's artistic concept consisted in the abnegation of any desire to depict the world of objects, but rather to explain their basic structures in a clear geometric system.

## Gerrit Thomas Rietveld, *Schröder House,* Utrecht, 1924

The cabinet maker Gerrit Thomas Rietveld, creator of the red and blue chair, was given one of the few chances granted the De Stijl group to translate their ideas into buildings. Following the principle whereby In 1917 he deconstructed the armchair into boards and squared pieces of wood, then put it together again, he and Truus Schröder, a woman architect specializing in interiors, deconstructed the cubic form of a house. The planar walls are arranged as a composition of independent rectangles, which project beyond the points at which they join. The flat roof and the balustrade of the balcony seem to be floating on air. The impression is heightened by the large panes of glass at the corners of the building. But the real revolution was the replacement of solidly divided rooms by a freely transformable ground plan. The walls throughout the first floor could all be folded up or pushed round, so that the inhabitants could vary it like children's building blocks, including having an uninterrupted open space.

The ideas that Mondrian had developed in abstract painting were now taken up by the architects Theo van Doesburg and Gerrit Thomas Rietveld, who was also a cabinet-maker, in three-dimensional form. In 1917, with some other artists, including the architects Jacobus Johannes Pieter Oud and Jan Wils, they formed the De Stijl group, whose organ was the periodical of the same name, which appeared up till 1932.

The name means simply "The Style," which expresses how the group saw themselves: in contrast to the historical *styles* of *Classicism* or the *Baroque*, the artists of De Stijl saw their language of forms – abstract, unadorned, constructivist – as Style itself.

In a manifesto that appeared in 1918 in the second issue of *De Stijl*, the intellectual leader of the group, Theo van Doesburg, gave a broad outline of their complex theoretical goal. The dominance of the individual, which had reigned in the art of the 19th century, should be relinquished in favor of an equilibrium with the universal. The condition for the realization of De Stijl's new world, which they called "consciousness of the times," was the removal of all the fetters of tradition.

The vision that van Doesburg and De Stijl conjured up for artists was of a renunciation of all traditional ornamental decoration as it had been cultivated by *historicism* or even *Expressionism*. Instead, buildings should be as radically simplified as Mondrian's pictures.

Starting out from the principle of the right angle, interpenetrating cubic volumes would create a complex, quasi-sculptural experience of space. The color scheme of the buildings, which were indeed treated very like sculptures, was bright, but reduced to primary colors only. The result of this artistic concept, which was driven primarily by van Doesburg, was the neo-plastic art of De Stijl.

The influence of the De Stijl group, which was of a constantly changing composition throughout its existence, was by no means confined to Holland. In particular van Doesburg had a direct influence on the Bauhaus, founded by Walter Gropius after the First World War. Gropius invited him there as a guest in 1921.

The first famous embodiment of the ideas of De Stijl was the red and blue chair made by Gerrit Thomas Rietveld. Once again taking inspiration from Mondrian's pictures, in 1917 Rietveld designed a framework of black pieces of squared timber, which were joined to each other in strict right-angles.

Into the load-bearing frame of wood thus created, brightly colored sheets of wood were inserted to make the seat and the backrest, which were both given a slope by placing the squared timber at different heights.

As van Doesburg's architectonic sketches of this period remained unrealized, it once more fell to Rietveld to give the first practical expression to the aesthetic conceptions of De Stijl, this time in the field of architecture.

# THE BAUHAUS

Even today the Bauhaus is synonymous with the radical modernization of art. There was no area of life that Bauhaus art was not out to reform or redesign. Far from being confined to fine art and architecture, its principles extended to dance, theater, photography, and design. Even toys (the *sailing boat*) were designed in its workshops. In having such a comprehensive brief, the Bauhaus resembled its predecessors, the English *Arts and Crafts movement* and the *Deutscher Werkbund*. Even today many of its products feature among the classics of design in their uncompromising modernity, such as Marcel Breuer's tubular steel chair or the Bauhaus table lamp.

In March 1919, when Walter Gropius took over the leadership of the Weimar Art School founded by Henry van de Velde, and united it with the former Art and Craft School to form the "staatlicher Bauhaus Weimar," his aim was to create a new unity between art and craft. The purpose itself points to the sociopolitical meaning acquired by the Bauhaus in postwar Germany. Gropius wanted to join all the creative forces into a unified "house of building", in which building not only implied architecture but a lot

*A classic of Bauhaus design: Marianne Brandt's teapot with internal strainer (1924)*

more besides. Gropius was entirely in tune with his time when following the catastrophe of the war and the collapse of the old order to erect a new society, he aimed to use his art to build a new mankind.

In order to achieve these elevated, socially utopian aims, all the masters at the Bauhaus followed a preordained sequence of courses with their students. A preliminary course introduced the students to working with the most various materials: wood, metal, textiles, glass, coloring materials, clay, and stone. The preliminary course was run by Johannes Itten in the early years in Weimar. It was largely due to Itten that the Bauhaus had at first a strongly Expressionist direction, and was formally modeled on the organization of the medieval guilds.

In mid-1921 Theo van Doesburg, the first and leading thinker of the Dutch De Stijl movement, came to Weimar. Under his influence the Bauhaus underwent a radical change to a technical, constructionist concept of art, which conditioned the second stage of its development. Marcel Breuer was stimulated by the red and blue chair created by the De Stijl artist Gerrit Thomas Rietveld to develop his tubular steel chairs.

But of all the masters at the Bauhaus, the new trend in art education is most clearly associated with the Hungarian László Moholy-Nagy, who

took over the introductory course from Itten. Dressed in a workman's boiler suit, he left no doubt that modern artistic production must be carried out from a technical point of view suited to the time. How broad the artistic spectrum of the Bauhaus remained, even under the influence of Moholy-Nagy, can be seen from the activity there of such diverse artistic personalities as the painters Oskar Schlemmer, Wassily Kandinsky, and Paul Klee.

While the Bauhaus was becoming the leading cultural force in the German – indeed the European – avant-garde, it was also coming under increasing political pressure. The progressive art school, which wore its political commitment on its sleeve, was a thorn in the flesh of the conservative forces that were once again gathering strength. In 1925 the Weimar Bauhaus had to close. A new beginning was undertaken in Dessau.

In Walter Gropius's Bauhaus building, the art school at last had an architectonic frame to match its inner concept. The architecture clearly expressed the various functions of individual parts of the building. So the workshop area was dominated by an uninterrupted wall of glass, providing the optimal amount of light. The façade of the students' living quarters on the other hand was characterized by an individual balcony for each room. It went without saying that Gropius's new building should have a flat roof, which in the 1920s was synonymous with modern architecture.

In 1928 Walter Gropius resigned as director of the Bauhaus. His successor was a Swiss, Hannes Meyer, who, like Gropius, was an architect. Under Meyer the social orientation of the Bauhaus became even more pronounced than under Gropius. Constructivism with an aesthetic bias was replaced by a style of artistic production that proclaimed itself to be strictly scientific. The components of this were an increasing standardization in the production of art-objects, and a growing collectivization of the production process that took the place of individual craftsmanship. The conscious politicization of the Bauhaus mobilized the right-wing press, which led in turn to the dismissal of Hannes Meyer by the mayor of Dessau.

It then became the task of Meyer's successor, the established architect Ludwig Mies van der Rohe, appointed in 1930, to steer the school into quieter waters. Political agitation had never been Mies's style, but even his move to concentrate on craft training could not prevent the Dessau Bauhaus from being closed down at the instigation of the Nazis. Mies's subsequent attempt to re-establish the Bauhaus in Berlin also failed.

*Demonstrating the Expressionist roots of the Bauhaus: Lyonel Feininger's woodcut for the title page of the 1919 Bauhaus manifesto Cathedral*

*Architecture that corresponds to content: the Bauhaus building erected by Walter Gropius at its new site in Dessau in 1926*

**Vladimir Tatlin, *Sketch for the Monument to the Third International,* 1919**

The victory of the Bolshevik revolution and belief in technical progress gave wings to the dreams of the Russian avant-garde. One of their boldest designs was by the constructivist Vladimir Tatlin. The office and conference building of the communist world organization the Third International depicted in his sketch was not only dynamic in its aesthetic effect, but actually moved. A steel spiral 980 feet (300 meters) high was to enclose three transparent volumes: a square assembly hall, a pyramidal administration area, and a cylindrical press office.

**El Lissitzky, *Sketch for Cloud Props at the Nikitskiya Gate in Moscow,* 1923–26**

The discussions about town planning that took place in the Soviet Union in the 1920s raised the need for designs for the new towns demanded by the stepped-up industrialization of the first Five-Year Plan. El Lissitzky's plan for a "horizontal skyscraper" for Moscow, which never got beyond the design stage, expressing both belief in progress and fascination with technology, is an attempt to transpose his Proun compositions into architecture.

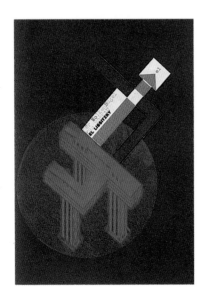

A traditional 19th-century house had to satisfy certain conceptions of grandeur and monumentality in the minds of its inhabitants. But it was quite other aspects that Rietveld was interested in expressing in the Schröder house. How new and unusual it was, with its flat *roof* instead of the usual pitched or hipped roof, can be appreciated by comparing it with the rest of the conventional terrace of which it was to be the end house.

Among the radical innovations in the Schröder house, besides the startling façade with its flat white plaster and the walls that intersected and reached out into space, were the wide expanses of window-glass. The inside, too, was full of revolutionary design solutions. On the first floor it was possible to remove the walls that divided the rooms, producing a completely open space, very different from the immutable sequence of rooms imposed by solid walls.

The Schröder house was a fundamental challenge to conventional house-building. Its variable layout, its inconspicuous flat roof, and the almost industrial sobriety of its façades set an entirely new standard, which were from then on regarded as milestones of modern architecture.

## CONSTRUCTIVISM

### Revolution and avant-garde in the Soviet Union

While the Bauhaus in Germany and the De Stijl movement in the Netherlands were centers of progressive activity, it was above all the avant-garde of the young Soviet Union that gave artistic and architectural expression to the revolutionary political changes that occurred after 1917.

Russian art in the 19th century had been narrowly dependent on developments in western Europe. It was only able to free itself gradually from this dependence toward the end of the century by going back to themes and forms derived from folklore and traditional Russian models from the Middle Ages. But by the beginning of the First World War, art in Russia had not only connected with the developments in avant-garde art in western Europe, it was even taking a leading role in them.

Kasimir Malevich's 1918 painting *White square on a white ground* reduced painting

absolutely as far as possible, to point zero, creating thereby an icon of modern art. Malevich advocated a "pure abstraction" in which feeling must have the prime role. Accordingly he named his work Suprematism (from the Latin *supremus* – "the highest"). This style of painting, which reduces art even more than does Cubism to basic geometric structure, influenced the De Stijl group and the Bauhaus. In Russia it was El Lissitzky who developed his own brand of the abstraction prescribed in the works of Malevich. With Vladimir Tatlin, El Lissitzky became the leading representative of a current in art that, like De Stijl, advocated a synthesis of painting and architecture.

In 1920 Lissitzky developed his famous "Proun" (a shortening of Pro UNOWIS, from the Russian words meaning "project for the creation of new forms in art"), abstract compositions made up of various geometrical elements that could be realized in both two and three dimensions, clearly showing the influence of Malevich's supremacist painting. Lissitzky saw his Proun as a contribution to the continuous search for new forms in art. His definition was therefore deliberately vague, so that it could be adapted to the constantly changing conditions of artistic production.

The concept was by no means confined to two-dimensional paintings; he also applied it to interior design and to architectonic sketches. It was Lissitzky's view, derived from painting and at first expressed only in painting, that architecture should be pared down to only its most necessary functional elements, so that it was dominated by construction. This view he shared with his contemporary Malevich.

Like the Italian Futurists of the prewar period (see page 29), the members of this Russian art movement were characterized by a belief in progress and fascination with technology. This new, avant-garde concept of art expressed the view that the young Soviet Union had of itself after the communist revolution of 1917, an ideology that had broken with everything outdated and belonging to the past. Accordingly the Soviet state used Constructivism for its own propagandist purposes for a few years, up to the consolidation of Stalin's power.

The most important architectonic project of these years was "Cloud Props", which El

Lissitzky, who had joined the De Stijl group in Amsterdam in 1922, designed with Mart Stam, who was Dutch. This sketch for a giant office complex, which was never built, presents a technicist-looking building, resting horizontally on very few supports and apparently floating almost weightlessly in space.

That another famous constructivist project, Vladimir Tatlin's Monument to the Third International, also proceeded no further than the design stage, is very understandable in the light of the politically still confused and above all economically strained situation in the post-revolutionary Soviet Union. In a similar way to Lissitzky, Tatlin was concerned not only with architecture but with sculptural form, and consequently his design for the Moscow monument is a synthesis of both architecture and sculpture.

The building was to consist of a structure of metal girders standing at an angle of nearly 45 degrees. It was intended to bore upwards into the heavens in a tapering spiral 980 feet (300 meters) wide at the base and higher than the Eiffel Tower, thereby emulating the old human dream of the tower of Babel. Three transparent volumes were to be suspended within the structure: a cylinder, a pyramid, and a smaller cylinder (with an extra hemisphere attached). Tatlin intended these edifices to be used by various state organizations.

The cosmic dimension to this monument only becomes apparent when you take into account the fact that the individual edifices were all intended to rotate on their axes in different rhythms: individually, once a year, once a month, and once a day. The planned monument thus united constructive as well as dynamic aspects in an entirely original way. Through the work of the Soviet institutions in the various edifices within the structure, and because of its transparent sculptural form, the Monument to the Third International would have been much more than a revolutionary constructivist building, in essence it would have represented the revolution and consequently the new order established within the Soviet Union itself. But whereas the model Tatlin had put together for the monument had been constructed out of old cigar boxes and tin cans, the actual realization of the gigantic building would, like that of Lissitzky's Cloud Props skyscraper, have

swiftly turned out to be beyond both the technical and financial capacity of its time.

Just as revolutionary as Lissitzky's and Tatlin's work was the Wesnin brothers' plan for a building for the newspaper *Pravda* in Leningrad (St. Petersburg). It was their intention to build a skyscraper out of basic cubic blocks, on a site just 20 feet (6 meters) square. The plan included a sign saying *Pravda* (as it appeared on the newspaper), in huge letters. Glass lift-shafts added an additional futuristic note to the plan.

A notable aspect of the utopian and revolutionary works of Soviet Constructivism was that, although they were embodied in a wide and ambitious program and were extensively and vigorously disputed among Russian intellectuals, only a very few of them were ever realized.

One of those that was realized was the Rusakov workers' club in Moscow, built of concrete, which was designed by Konstantin Melnikov. The heart of the building is an assembly hall for 1,400 people. The cubic blocks housing the seating stick out sharply between the vertical strips of windows in the façade, giving the building a dramatic as well as a dynamic feel.

However, Constructivism, in a similar way to modern art in general, was allowed only a relatively short flowering. As early as 1931, when a competition was held for a "Palace of the Soviets" in Moscow, all the Modernist submissions, including those of Le Corbusier and Walter Gropius, were rejected in favor of a

**Konstantin Stepanovitsch Melnikov, *Rosakow Workers' Club,* Moscow, 1928**

Most of the dreams of the Russian avant-garde never got beyond the drawing-board. One of the few buildings to be completed was the Rusakow workers' club. Appropriately for a building that was to serve as a center of cultural education for the proletariat, Konstantin Melnikov gave it a semi-industrial appearance. Like Melnikov's Soviet Pavilion for the Exposition des Arts Décoratifs in Paris in 1925, the reinforced concrete building was dominated by intersecting irregularly shaped geometrical volumes and sharp diagonals. Hidden within the cubic shapes that project far out from the façade of the Moscow building is seating for an audience of 1,400.

**Giuseppe Terragni,** *Casa del Fascio,*
Como, 1932–36

In Italy, which was less developed than
Germany, it was easier for the fascists to
see themselves as the party of
modernization, and Rationalism was
sanctioned as the official architecture of
the state. The purest example is the Casa
del Fascio, erected in Como by Giuseppe
Terragni. In accordance with the classical
theory of proportion, Terragni designed
the headquarters of the local fascist party
as a square whose elevation, 54 feet (16.5
meters), was exactly half the length of
each side of the plan. The visibility of the
structural grid of *columns* and beams on
the entrance side was a modern
interpretation of the façade of the
Colosseum and gave the community
building a symbolic transparency. The
alternation of dazzling white marble and
hollow spaces unfolds a dramatic play of
light and shade. The Casa del Fascio
demonstrates that modern and classical
architecture in Italy, unlike many other
European countries, were not inimical
opposites.

neo-classical design corresponding to what
was to become the favored Stalinist form of
state architecture.

## RATIONALISM VERSUS NEOCLASSICISM

### Giuseppe Terragni and Italian Rationalism

As in many European states, the political
situation after the First World War in the
kingdom of Italy was far from stable. Society
was polarized at the extremes of the political
spectrum. There was a strong communist
party, and there was also a fascist party
which was rapidly gaining influence. Benito
Mussolini's march on Rome in 1922
established the first fascist regime in Europe.
Aside from the futurist projects of the prewar
period, which never got past the drawing-
board, Italy had no tradition of modern
architecture worth the name. Whereas in
Germany between 1918 and 1933 the
Neues Bauen movement was both reforming
and predominantly socialist in aim, new
building in Italy was by no means anxious
to outlaw traditional architecture. The cause
for this may have been that Modernism
was only able to become established in
Italy under the fascist system. This also
explains the circumstance that, unlike in
Germany where after the Nazi seizure of
power in 1933 the modern buildings of
the Weimar Republic and their architects
were widely despised, in fascist Italy modern
architecture was part of the innovatory

character of the system, and was even
attributed a certain role in the upholding of
the state.

In general terms, fascist Italy between 1920
and 1940 can be said to have had two
competing architectonic currents, both of
which based themselves in different ways
upon the heritage of classical Rome. Both
currents can be personified in their main
protagonists: on the one side there was
the *neoclassicist* Marcello Piacentini, and
on the other Giuseppe Terragni. The latter
joined up with six other architects from Milan,
who gave themselves the name "Gruppo 7"
and called for a radical modern architecture.
In so doing, Terragni saw no contradiction
between maintaining the traditional Italian
heritage of building that had been in
existence since antiquity, and developing a
new architecture. In their *Manifesto of Italian
Rationalism* which the group published in
1926–27, they demanded an architecture
based strictly upon the laws of logic and
proportion (otherwise named "ratio," which
caused the movement to be called
"Rationalism"). Influenced by the machine
aesthetic of the Futurists and the revolutionary buildings of Le Corbusier, Rationalism
established itself chiefly in the north of
Italy with its flourishing commercial and
industrial centers in Milan and Turin, where
the increasingly important car industry
was based.

The clearest expression of Rationalism's
formal and aesthetic priorities is to be found in
the Novocomum building, a block of rented
apartments in Como built in 1928, and in the
famous Casa del Fascio, the local office of the
fascist party in Como, which like the
Novocomum was built by Giuseppe Terragni.

The buildings incorporated an equal
balance between the aesthetic demands of
modernity and the classical theory that had
dominated the architecture of the Italian
peninsula since the days of the Roman
Empire. Terragni's grid of *columns* on the
entrance side of the Casa del Fascio is an
updating of the classical *portico.* His ground
plan, 110 square feet (33 meters), with an
elevation of 55 feet (16.5 meters), exactly half,
relates to the idea of *proportion*, already held
to be decisive by Vitruvius, whose influential
theories on building date back to Roman days.
At the same time the Casa del Fascio took up

the theme of transparency, an important aspect of the party's public image, by a symbolically open-looking façade.

Although Terragni's Italian Rationalism continued on into the 80s (see pages 94 ff.), it gradually lost influence after 1935. It was pushed aside by the classicist monumentalism of Piacentini. If Terragni's work presented a balanced synthesis of classical and modern, which came out in the fine detail and aesthetic sensitivity of his buildings, no such sensitivity is present in the stiff classicism of Piacentini, which became the preferred state architecture of Italy.

# NEW BUILDING IN GERMANY

### Housing developments in Berlin and Frankfurt

One of the most pressing problems facing the democratic Weimar Republic after 1918 was to find a solution to the housing shortage, which was one of the main causes of social distress. Even before the war there had been some initial moves to change the way in which new housing was constructed, especially in the largest German city, Berlin. The aim had been to replace the speculatively built working-class tenement blocks, with their warrens of dark, damp courtyards, with dwellings offering better conditions and an improved style of life. Instead of the large, dark apartments without adequate sanitary facilities, which were shared by several different groups of tenants, smaller units were to be constructed with increased light and ventilation.

But it was only from 1924 that the economic situation in Germany, which had been severely hit by the payment of reparations to the victorious Allies, began to pick up. This consolidation provided the conditions for a scheme conducted by the city architect for Berlin, Martin Wagner, which was unique in Europe: a *popular housing program*, providing tens of thousands of new homes in Berlin, and ending only with the world economic crisis of 1930.

Hans Scharoun, Walter Gropius, Ludwig Mies van der Rohe, and Bruno Taut were among the most important architects of these Berlin housing schemes. They found ways to unite the social purpose inherent in the often cooperatively built apartment blocks, with a language of forms that was as functional as it was modern. A flat *roof* and white or brilliantly-colored façades characterize their buildings, as do quotations (such as round windows) from naval architecture, which Hans Scharoun in particular uses very frequently, following the lead given by Le Corbusier. In order to meet the challenge of producing serviceable buildings at low cost, thereby ensuring a low rent, the architects had to make them as standardized as possible and needed to use the most economical building materials.

These housing projects of the 1920s did not produce a multitude of single houses, like the Garden City movements at the turn of the century in England and Germany (see pages 40–41). They produced small, complete districts, laid out in an unstructured way with a great variety of apartment blocks. The social impetus that underlay these housing projects was notably expressed in the inclusion of communal facilities such as laundry rooms and roof-terraces. This, like the green environment in which the buildings were placed, was intended to promote healthy living and a sound social relationship among the inhabitants.

Apart from Berlin, the other big German city to face up to the general lack of housing by launching a systematic housing development scheme was Frankfurt, under the supervision of the city architect Ernst May. By building

**Hans Scharoun,** residential block, *Siemensstadt Estate,* Berlin, 1931

The revolutionary upheavals following the First World War engendered strenuous efforts, in Germany as elsewhere, to solve the housing crisis. Hans Scharoun's residential blocks on the Siemensstadt estate, constructed as part of the state housing development scheme, are a prime example of the Modernist promise of a living space full of light and air for the working masses. Scharoun was one of the few architects of the modern movement to inhabit one of his superbly crafted apartments himself.

**Margarete Schütte-Lihotzky, *The Frankfurt Kitchen,* 1928**

Margarete Schütte-Lihotzky designed the prototype of all the fitted kitchens produced in the decades that followed. The elements are positioned to suit kitchen routines, and are fitted into the smallest possible space. A step that was intended to make light of housework also transformed the kitchen from a family living area into a purely functional space – all with the purpose, however, of giving the housewife more leisure or enabling her to go out to work.

with industrially prefabricated parts, the cost of the scheme – and thus the level of rents – could be kept down. The apartments were relatively small, but they had the benefit of the space-saving "Frankfurt kitchen" designed by a female architect, Margarete Schütte-Lihotzky, which created a supremely rational work space making the cumbersome kitchen dresser a thing of the past. Schütte-Lihotzky's creation, which was the forerunner of all modern fitted kitchens, was the first to be mass-produced and ready-made, and until 1930 was fitted into 10,000 apartments in the Frankfurt housing schemes. Into a space of just 21 square feet (6.5 meters) the architect fitted everything necessary for a fully working kitchen, from the sink to the cooker.

Architects like Ernst May and Margarete Schütte-Lihotzky believed they had found the social model for the future in the revolutionary USSR. So, when the world economic crisis

practically put a stop to building in Germany, they tried briefly to put their architectonic ideas into practice in the USSR. However, these plans came to grief because of the totally inadequate infrastructure in the Soviet Union, which made a building program like that which had been achieved in Germany quite impossible.

### The modern as program: the Weissenhof estate in Stuttgart

Like a magnifying glass placed over a page, the building exhibition of 1927 organized by the *Deutscher Werkbund* in the Weissenhof housing development in Stuttgart highlighted what was newest in the architecture of the day. For one more time, before National Socialism outlawed it, the Deutscher Werkbund was able to offer foreign practitioners of Modernism such as Le Corbusier and Jacobus Johannes Pieter Oud, and German architects such as Scharoun, Gropius, Behrens, and Mies van de Rohe, a forum in which to present the new building styles and their rationale systematically to the public. Flat roofs, white façades, glass, and metal were as much a part of the picture presented by the exhibition as the functionality and the stacked-cube construction of the buildings. Even today the Stuttgart estate, despite the extensive rebuilding that has occurred, gives an impression of the idea behind this new residential housing.

But in contrast to the *housing schemes* in Berlin and Frankfurt, it was not the working classes who were being offered a new lifestyle with the new architecture. In comparison, the Stuttgart Weissenhof estate, which started out under the direction of Ludwig Mies van der Rohe, was aimed at a well-off, university-educated public of bourgeois origin, as is apparent from the presence of the servant's room that is included in the ground-plans of the apartments.

This concentrated display of modern architecture at a time when it was still unusual evoked as much passionate enthusiasm as emphatic dislike. The white cubic shapes were compared to African buildings, and a humorous postcard shows them surrounded by dromedaries, palms, and people wearing turbans. Behind such criticism lay a deep and not unfounded mistrust of what was seen as modish architecture cut off from regional traditions. The *heritage protection movement*, which was very well represented in Germany via the architect Paul Schmitthenner and the Stuttgart school, accused the scheme of not having taken account either of the landscape or of the traditional buildings around it.

Astonishingly enough, in view of the large number of architects involved and the recognizably different styles that went into the details of their buildings, taken as a whole the buildings form a remarkably homogenous group. Although the architects came from different countries, bringing with them a highly diverse architectonic heritage, and were also all of different ages, the forms and materials they employed were broadly of a kind.

In the few years since the First World War a completely new architecture had developed, and in the Stuttgart Weissenhof estate it became clearly evident for the first time that this was not a specific style with a regional stamp, but a worldwide development.

## CIAM and the International Style

In reaction to the stir caused by the Weissenhof scheme as an entity and as the product of an international team of architects, in 1928 Le Corbusier and Siegfried Giedion created the CIAM (Congrès Internationaux d'Architecture Moderne), to be a yearly forum for Modernist architects. It carried on until 1956, having met a total of ten times, each session being devoted to different social and architectonic themes. For example, under the leadership of Ernst May there was a debate on the theme "the minimal living unit," Gropius insisted on a debate about "rational building methods." But there were also debates on such themes as "the new city."

In face of the rapid worldwide triumph of the new building style exemplified by the Weissenhof estate, it is not surprising that it was christened the "International Style" by the architectural critic Henry-Russell Hitchcock on the occasion of an exhibition of recent Modernist architecture in the Museum of Modern Art in New York in 1932. This international style conquered almost the whole world in the years before the Second World War. With its cubic units in cement, steel, and glass it unified the visual aspect of cities, and dominated almost the whole of architectural development right into the 60s.

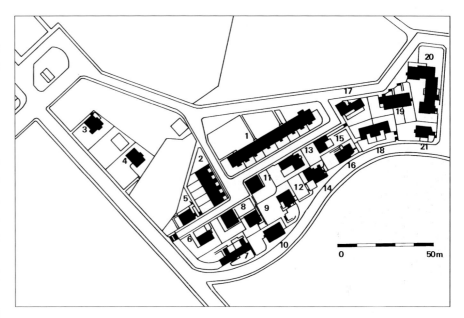

*The Weissenhof estate,* residential block by **Ludwig Mies van der Rohe,** Stuttgart, 1927, and **general plan**

Mies van der Rohe, who had the idea of laying out the scheme on an overall basis of cubic elements, also designed the apartment block that dominates the estate. The *steel skeleton construction* has all the advantages of the variable-plan interior. The Weissenhof exhibition is regarded as the final breakthrough for *Neues Bauen* in the Weimar Republic, when 21 different models of houses by various architects were on display.

Buildings, numbered by architect:
**1** Ludwig Mies van der Rohe, **2** Jacobus Johannes Pieter Oud, **3** Victor Bourgeois, **4/5** Adolf Gustav Schneck, **6/7** Le Corbusier, **8/9** Walter Gropius, **10** Ludwig Hilberseimer, **11** Bruno Taut, **12** Hans Poelzig, **13/14** Richard Döcker, **15/16** Max Taut, **17** Adolf Rading, **18** Josef Frank, **19** Mart Stam, **20** Peter Behrens, **21** Hans Scharoun

Revolution on a grand scale

# TOWN PLANNING IN THE 20TH CENTURY

## 1850–1930

For centuries the town had functioned so well as an almost unchanging, easily comprehensible, coordinated fabric of relationships that its laws had become invisible. Then with the industrial revolution of the 19th century it turned almost overnight into a Moloch. The flight from the land brought an urban explosion. The problems arising from this could not be removed by technology or architecture alone. So a new discipline was born: town planning, which looked at the city as a whole for the first time. The planners found their first models in the place where the people who had caused all these urban problems had come from: the country. There they designed new towns as antitheses to the old ones.

### The urban crisis at the end of the 19th century

During the 19th century the balance between town and country, which had until that time generally been fairly harmonious, suffered a dramatic change. The town became the theater of the industrial revolution. Its new economic structure produced an enormous growth in population. The country became depopulated; the cities exploded. In Great Britain, which spearheaded the change, there were fewer than 9 million inhabitants in 1800, 80 percent of them living in the country. Some 100 years later there were 36 million, 72 percent of them clustered in the big cities. In Germany over the same period the number of inhabitants shot up from 24.5 to 65 million. When the German state came into being in 1871, two-thirds lived outside the main centers of population, but scarcely half a century later this had dropped to 37 percent.

This unprecedented growth led – in cities whose structure dated back to anywhere between medieval times and the 17th century – to indescribable problems. The technological infrastructure could not keep pace with the change, the narrow streets could not contain the massively increasing pressure of traffic. New transport systems such as the railway could only be placed at the edges of towns because of the enormous amount of space they took up. Unregulated economic forces created a jungle of different usages, with factories wedged into living areas. These became so overcrowded due to the constant influx of people, that the most elementary necessities of life were no longer guaranteed. In the English city of Bristol, for instance, 46 percent of families had only one room between them. People who had to live in houses that backed onto lightless, airless yards were becoming ill. Infectious diseases spread through the tenements. Child mortality was high. There were no compensatory open spaces, parks, or squares. The housing question became a question of power. Economic freedom led to a widening gulf in city life between rich and poor, causing people to challenge the existing model of the city, and ultimately, the political order itself. The pressure of circumstances led in about 1900 to a new discipline – town planning.

### Town planning

Town planning is a young discipline that looks back over a long tradition. The term was not used until the late 19th and early 20th century. But as long ago as the first urban groupings of distant antiquity, people began thinking about the most advantageous organization and structure for these residential and economic centers, taking into account strategic and climatic factors. While many towns were springing up "naturally," the first planned towns were coming into being, most according to a geometrical chessboard-like schema (Milet, Priene). Certain functions, as for instance that of the marketplace (the Greek agora), were allotted a specific position in the Greek city of antiquity. At the same time, standardized dwellings were erected according to a unified design.

The notion of the ideal city built according to a geometrical plan occurs over and over again in architectural theory over the centuries. It was in the era of the baroque that plans for an ideal city were transformed into buildings (Freudenstadt 1599, Mannheim 1607), in cities shaped by the ruling concept of society.

In Europe in the 19th century the flight from the land and the overall growth of the population led to

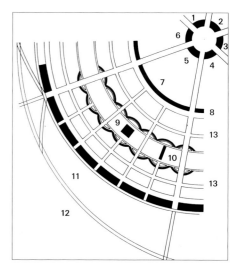

*Ideal plan for an English Garden City, 1902*

**1** Hospital, **2** Library, **3** Theater, **4** Concert hall, **5** Town Hall, **6** Museum, **7** Central park, **8** Crystal Palace, **9** School, **10** Church, **11** Allotments, **12** Large farms **13** Residential area

ever greater urban concentrations, which made a serious reconsideration of the structure of the city essential on social and public health grounds. The initial steps in that direction look rather modest, in that they sought to enlarge and improve the organization of what already existed.

The first move was the "Commissioners' Plan" proposed for New York in 1811. It increased six-fold the area to be covered by the commercial settlements which had until then been concentrated at the southernmost point of Manhattan, and laid a regular grid over the whole island. From east to west ran 155 narrow Streets, all exactly 3 miles (5 kilometers) long, and from north to south ran 12 wider Avenues, all exactly 12 miles (20 kilometers) long. As befitted the ideal of an egalitarian society each of the 2,082 blocks measured 650 by 2,600 feet (200 by 800 meters) and each plot was 25 by 100 feet (7.5 by 30 meters). Only in 1853 was it decided to leave Central Park as a public space, only in 1916 was

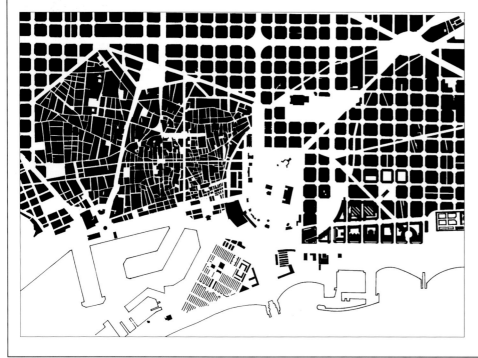

*Inner-city Barcelona today: bottom, the sea; left, the confused network of streets in the old city; right and above, the grid of blocks created by Cerdà's extension of the city in 1859. It has grown outwards a great deal since then.*

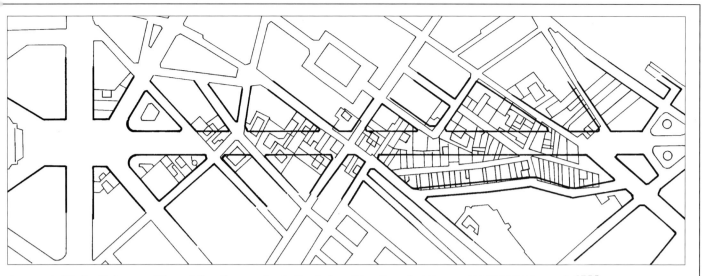

*Avenue de l'Opéra, Paris, carved through the city according to the design of the city prefect Georges Eugène Haussmann in 1862*

the zoning law enacted to regulate the height of buildings, and only in 1961 was any law regarding land usage laid down. There is no traffic plan to this day. The "Commissioners' Plan" designated a terrain on which the forces of growth could develop freely and took no measures to prune them if they got out of hand.

The first attempt to address social needs was made by Ildefonso Cerdà, with the enlargement of Barcelona. In order to gain public space, his plan, which divided the city up into a grid of boulevards 165 feet (50 meters) wide, also sliced off the corners of the 440 by 440 feet (133 by 133 meter) blocks so that the intersections took on the character of public squares. But his idea that each block should only be built up on two sides failed because there were no mechanisms for enforcing it. Private owners continued to use their land as intensively as possible. Instead of buildings with courtyard spaces between them full of greenery, a crowded mass of blocks arose, which are still a dominant feature of the city.

It was with very much greater powers at his disposal that the Paris prefect, Georges Eugène Haussmann, undertook the transformation of that city. He proposed building a network of new boulevards which would give the city a "pleasing aspect," solve traffic-problems, and get rid of sources of infection in the poor quarters (and also increase the mobility of the army, enabling it to nip social disturbances in the bud). But the pressure for change was beyond the control of the existing city and state. Insurrection – the Paris Commune of 1870 – brought down the Empire. Though demolition and rebuilding under government control had at least been established as a method, nothing at this stage was able to resolve the city's problems. Radical concepts which also took issue with society were the order of the day. Even when socialist thinking did not result in a revolution, it changed the self-image of the state and its functionaries. The socially oriented state arose, taking responsibility for the lives of its citizens in all kinds of areas. The builder of cities changed into the technician of the city, and finally to the builder of a new society.

### A new society

All the utopias that were developed at the beginning of the 20th century said goodbye to the old city and tried instead to remove the tensions between town and country. In 1898 an Englishman, Sir Ebenezer Howard, developed the idea of the garden city. He proposed the creation of new towns independent of the old cities, of limited dimensions and whose inhabitants would be self-supporting through arable farming and cattle-rearing. A settlement of a maximum of 32,000 people was to radiate out from a central park. The garden city was to be fully 400 hectares in total, of which half should be for productive use. The first garden city, Letchworth, was created some distance from London in 1903 by Barry Parker and Raymond Unwin. The age-old ideal of a rural commune did not, however, fit with the contemporary economic system. The garden cities failed as self-sufficient entities, but they succeeded outstandingly on the export market as a model for living. Many smart agglomerations of private houses were built in Germany under the name of garden cities, and in England the idea gave rise to the "new towns" of the 1960s, which were actually nothing but collections of houses.

Of greater success were the American Frank Lloyd Wright's anti-urban reflections (see page 16). He gave the name "Usonia" to the utopia in which the architect brought individual and countryside together to live in organic unity. His most extended elaboration of the idea was in his plans for Broadacre City (1935). Here city space becomes landscape. The primary building block of Broadacre City was the Usonian house, dovetailed into the landscape, in which people were to live and work. Every family was intended to cultivate their garden, so houses were built on large plots of land. Wright's demand for half a hectare per family was not at all unrealistic in view of the size of America. The whole population of America at that time could have been housed in

the state of Texas. All the usual public buildings were to be placed in open countryside. Complexes comprising school, library, administration and meeting halls would form the social center of a neighborhood. Industry was to be accommodated in separate industrial parks. At the nodal points for traffic, skyscrapers housing offices would be built. Here Wright placed market centers where every citizen would offer his produce for sale.

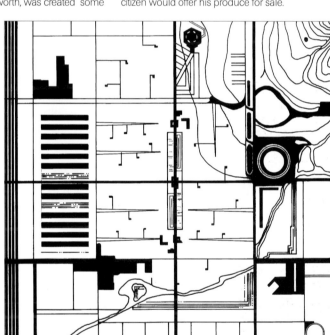

*Instead of overcrowded working-class areas, single houses for free individuals. But the scheme that was intended as a replacement for the old metropolises developed not in opposition to them but with them: Broadacre City (above, part of the "Broadacre" project, Frank Lloyd Wright, 1935) became a model for suburbs everywhere.*

This new style of building was the ancestor of the malls of today. The functional buildings, which were set at a distance from each other, are joined by a hierarchical street-system. Without the car, one of which Wright intended every citizen to own if at all possible, Broadacre City would not work. Today Wright's vision seems to have been realized in the worldwide phenomenon of the suburb, except that in practice Wright's individualistic ideal was to prove incompatible with his projections of a centralized plan (see pages 66–67).

The way to the skies

# American Architecture

1920-1940

**Cass Gilbert, *The Woolworth Building*,**
New York, 1913

Frank Woolworth, the founder of the retail chain, gave Cass Gilbert the task of designing an imposing symbol of his power. The architect faced the challenge of seamlessly welding traditional aesthetics with the demands of a very tall new office building.
The result was for 17 years the tallest building in the world. Gilbert chose to make it in the *Gothic* style, with its arches, little towers, flying buttresses, which had already adorned the French cathedrals of the Middle Ages: historical vocabulary camouflaging technical innovation.

## LAND SPECULATION AND ARCHITECTURAL ENGINEERING

### The roots of the American passion for skyscrapers

To this day the fascination of the skyscrapers in American cities continues unabated. They dominate the skyline, majestic symbols of economic power and social prosperity.

It only took a few years at the end of the 19th century to establish the basic preconditions for building skyscrapers several hundred yards high, and to resolve the complex technical and static problems that the new type of building posed for architects and engineers. Fireproofing was a particular concern, as were the problems relating to the access to such tall buildings.

Yet, however great the aesthetic fascination of these masterpieces of *architectural engineering*, their creation was by no means an end in itself. Economic causes had led almost inevitably to ever taller buildings, since increasing land prices in the thrusting centers of American economic activity necessarily led to the exploitation of every single square foot of a plot of land. After the problems of constructing tall buildings had been solved, a price spiral set in: the more effectively a piece of land could be exploited through ever taller buildings, the more gigantic the sums which could be earned from it on the real-estate market.

### The Chicago fire

If New York, the throbbing heart of economic life, was the first center of this new architectural movement, it was soon more than rivaled by Chicago. The all-engulfing fire which raged there between 8 and 10 October 1871 had razed large tracts of the city to the ground. Yet, terrible though the consequences of the fire were, it also acted as a trigger for the construction of a new city, of which the skyscrapers, mounting story upon story, were the most distinctive component. Chicago saw the creation of such extraordinary early skyscrapers as the *round-arched* Marshall Field Warehouse by Henry Hobson Richardson (1885–87) or the first building with a steel skeleton, the Home Insurance Building by William Le Baron Jenney (1883–85). One of the leaders of the American skyscraper culture at this time was

Louis Sullivan, the chief representative of the *Chicago School*, the general label given to the most important architects of the new Chicago.

Although Sullivan did add some ornamental decorations to his buildings, at the turn of the century he was already beginning to formulate one of the leitmotifs of modern architecture in his tall buildings: the strict grid-like articulation of their façades. In this way the façade of the Garanty Building in Buffalo (1894–95) looked as though it was striving heavenward, an effect that was heightened by the perpen-dicular strips of masonry between the rectangular windows. By contrast, the Carson, Pirie & Scott Store in Chicago (1899–1904), also by Sullivan, displays an energetic balance between horizontal and vertical elements. Whereas the two parts of the store facing on to the street tended to create the impression of a grid of horizontal layers, the rounded corners clearly expressed verticality.

### Neo-Gothic cathedrals of consumerism

Although it was an unheard-of innovation to have as many people as would normally inhabit a small American town suddenly all working and shopping in the same building, surprisingly enough no specific new architectural language was at first evolved for the new genre.

Most of the leading American architects did not take much note of the debates on architectural reform in Europe, dismissing them as intellectual. So the development of architecture in the United States between 1900 and 1925 proceeded, with a few exceptions, along its own path. Instead of relating to modernist work in Europe, American architects rifled the store-cupboard of historical models and dressed their technically highly innovative tall buildings with *historicist* façades which often seem to us today quite inappropriate to their time. Although Louis Sullivan in Chicago had already started the breakthrough into a new skyscraper architecture, other American architects of the same era were unceremoniously mingling *Art Nouveau, Classicism, Romanesque,* and, especially, *Gothic*. The end result of this was that many American tall buildings did not differ much from their historical forebears, the Gothic cathedrals of Europe, the "skyscrapers of the Middle Ages," which had the same ornamental repertoire of tracery around their windows, the same crockets and merlons.

The high point of this *eclectic* skyscraper architecture remained for many years the Woolworth building, erected in 1913 by Cass Gilbert for the American retail chain. At 850 feet (260 meters) it was the tallest building in the world for 17 years. The tower of the Woolworth building not only dominated the skyline of the city, it also powerfully expressed the enormous wealth and the economic might of the concern which had commissioned and now possessed it. In the consumption-oriented society of the United States, skyscrapers were not only signs of technical and social progress. They served, years after their construction, as important status symbols and advertisements, sometimes to the point of being modeled, as with the Chrysler building, on parts of the product being advertised.

## The *Chicago Tribune* competition

In 1922, the *Chicago Tribune* announced a competition for a new building for the newspaper in that city. The requirements were not exactly modest; the terms of the competition demanded that it should be the most beautiful building in the world – and naturally it would be another skyscraper.

Surprisingly enough, European architects also took part. Previously they had been hindered from constructing very tall buildings by the mature, often medieval structure of European cities, but after the First World War, the longing to build "towers" had awakened. Many representatives of the *new building* movement saw the American competition as an opportunity to use the formal language of European Modernism in a skyscraper. Eliel Saarinen from Finland, the group composed of Walter Gropius, Adolf Meyer, Adolf Loos, Bruno and Max Taut, and Hugo Häring were among the best-known European architects who submitted designs for the newspaper building. Yet despite the epoch-making quality of the contributions – discussed many times thereafter in architectural publications and used as models by many other architects – the Americans opted for an utterly conservative design, that of Raymond Hood and John Mead Howell's *Gothic-inspired* skyscraper, whose climbing tracery seemed to mock the development of European architecture.

**Eliel Saarinen, *Chicago Tribune Competition,*** design drawing 1922

Saarinen's entry for the competition to design a building for the *Chicago Tribune* newspaper was consigned to second place, but even the winner, Raymond Hood, thought it better than his own design. Saarinen's thrusting conception, monumental yet mobile, exerted a strong influence over the later development of skyscraper architecture.

**Raymond Hood, *McGraw Hill Building,*** New York, 1928–29

Hood concentrated all the impact of this skyscraper into the horizontal strip windows and glazed windowsills, which was immediately interpreted as an engagement with European Modernism. But the symmetry and ziggurat shape of the building are entirely in the tradition of American skyscrapers.

Nonetheless, it was a representative of European architecture, Eliel Saarinen, who was awarded the second prize. His sketch was quite without frills, achieving a distinctive vertical effect through the articulation of the façade, with its emphatic corners, by masonry bands, a device previously used by Sullivan. This effect is further emphasized by the skillful stratification of volumes in the sky-scraper. Through the use of narrowing steps at increasing intervals, Saarinen creates a pyram-idal effect. The building narrows as it goes up, culminating in a tower which appears to rise from out of the building and dominates the whole complex.

### From the Gothic to the Modern: the skyscrapers of Raymond Hood

In the years that followed, Raymond Hood set about becoming the uncrowned king of the American skyscraper. In the forceful 21-story, black and gold Radiator Building (1924) he once more gave free rein to his Gothic fanta-sies. But the vaguely Gothic formal language of the building that seems to rear up in the way of something from a painter's imagina-tion, crowned once more by a tower-like struc-ture, had now clearly become more abstract than his design for the Chicago Tribune building had been.

The versatility of Hood's architectural language can be seen from the steel skeleton construction of the McGraw Hill Building (1928–29). Suddenly all the "Gothicism" was gone, and in its place came borrowings from the treasury of contemporary European archi-tecture. The absence of rich ornamentation on the façade, the quieter formal language, the stratified rectilinear volumes all agreed with the conceptions of Modernist architects, as did the horizontal strip-windows, which had become the trademark of big-city avant-garde architec-ture in the 1920s. All of which may have been why Hood's McGraw Hill Building was the only American skyscraper awarded the distinction of being included in Henry-Russell Hitchcock and Philip Johnson's 1932 exhibition "The International Style."

Articulated into clearly defined grids, the stories of the greenish McGraw Hill Building were stacked in tiers. The only reminder of Hood's earlier passion for richly detailed deco-ration is the tower which crowns the building, giving it a monumental appearance.

In the Daily News building in New York which Hood designed only a little while later (1930) he changed his design principles yet again. Instead of the tiers of the McGraw Hill building, he now ordered the building in a strictly vertical direction. Only the stepping of the volumes, which Saarinen had already proposed in his design for a tall building for the Chicago Tribune, gave some life to the shiny façade of the skyscraper.

## EUROPE MEETS USA

### Residential buildings by Schindler and Neutra

It was only towards the end of the 1920s that Hood reacted to modern architectural developments in Europe and took leave of his neo-Gothic formal language. By then two young Austrian émigrés, Rudolph Schindler and Richard Neutra, had already given Modernism a toehold in America. Influenced by the country houses of Frank Lloyd Wright, in whose studio Schindler had worked for a time, they did not, interestingly enough, break into the American domain of the skyscraper but started with private houses, where they dev-eloped new architectural concepts that, in many respects, went further than the con-temporary buildings of Le Corbusier or Mies van der Rohe.

Rudolph Schindler was strongly influenced by the abstract *Cubist* formal language of his teacher Otto Wagner and the buildings of the Vienna *Secession.* In 1921 he built his own house in California, which also had room for two friends – a married couple. As an experi-ment in communal living Schindler created private as well as communal areas for both couples. Like Rietveld in the Schröder house in Utrecht (see page 32), Schindler entirely abandoned the sequence of rooms that had been traditional for prestigious homes in the 19th century. Instead he aimed for an inter-penetration of interior and exterior. Large sliding doors opened out onto the garden, thus creating a relationship between the inhabitants' studios and the natural world around. An interior courtyard with an open-air hearth took over the function of the traditional living room. The bungalow-like building was unusual even in its use of materials. The walls were constructed from thin prefabricated concrete slabs. Ceilings and window frames were of dark wood, which, in conjunction with the simple interior fittings also designed by Schindler, gave the building a feeling of being both natural and close to the earth. In its spare sobriety and reserved charm, with its sliding doors and horizontal window bars, and its mingling interior and exterior, the house bears witness to the influence of the traditional home culture of Japan.

Schindler was constantly experimenting in his buildings with new materials and forms, as can be seen in the famous Lovell Beach House, which he built for a doctor client, Phillip Lovell, as his holiday house by the ocean.

The unusual appearance of the house, almost reminiscent in its formal language of technical buildings, is simply a playful conceit of the architect's. Schindler erected the modern holiday house upon five concrete stilts, cast in the form of a figure of eight, which served many purposes. The upper story, which was almost fully glazed, had an uninter-rupted view over the neighboring buildings to the sea, and since the upper story overhung the bottom story there was a protected roofed area at the front of the house which could be used for the children to play in. The decisive advantage of this construction, which was expensive to build, was its safety in the event of an earthquake. California is one of the most endangered areas of the world as regards earthquakes, and in fact the Lovell Beach House, standing as it did on stilts, with-stood one such quake only a few years after it was built, during which nearby buildings were destroyed.

For the same client, Richard Neutra, who had worked for a while in Schindler's office, built the Lovell Health House. The entrance to the building, situated on a slope in Beverly Hills, is via the top floor. The living area, with its lavish use of glass, works like an enclosed space that has been placed in a frame composed of horizontal strips of concrete, painted a bright white, and the vertical steel skeleton. This latter was put up in only 40 hours. The close relationship of the house with the natural world around, which is spread out in an overwhelming panorama in front of the building, is also reflected in the outward reaching concrete walls which serve now as windowsills and now as roofs to terraces, but also compose an abstract spatial boundary, an extension of the building line.

Neutra's façades, in the same way as Schindler's, have the quality of an abstract multi-dimensional sculpture, a design which is continued in the interior through the interpen-etration of individual living areas.

The two Austrians did not simply reproduce the work of their teacher, they developed it further in their own architectural language, at the same time opening up American architec-ture to contemporary European developments.

## ART DECO

### Advent of a new taste

In 1925, the "Exposition internationale des arts décoratifs et industriels modernes" was held in Paris, France. It was an international exhibition of work in progress, covering the various contemporary developments in the areas of decorative art and design and

**Rudolph Schindler, _Lovell Beach House,_** Newport Beach, California, 1926 (top)

**Richard Neutra, _Lovell Health House,_** Beverley Hills, Los Angeles, 1929 (above)

Rooms and landscape flow into each other. Taking a lesson from their teacher Frank Lloyd Wright, Rudolph Schindler and Richard Neutra made the dream reality. Instead of conventional walls, they used modern construction methods: In the case of the house built for Phillip Lovell, a doctor, five figure-of-eight shaped concrete supports sustain an upper story that is almost entirely of glass. From every point of the open, interconnected space there is a dreamlike view of the Pacific ocean.
The same effect was achieved by Richard Neutra in the hills of Los Angeles with an entirely different construction. In the Lovell Health House each story-level is suspended on a light steel skeleton by steel cables.

architecture. This concentrated presentation of new trends brought a change in the artistic landscape. The great influence which the Paris exhibition of "arts décoratifs" had on art in the 1920s and early 1930s can easily be gauged by the fact that it gave its name to a new style: Art Deco.

From clothing and jewelry to cutlery and cars, and even architecture and painting, the geometric shapes of Art Deco with their semi-circular forms and rounded corners were to be found everywhere. A touch of *Cubism*, a pinch of *Expressionism*, a little of the practicality of the *Neues Bauen*, and some of the technicity of the machine aesthetic – this was Art Deco's successful recipe for catching the tone of the times. The style is not always elegant; sometimes there is a certain amount of clumsiness about it, deriving in part for the preference for heavy materials such as steel, silver, and especially brass.

In America as well as Europe, Art Deco quickly became the symbol of the Roaring Twenties with their elegant charm but also their decadence. Advertising, which burgeoned with the American economic boom of the 1920s, was filled with the streamlined, glittering chrome of Deco. Advertising awakened in the prosperous classes of society, especially in towns, a continual longing for new products, which stimulated demand and increased production and sales.

But right next to this glittering world there was the America of the poor. Poverty was at its most visible in the slums which were a by-product of the continued rapid growth of the big cities, where hundreds of thousands of immigrants and black Americans lived in hope of a better life – all too often in vain.

In the United States it was the era of Prohibition, the infamous Al Capone and the Mafia, and the rise of the film industry in Hollywood, which challenged the European cinema and brought in new stars for the sound movies which were gradually replacing the old silent pictures. The public loved to see Harold Lloyd, at once comic and tragic, hanging terrified but still witty from the dizzy height of a skyscraper façade, the street like a narrow ribbon below with cars, oblivious of his plight, racing along it like toys.

The boom, which inspired the massive demand for cars and was synonymous in its early stages with the name of Henry Ford (whose architect was Albert Kahn), continued on its way with the automobile company of Walter P. Chrysler. The Chrysler Building was to be the visible expression of the seemingly unlimited might of the car magnate. Originally designed for another client, William van Alen's 77-story skyscraper, which bores 1000 feet (319 meters) up into the sky over New York, was not only for a short while the highest building in the world; it also became an icon of Art Deco and was reproduced thousands of times over.

To what irrational and technically complex lengths architects were prepared to go in their competition to erect the tallest building in the world in New York City is illustrated by the story of the top of the Chrysler tower. In order to prevent his competitors from garnering the coveted title of builder of the world's tallest skyscraper, van Alen had the seven-story tower which was intended to cap the building constructed inside the building. In a surprise coup which trumped the opposition, he then anchored the complete tower within a few hours on to the top of the skyscraper.

The top of the Chrysler Building, with its pinnacle, is, in fact, a splendidly theatrical crown to the building. Its semi-circular segments of decreasing size rise one on top of each other like a telescope to a sky-piercing point, so that it seems even today to be striving up and up into the clouds. The three-cornered window openings in the semi-circles add a dynamic, jagged quality to this dramatic structure, which could almost be part of a film set such as is seen in Fritz Lang's visionary classic *Metropolis*. On top of all this there is the delicate coloring of the tower-top, which is covered with reflecting, glittering steel, and offers an extraordinary spectacle when illuminated at night.

However, the Chrysler Building was not just the tallest construction in the world. It also functioned as a giant advertisement for the automobile company. Original wheel caps from Chrysler cars were used on the façade, and giant radiator mascots imitated *Gothic* gargoyles at the corners of the building. But it is the slightly decadent elegance which the Chrysler building continues to exude in defiance of the changing face of fashion which gives it its unique charm. It is this charm which secures its leading role among the numerous skyscrapers of New York, even though the Empire State Building took its place as the highest building in the world only a few years after it was constructed.

Although the Empire State Building, which for years dominated the staggering New York skyline, has long since lost the title of tallest building to the skyscrapers of southeast Asia, it retains its position as the star of New York's tourist attractions, a myth which Hollywood played a considerable role in cultivating and propagating. What would King Kong be, without his pose at the top of the (then) tallest building in the world? And the building still plays an unbilled lead in many films , like *An Affair to Remember* or *Sleepless in Seattle*, where decisive encounters take place on its observation platform, with New York lying at the actors' feet.

With its somewhat cool effect, and its use of noble materials, the Empire State Building was the parting shot of the American variety of Art Nouveau. It was an act of daring in the face of the growing economic problems in the United States at the end of the 1920s, to erect a building that makes such a bold statement. In fact it was impossible to find tenants for the offices for a long time, and it quickly became known to a mocking general public as the "Empty State Building."

The Chrysler Building and the Empire State Building were essentially visions in stone of the "American Dream" of the 20th century, whereas in the MacGraw Hill Building and the Daily News Building, Raymond Hood showed himself open to the formal language employed by the European avant-garde. In their skyscraper for the Philadelphia Savings Fund Society (PSFS) in New York (1926–31) George Howe and William Lescaze tried to effect a synthesis between the demands of European Modernism and the traditional American skyscraper. The strip windows girdling the building are given a rhythm by the supporting elements; this brings the whole into an interesting balance. The functionality, which was the chief aim of the PSFS building, was visibly expressed in the structure of the façades. Howe and Lescaze used dignified materials throughout, except for the mechanical services floor,

which made a clear break in the façades' composition.

## Dance on the volcano

Just how fragile the hard-won postwar prosperity of the 1920s was – not just in the United States – was shatteringly revealed by the world economic crisis. Worldwide, the 1920s were both economically and socially a "dance on the volcano," a tight-rope walk over the abyss without a rope or a safety net.

This dangerous situation is strikingly captured by Louis W. Hine in his photographs, which document the construction of the Empire State Building. Surrounded

**William van Alen, *Chrysler Building,*** New York, 1930

A gleaming needle pierces the New York sky. With its steel-covered, telescopically narrowing point, the Chrysler Building seems to grow out from itself. It was the tallest building in the world when it was erected, and even today it remains the most symbolic, an advertisement for skyscrapers as well as for the company that commissioned it. Wheel caps and radiator mascots from the products of the car manufacturing giant decorate the Art Deco façade of the 1000-foot (319-meter) building.

**Shreve, Lamb & Harmon,** *Empire State Building,* New York, 1931

The Empire State Building broke all conceivable records and its height was only one of them; at 1250 feet (381 meters) it was to remain for more than 40 years the tallest building in the world. Immediately after its construction the world economic crisis ended the struggle to beat the record for height. People shrank from putting up buildings whose use was symbolic rather than practical. That the Empire State Building, which is certainly not architecturally breathtaking, became synonymous with the idea of the skyscraper, was undoubtedly due to its media image. Millions of cinema-goers saw King Kong fall to his death from its roof – a symbol of the downfall of the mighty.

by steel girders and cables, iron, and cranes, the building workers seem almost to hover over the city, which stretches out hundreds of feet below them. Man and technology seem to have entered into a daring pact: one false move, one wrong step and the harmony of the moment would break, and they would hurtle into the abyss. This is exactly what happened on 24 October 1929, when the bottom fell out of the stock market on Wall Street, the financial center of New York, turning millionaires into beggars within the space of a few hours.

The effects of the Wall Street Crash were felt across the world, and in the wake of the ensuing economic crisis, unemployment and inflation, which it had taken immense efforts to combat, began once again to rise. The economic existence of workers and middle classes alike was threatened, leading to more political radicalization, against which in many countries no adequate countermeasures could be found. The brief postwar boom gave way to a deep depression, the "dance on the volcano" ended in a fall.

That such extensive building projects as the Empire State Building or especially the Rockefeller Center were nonetheless undertaken in this economically and politically

tense situation, was largely due to the fact that they had been planned and begun before "Black Friday," as the day of the Wall Street crash subsequently became known, and that basic changes in concept were accepted in order to complete them. In the case of the Rockefeller Center there was also the knowledge that despite all the economic problems there was nonetheless a financier – John D. Rockefeller – in the background, who had a large and solid fund of capital.

The plans for the Rockefeller Center had begun in the late 1920s. Numerous architects were originally employed on the project, once more among them was the highly successful Raymond Hood. Hood was responsible for the actual focal point of the enormous site, the thin slab that is the 70-story RCA Building. Stepped at the sides, it rose elegantly from among the numerous buildings of lesser height that surrounded it. These had various functions: the Rockefeller complex was a predecessor of modern media centers – a city within a city – including the Radio City Music Hall which could accommodate as many as 6,200 visitors, and a movie palace for an audience of 3,500.

Yet the length of time that it actually took to build the Rockefeller Center – it was finally completed in 1940 – also serves to make clear the serious problems that such an ambitious project had to face in those economically difficult times.

## The New Deal

Under the leadership of President Franklin D. Roosevelt the United States began in 1933 to master against the economic crisis that had been brought on by the stock market crash with a whole catalog of national measures. These had decisive consequences for the economy, for communities, and for the social whole. The breakthrough was the New Deal introduced by Roosevelt. The heart of this economic program was a range of economic measures designed to combat unemployment in industry as well as in agriculture, while at the same time targeting homelessness and urban slums

A gigantic work-creation program provided for the construction of canal systems, streets, theatres, gardens and parks, schools, law courts, town halls, and hospitals. Since there were enough workers, materials, and supporting funds, and no time constraints, the simplest technology and the most basic of working methods were used.

Important technical projects such as the building of a total of 32 cofferdams, headed by the architects and engineers of the Tennessee Valley Authority did not just create work. Realized in a forward-looking and ambitious formal language, they expressed the dynamic new start taken by the American economy, and demonstrated the gradual return to national self-confidence after the shock of the economic crisis.

For prestige buildings on the other hand, the traditional forms of *Classicism* were preferred, giving a reassuringly familiar image in these uncertain times. For example, the classical monumentality of the United States Mint erected in 1937 by architect Gilbert Stanley Underwood in San Francisco leaves no doubt that the stability of the dollar is once again now guaranteed.

The measures for economic advancement undertaken by President Roosevelt in the New Deal also had the effect of laying the foundations for the successful rise of the United States to the position of top industrial nation after the Second World War.

**Reinhard and Hofmeister; Corbett Harrison and MacMurray; Hood and Fouilhoux,** *Rockefeller Center,* New York, 1931–40

The American millionaire John D. Rockefeller was the only man who dared, at the time of the world economic crisis, to commission a gigantic project such as this one: a complex of 15 buildings including a skyscraper (seven more buildings had been added by 1973). This city within a city built primarily as a business center offers a wide range of arts events and services for the general public. Faced throughout in limestone, the complex bears witness to Rayond Hood's concept of building a coherent group of tall buildings which would stand out as a self-sufficient entity against the rest of the city, both reducing the chaos of the New York traffic and improving the quality of life.

Modernism under Siege

# Architecture and Power

1930–1945

## THE RULE OF FORCE

### The Europe of the dictators

The establishment of dictatorial regimes in numerous countries between the two world wars is one of the distinctive phenomena of the 20th century. In their contempt for human beings, and their ultimate willingness to destroy great numbers of them, these regimes differed from each other only in one aspect, whether they were situated on the left or right of the political spectrum.

Why this political polarization was able to take hold in so few years in so many countries has many reasons. While it is true that the responsibility cannot be laid uniquely at the door of the tense economic situation present in the inter-war years and the post-1929 economic crisis and the concomitant housing shortage and high unemployment, nonetheless they were the ground in which extremism could flourish. The roots were already there, in the nationalism of the 19th century. In most countries that had been monarchies before the First World War, there was now an absence of democratic tradition which favored the establishment of dictatorial systems. In a world which had been shaken to its moral foundations, many individual citizens found political freedom too much of a burden. Because of their frequently unthinking faith in authority, the tide of radicalization to left and right was not stemmed either vigorously, or early enough. The ominous progression towards dictatorship began.

The high-flying dreams of a new mankind that had accompanied the October Revolution of 1917 in Russia evaporated. In their place came a communist reign of terror under Josef Stalin, which systematically eliminated all opponents and persisted until he died in 1953. As early as 1922 the first fascist regime in Europe came to power in Italy under Mussolini. In Spain, after an extremely bloody civil war, the fascist General Franco finally wrested power from the Republicans. He was supported in the war by the German Condor Legion, which was responsible for the destruction of Guernica. It was in response to the sufferings of the civil population of that shattered village that Pablo Picasso painted his famous picture *Guernica* in 1937.

In Germany a National Socialist dictatorship was established in 1933 under Adolf Hitler. The persecution of Jewish citizens, political dissidents and intellectuals, and other minorities began immediately. Many of the leading architects of the Weimar era went into exile. The 1930s in Germany were one long trail of tyranny and the denial of human rights, beginning with the Nazi seizure of power, and proceeding through the burning of books, the night when Jews were beaten and their shop-windows broken, and the outbreak of the Second World War, to the decision at the so-called "Wannsee-Konferenz" of 1942 to

**1930**: National Socialists and Communists gain seats in the German parliamentary elections. The Frankfurt School, headed by Max Horkheimer and Theodor W. Adorno formulate the "critical theory of society." *The Blue Angel*, starring Marlene Dietrich, comes to the cinema. Death of Sir Arthur Conan Doyle, author of the Sherlock Holmes detective novels.

**1931**: Electoral victory of the coalition of left-wing parties in Spain. King Alfonso XIII abdicates. Spain becomes a republic. Clark Gable begins his film career in Hollywood.

**1932**: Height of the world economic crisis. Around 30 million unemployed worldwide. Thomas Beecham founds the London Philharmonic Orchestra. A star at four, Shirley Temple is the world's youngest film actress. Exhibition of international architecture at the Museum of Modern Art in New York.

*German sportswoman,*
**portrait photo of a javelin thrower, 1934**

**1933**: The National Socialists seize power in Germany. Adolf Hitler appointed chancellor. Franklin D. Roosevelt becomes President of the United States. Beginning of the New Deal program of state economic planning. Federico García Lorca's play *Blood Wedding* performed in Spain.

**1934**: Death of the English composer Edward Elgar. The Polish-born French chemist and physicist Marie Curie dies. She had been awarded the Nobel Prize for physics in 1903 and chemistry in 1911.

**1935**: The Nobel Peace Prize goes to Carl von Ossietzky. Elias Canetti's novel *Auto da Fè* published. First performance of George Gershwin's opera *Porgy and Bess*.

**1936**: Beginning of the Spanish Civil War (ends 1939 with the victory of General Franco). Margaret Mitchell's novel *Gone with the Wind* published.

**1937**: Picasso completes *Guernica*. In Germany, Nazi exhibition of so-called "Degenerate Art" vilifies modern art.

**1938**: "Swing" reaches its peak under jazz musician Benny Goodman. The 40-hour week introduced in the USA.

**1939**: German troops attack Poland on 1 September. Start of the Second World War.

**1940**: Massive German air attack on the English city of Coventry. Leon Trotsky murdered in Mexico. Chaplin's film *The Dictator* comes out.

**1941**: Japan enters the war by attacking the US Pacific naval base at Pearl Harbor. Konrad Zuse builds the first program-driven electromechanical digital computer.

**1942**: In Berlin the Wannsee Conference is held to make technical and administrative plans to exterminate the Jews in Europe. Astrid Lindgren's *Pippi Longstocking* published.

**1945**: Capitulation of Germany. The United States drops atomic bombs on Hiroshima and Nagasaki.

murder European Jews. At the end of this long
decade (1945) millions were dead and a wave
of destruction had passed over central and
eastern Europe.

## Memorial architecture

The 1920s and 1930s were not only the
time of a new departure in search of a modern
society, they also constituted an epoch whose
population were still suffering from the shock
of the First World War.

All the people from both sides who had
lost relations or friends in the conflict had to
work through their grief. In national terms, all
the ex-belligerents felt the need to remember
and commemorate.

Once again there emerged an era of heroic
memorials, those national shrines that had
already figured so importantly in the architecture of the 19th century. It was a bizarre combination: remembrance of the casualties of the
first "modern" war, expressed by means of a
19th-century building concept in the architectural forms of the present.

As a result, innumerable war memorials
sprang up in almost every village in western
Europe after 1918. Particular importance was
accorded to monuments to the fallen erected
on battlefields. Within a few years these had
become the starting point for a regular tourist
industry based around the battlefields.

One of the largest and most impressive of
such commemorative monuments is that
erected by Edwin Lutyens at Thiepval near
Amiens in France, which is dedicated to the

nearly 74,000 British soldiers who went
missing at the battle of the Somme and whose
bodies were never identified. Lutyens's monument consists of a triumphal arch which goes
up in steps like a pyramid, dominated by the
color-contrast between the light areas in *freestone* and the red areas in *brick.* Through
linking a motif of architecturally historic significance – the *triumphal arch* (victory) – with the
motif of the *pyramid* (death), Lutyens created a
synthesis that is both full of interesting tension
and universally comprehensible. The over-
emphatically formal style of the monument
leaves no doubt as to its meaning: victory
legitimated the deaths.

Lutyens's monumental formal language
provides an interesting comparison with the
charnel house erected between 1923 and
1932 at Douaumont near Verdun, one of the
most fought-over sites of the war, by the architects Léon Azéma, Max Edrei and F. Hardy. The
monument holds the bones of 10,000 French
soldiers killed at Verdun. The building is long,
with rounded corners, but in the center it has a
structure similar to a church tower which, like
a lighthouse, lights up the battlefield at night.

In Germany it was not on the Western Front
(where most of the German losses actually
occurred) but on the Eastern Front – where
the war against Russia was won – that a
nationalistic war memorial was built. The
Tannenberg national monument, designed by
Walter and Johannes Krüger, was dedicated
in 1927. The octagonal, fortress-like building
was dominated by eight unfriendly-looking

towers in bluish-red brick, enclosed linked by a pleasant and quite modern looking glassed-in walkway. Tannenberg was a site which could serve a variety of purposes, but the omnipresent cult of the dead was at its center. Under a tall and monumental cross of bronze was the grave of 20 unknown soldiers killed in the battle at Tannenberg in August 1914.

However different these three memorials to the war dead were from each other in formal terms, they were closely related in purpose. They were all places of national significance, dedicated to the memory of the war and its dead, but above all to the glorification of death in battle and so to the formation of myths of the nation-state.

### Forward to tradition

At the beginning of the 1930s modern architecture was radically split. While the towns had seen the introduction of many exemplary projects – public housing schemes, private houses, schools, town halls, and factories – covering the whole spectrum of Neues Bauen from Expressionism to New Objectivity, there had always been a group of clients and architects who – as with the war memorials – clung determinedly to traditional forms.

Whereas in the United States at the start of the 1930s Modernism was gradually beginning to influence the building of skyscrapers, in Europe it was under increasing political attack. In the Soviet Union under Stalin the Constructivists lost their influence. In Germany, where at the end of the 1920s, projects such as the Stuttgarter Weissenhof estate had set out to make a splash and did, more critical voices were now interrupting the chorus of acclaim. Neues Bauen was castigated as "Bolshevik architecture imported from the USSR," without any consideration of the fact that only a very few of the Modernist architects did indeed support the communist ideology. Along with such political polemics which belonged to the social polarization of the times, there were also professional criticisms. The flat roofs of the Neues Bauen were unfavorably compared – on the grounds that they fell in easily and were not waterproof – with the traditional hip or saddle roofs; the whitewash favored by modern architects peeled off and their steel window frames rusted, whereas the original wooden ones did not. There were indeed some technical faults in Modernist architecture, but what actually brought it down was the world economic crisis. Another phenomenon was also taking shape: influenced both by political events and wide-ranging economic constraints, a number of architects in Germany and elsewhere turned, in around 1930, to a harder, more monumental language of forms, with a different arrangement of rooms and new dimensions. Instead of friendly white stuccoed exteriors or uncovered cement, suddenly façades started being clothed in freestone, usually granite or limestone. There might well be a building with a modern structure and shape underneath, but the stone façade linked the building to traditional values, and thus to security and stability.

### The start of Gigantism

One of the projects that stands very clearly on the cusp between the first period of Modernism and the swing back to conservative ambitions in Germany, was the competition for an extension to the Reichsbank in Berlin in 1932, which was announced on the eve of the Nazi seizure of power. It was not only traditional architects who took part; there were also important representatives of Modernism such as Ludwig Mies van der Rohe, Heinrich Tessenow and Hans Poelzig. But even in their submissions one can trace an inclination to monumentalism. The building that was finally erected, designed at Hitler's wish by the house architect for the bank Heinrich Wolff, can be seen as the first official Nazi building. It is in fact an only moderately monumental office building, characterized inside and out by boldness in conception and functional quality. The decor was comparatively sparing, so that there was no excessive "ornamentation" with Nazi emblems.

Very different to this was the case of the new Reichskanzlei (Chancellery). The prestigious new building faced on to the Wilhelmstrasse in the middle of the old Berlin governmental quarter. A grandiose hall over 160 feet (50 meters) long led to the main entrance, which was adorned by a portico with four gigantic Tuscan pillars.

But not only were the sheer size of the building and the scale of its pillars impressive, the visitor was also intended to be impressed by the two bronze sculptures by Arno Breker flanking the entrance: two naked male figures, one holding a torch and the other a sword, symbolizing "party" and "army." The sculptures,

in conjunction with the architecture of the building, represented the self-image of National Socialism: the Nazi party and its various sub-organizations, and the army were the most important pillars of the Nazi regime in Germany up to and including the moment when Hitler unleashed the Second World War. The inside of the building continued in the plain monumental style preferred by Hitler. Painting and mosaics, valuable fittings in wood and stone, all of an intimidating magnitude – everything combined to present the visitor with an unambiguous picture of the limitless ambition for power of the National Socialists and their leader Adolf Hitler.

But the new Chancellery, the building which was meant above all other to incorporate Hitler's "thousand-year Reich" was not granted a long life: what was left of it after bombing in the Second World War was forcibly removed by the Soviet victors. The costly marble of the Chancellery, where Hitler committed suicide in an underground bunker in 1945, was used by the victors for their memorials.

The monumental buildings of Albert Speer and the reactionary politics of the National Socialists, however, presented only one side

of the picture. On the other side, there were thoroughly modern aspects of the realm of architecture, exemplified, for instance, in the Luftwaffe buildings. These were designed chiefly by Ernst Sagebiel, who had previously been in charge of Erich Mendelsohn's office. Sagebiel's central airport building at Berlin-Tempelhof, which unites modern construction with a feeling of grandeur, remains one of Europe's greatest buildings.

The same principle is to be seen in the 1938 buildings for the German KdF ("Kraft durch Freude" – "strength through joy") car – the Volkswagen. After 1945 the car enjoyed worldwide success as the VW Beetle. The south façade of the factory buildings, which is just less than one mile (1.3 kilometers) long and is reminiscent of a city wall, is given not only a monumental, but an astonishingly modern appearance by the characteristic towers housing the stairwells, which stand out from the building line.

In contrast to this there is the residential architecture of the KdF town, which is today called Wolfsburg. The buildings there, planned by Speer's protégé Peter Koller, were in the *heritage protection style* that had been

**Albert Speer, *New Chancellery,*** Berlin, seen from the Vossstrasse, 1936–39

With its quarter-mile (422-meter) length, the New Chancellery, inaugurated in January 1939, gave a foretaste of the architectonic *megastructures* which Albert Speer planned for the rebuilding of Berlin under the direction of Hitler. The impression of size created by this *neo-classical* building with its long tracts of offices is mitigated by the way in which the height of the eaves 72 feet (22 meters) is designed to fit in with buildings of the neighborhood, and by the modeling of the façade with its projecting and set-back areas.
It was only on the garden side, not accessible to the public, and above all in the interior that the New Chancellery showed the intimidating face of Nazi official architecture. With their extravagant marble mosaics and tapestries, the giant halls documented Hitler's drive towards ever greater power. In 1949 the Chancellery, which had been war-damaged, was pulled down.

**Jacques Carlu, Louis Boileau, and Léon Azéma, *Palais de Chaillot*, exhibition** pavilion for the International Exhibition, Paris, 1937

The two 600-foot (195-meter) long, slightly curved wings of the Palais de Chaillot, which now houses several museums, culminate in two symmetrical buildings with towers on top, between and in front of which there is a paved square. Built in 1936 as the foreground to the exhibition, the Palais, in its slightly raised position, forms the visual conclusion to the long reaches of the Champ de Mars. With its monumental linked rows of *pillars* and its lavish decoration with mosaics, the complex is an example of the international *Neoclassicism* of the 1930s, which was influenced by Art Deco.

widespread since the turn of the century, with saddle roof, wooden veranda and sash windows. Wolfsburg is a good illustration of the very varied aims of National Socialist architecture. It also illustrates the unbroken success in West Germany of architects of the National Socialist system after 1945: Peter Koller was once again responsible for town planning after the war.

## Cult and seduction

Nowhere are the mechanisms of the regime clearer than in the memorials and places dedicated to the Nazi cult. The effect that an impressive architectural backdrop to a semi-religious cult can have in seducing the masses is particularly evident in these places. Albert Speer's setting for the Nuremberg rally or Paul Ludwig Troost's arrangement of the Königsplatz in Munich were such places, and their main purpose was to provide a suitable site for mass events.

The stone paving, the flanking buildings in granite, the axial direction of the installations towards the Führer: this was the constantly recurring setting of Nazi rituals, which were carried out with military precision. They were accompanied by impressive theatrical effects, such as Speer's "cathedral of light," which caused a "building" created by anti-aircraft searchlights to appear over the assembly.

The culmination of National Socialist architectural ambition would doubtless have been the transformation of Berlin into the new capital "Germania." But the gigantic plans that Hitler and Speer had made, and were now ready to start realizing, were overtaken by the fall of Germany and got no further than the first stage. Speer had planned a monumental, memorial-like north-south axis, along the lines of what he had designed for Nazi rituals, the focal point of which was to be the "great hall."

Its technically innovative cupola, much larger than St Peter's in Rome, was intended to have a classical appearance. The dome was to be 820 feet (250 meters) in diameter, and there would be room for 100,000 people inside the gigantic hall. Beside the "great hall" the old German Reichstag, which had been a ruin since the 1933 fire, would have looked like a tiny relic of a bygone era.

Part of the plan for Germania included confiscating the property of Jewish citizens of Berlin who were deported to concentration and death-camps. But only a small part of the destruction of the historic fabric of the city meticulously planned by Speer and his staff took place at their hands. The rest was taken care of by the war, which destroyed Berlin almost completely.

## Between worlds

The Paris international exhibition of 1937 was the last time between the wars that the political systems and their respective architectures met. There were buildings planned for the exhibition that were firmly based in the Modernist tradition of the 1920s, such as the Spanish pavilion by Josep Lluís Sert, with its clear grid construction. However, it was *Classicism* of the simplified international kind characteristic of the 1930s, which had the upper hand.

With their monumental language of forms and colossal pillars, the Palais de Chaillot and the nearby Palais de Tokyo, built in 1937 on the right bank of the Seine, formed a significant backdrop for the exhibition. But it was in the architecture of the German and Soviet pavilions that the claims to universal power of both systems collided. In a skillfully devised *mise-en-scène*, the two buildings were placed opposite each other as the dramatic highlight of the Paris exhibition.

The Soviet pavilion consisted of a stepped building on a podium – almost streamlined in appearance – created by the architect Boris Iofan. But the sculpture by Vera Moukhina that crowned it was its dramatic climax. Storming forward with a challenging stride, two symbolic heroic figures – an industrial worker and a woman from a collective farm, – brandish the insignia of Soviet might: the hammer and sickle.

These figures, poster-like in style, with a generally accessible ideological message, were entirely in line with the pedagogical conceptions of the dominant style in art: *Socialist Realism*. This had completely suppressed the intellectually demanding art of the Russian Constructivists – though the latter, it must be said, had permitted their work to be misused as a means of propaganda directly after the October Revolution.

Standing opposite Iofan's relatively dynamic construction was the undeniably static tower designed by Albert Speer, which the architectural critic Paul Westheim ironically described as "a cardboard box with pillars." As with the Soviet Pavilion, the sculptural embellishment played an important ideological role, in this case the national symbol, the eagle of the Reich, holding a swastika in its claws.

However great the influence of Speer and his buildings was, they should not be regarded as synonymous with National Socialist architecture. The highly official pavilion for the Paris exhibition should not lead one to make generalizations about building under the Third Reich, despite the strict boundaries within which it had to work. There was a hierarchy of building tasks on offer between 1933 and 1945, from the prestige building down to the factory, with a choice of solutions permitting a real, if limited, breadth of stylistic choice.

## Classicism in Italy

The situation was rather different in Italy. Avant-garde Modernist architecture had been able to develop early there, in spite of the fascist regime. But even here it was increasingly pushed into the background in the 1930s by the general spread of Classicism.

A good example of such Classicism, based on Roman models, are the buildings for the University of Rome begun in 1932 by Marcello Piacentini, who had been at Mussolini's side as his building adviser since 1922.

His marble-covered rectoral building of 1935 is notable for its monumental *pillared portico*, which extends over the whole height of the building. Taken as a whole, the building displays the features of that type of Classicism reduced to its basic stereometric forms that Heinrich Tessenow had employed at the turn of the century for his Festspielhaus in Hellerau, near Dresden (see page 24), and which was soon to be deployed in France in the Palais de Chaillot.

Piacentini's rectoral building can, however, also be seen as an Italian approach to the architectural vision that was being developed by Mussolini's allies north of the Alps.

Boris Iofan, *Soviet Pavilion* and Vera Moukhina, *Sculptural Group,* International Exhibition, Paris, 1937

Vera Moukhina's two monumental bronze figures (an industrial and a collective-farm worker) seem to be flying almost weightlessly towards a glowing socialist future. Hammer and sickle raised victoriously above them, the powerfully dynamic group was created to serve Stalin's reign of terror.

The future begins

# The Globalization of Modern Architecture

1945–1960

## VISIONS OF A CIVIC ARCHITECTURE

### A shattered world

The devastation of the First World War had led to radical changes in political, economic, and social thinking all over the world, but the situation at the end of the Second World War was even more dramatic. The world of 1945 was very different from that which had existed, still, in 1939.

Hitler's Nazi reign of terror in Germany had led to millions of deaths all over the world, culminating in the horrific crime of the Holocaust. Never before had a war taken so many civilian lives, never before had a war so radically destroyed both cities and country-sides, and thus the foundation of the people's lives. The increasingly technological nature of life in the 20th century brought with it a corresponding advance in the technology of war, which found its melancholy climax in the dropping of the first atom bombs on the Japanese city of Hiroshima by the United States, and a few days later on Nagasaki.

But the end of the war in 1945 did not bring peace to the world. While city and countryside still lay in rubble and ashes, in Europe, Japan, and the USSR in particular, people began to migrate in huge numbers, either because they wished to emigrate or they had been driven out. The map of the world had to be redrawn because of this displacement. France, England, and the United States had fought together with the Soviets against Hitler's Germany, but the alliance shattered soon after the end of the war. The world disintegrated into Eastern and Western power blocs, with the barrier between them running straight through Germany, which was divided into two.

The Western, capitalist-oriented power bloc was formed out of the democratic countries, headed by the United States as the world's most powerful economy. The Eastern power bloc, where communism was the determining ideology, was led by the USSR, where Josef Stalin exercised dictatorial power until his death in 1953. Like the USSR, the other socialist countries were officially "people's democra-cies," but the people did not have the basic right of every real democracy: to be able to cast their votes secretly in free and equal elections.

Up until the ending of the communist regimes in 1989, East and West stood in irreconcilable opposition to each other: this was the Cold War, which at times, such as the Berlin blockade, or the Cuba crisis, threatened to break out into open conflict. There was fear of a Third World War.

Architectural history was largely shaped according to a Western point of view, as can be seen from the fact that the architecture of the Eastern bloc, in its various phases, has come only gradually, into the public eye, and has begun to be researched only since the opening up at the beginning of the 1990s of the erst-while Eastern-bloc countries. It transpired that up till the death of Stalin in 1953 the "wedding

1945: Potsdam Conference between Truman, Churchill, and Stalin decides the postwar fate of Europe. Founding of the United Nations (UN). End of the hostilities of the Second World War after the capitulation of Japan.

1946: Posthumous publication of *Le Petit Prince* by Antoine de Saint-Exupéry. The US CARE organization begins sending aid packages into countries suffering from the effects of the war. Death of Damon Runyon, author of *Guys and Dolls*.

1947: Theodor W. Adorno's socially critical philosophy *Dialectics of Enlightenment* published. Maria Callas begins her brilliant career as an opera singer. Thor Heyerdahl sails on a raft from Peru to Polynesia to prove by following migratory routes that prehistoric societies were related. The "New Look" favors calf-length clothes making lavish use of material.

1948: Blockade of Berlin by Soviet Russia (lifted 1949), the Western powers supply the city by airlift. Ben-Gurion proclaims the new state of Israel in the area covered by the British Mandate for Palestine. George Balanchine founds the New York City Ballet. The UN General Assembly promulgates the Declaration of Human Rights. Gandhi assassinated. The Soviet film director Sergei Eisenstein dies aged 50.

1949: East and West Germany constituted as states either side of the boundary between the two blocs. The communist people's army under Mao Zedong conquers the whole of China; the Chinese People's Republic proclaimed. George Orwell publishes *1984*, his novel about a future totalitarian state.

**The Berlin blockade: the West supplies the city by air-lift**

1950: Armed conflict between communist North Korea and capitalist South Korea. Settled in 1953 by the superpowers.

1952: American fashion for jeans spreads rapidly in Europe.

1953: Workers' revolt in East Germany put down by the mobilization of Soviet tanks. The coronation of Queen Elizabeth II arouses worldwide interest through the use of modern news reporting techniques. Death of Stalin.

1956: Bloody suppression by Soviet troops of anti-Stalinist uprising in Hungary.

1957: The first artificial satellite

(Sputnik) circles the earth.

1958: Hendrik Verwoerd, prime minister of South Africa, makes *apartheid* (separation of the races) state policy.

1959: Victory of the revolution in Cuba under Fidel Castro. Federico Fellini's socially critical film *La Dolce Vita* comes out.

cake" style had spread through the whole bloc, and that it was only at the end of the 1950s that attempts could be made to realize a type of architecture appropriate to the ambitious goals which the socialist systems, with their concept of a "new" society, were propagating. Unfortunately, these initiatives, which often produced architecture that was both futurist as well as functional in tone, only lasted a short time. By the 1980s the economic problems of the Eastern bloc had become so great that there were only the resources available to put up what were standardized buildings in mostly prefabricated materials, and in a generally insipid architectural style.

The architecture of East Germany, and its capital East Berlin, had particular significance in the East-West ideological conflict, as East Berlin had to maintain a high profile in the face of West Berlin as the showplace of the Free World, and prestige projects were erected there such as the residential buildings in the Stalin-Allee (today Karl-Marx-Allee) and later the television tower.

## The new beginning and continuity

With the Second World War, most of the social visions which had been the mainspring of modern art and architecture in the 1920s had evaporated. In their place new ideals of a peaceful and just community quickly evolved, but these all too often proved to be of limited feasibility when faced with the confrontational reality of the Cold War.

It very quickly became clear after 1945 that, despite the drastic experiences of the Second World War, there was in art, as in politics, no such thing as a "clean slate." One style had certainly lost its credibility with the downfall of the Third Reich: the *Classicism* employed by Albert Speer and Paul Ludwig Troos for their Nazi prestige buildings. On the other hand, the Modernist *International Style* (see pages 30 et seq.), which had no undesirable political connotations, came alive again after 1945, particularly in the United States. German architects such as Walter Gropius and Ludwig Mies van der Rohe who had emigrated there were able to look back to their earlier work, and to take it further after 1945.

In addition, as lecturers in the universities they became role models for a complete generation of young architectural students. Despite the numerous cultural and political rifts caused by the Second World War, the language of forms associated with the International Style in architecture carried with it an important element of continuity from the prewar era.

Shattered countries had to be rebuilt, and *reinforced concrete* and glassy façades became the hallmarks of a new era. From south America to southeast Asia, architecture took on a unified style, which put its stamp to a greater or lesser degree on all cities, sometimes pushing regional architectural forms into the background, or causing them to disappear from the profile of the city altogether.

**Walter Gropius, *Graduate Center,*** Harvard University, Cambridge, Massachusetts (USA), 1950

In 1935 the architect and ex-director of the Bauhaus in Dessau (see page 33), Walter Gropius emigrated, via England, to the USA, where in 1950 he once again designed a building for educational use, this time for Harvard University, where he himself taught.

Although the arrangement of the volumes and the supports on which they rest have a clear affinity with the Bauhaus building, the spirit of revolt is gone. In the face of the horrors that heroic ideologies had brought upon the world, stylistic muteness seemed the proper response. The daring of Modernism had given way to the bland interchangeability of the *International Style*.

**Philip Johnson, *Glass House,* New Canaan, Connecticut (USA), 1949**

It is difficult to imagine anything more transparent. Living space and country space intermingle. All the exterior walls are completely glazed. The steel frame which supports the whole could not be more minimal. Only the bathroom unit is in a closed cylinder. But you could only live so openly if, like Philip Johnson in New Canaan, you could protect yourself from prying eyes by turning the surrounding countryside into your own private property. The high point of building in glass was a dead-end for residential building in general.

**Charles Eames, *Eames House,* Santa Monica, California (USA), 1949**

It looks at first sight like a system-made factory building. In reality it is a house. The villa, which director, furniture, and exhibition designer Charles Eames designed for himself, made no secret of the fact that it was made of industrially prefabricated parts: it became the prototype of industrial building and *high-tech architecture.*

## THE BAUHAUS TRADITION IN THE UNITED STATES

### Old masters – new buildings

Two of the leaders of the Bauhaus emigrated to America: Walter Gropius in 1935, followed by Ludwig Mies van der Rohe who finally left Germany in 1938. They brought its traditions with them: simplicity of construction and strict rationality, which had been characteristic of Bauhaus building since the 1920s and which struck a chord in postwar American society.

By the end of the 1930s, Walter Gropius had already taken part in several competitions for college buildings in the USA, and also produced a few buildings. When he built the Graduate Center at Harvard, where he also held a lectureship, he was able to refer back to these earlier designs, although he made a point of arranging the buildings to suit the courtyard system prevailing elsewhere in Harvard.

The Graduate Center casts light in many respects on Gropius's views on modern architecture and the way it is produced. He realized the Harvard buildings in cooperation with his studio TAC (The Architects' Collaborative) in which he saw the materialization of his ideas about creative teamwork. The Graduate Center is also a formal and personal link with the Bauhaus tradition in Germany. The elegant pillared buildings with their flat roofs and long strip windows, which he created for Harvard, were entirely in the tradition of the 1920s language of form. And for the artistic decoration of the complex he brought in old comrades in arms from his Bauhaus days such as Herbert Bayer, Josef Albers, and Hans Arp.

Ludwig Mies van der Rohe understood even better than Gropius how to adapt to American needs the basic principles of his classical-modern formal language, which he had employed in the late 1920s in the Villa Tugendhat, or in the famous pavilion for the international exhibition in Barcelona. His legendary maxim "less is more" was taken by a whole generation of architects not just as a brilliant sally, but as an article of faith.

### Johnson and Eames – in the footsteps of the master

Steel and glass were Mies van der Rohe's favorite materials and he knew how to use them – in both residential and commercial buildings – like no one else. The steel and glass mania which Mies unleashed in America found many imitators, including Philip Johnson. Johnson, who had worked for a time in Mies's office but later abandoned the plain language of forms cultivated there, went on to become one of the most brilliant figures of the American architectural scene in the 20th century. His publication, with Henry-Russell Hitchcock, of *International Style* at the beginning of the 1930s brought him instant celebrity. His Glass House in New Canaan emulates the strict purism of Mies.

The house was built, according to Mies's concept, on a steel frame which he *filled in* with nothing else but panes of glass. This highly fashionable house, elegant and aesthetic though it is, inescapably begs the question of how practical, how livable such architecture is. How are you supposed to live in a house made totally of glass?

The same, rather polemical question had been posed by many an architectural critic 20 years before in reference to the open ground plan developed by Mies van der Rohe for the Villa Tugendhat in Brünn. Looking at the Glass House, so clearly built to a program, one has the insistent feeling that this is less architecture for living in than a sort of architectonic confession of faith. This feeling is further confirmed by other buildings carried out later by the extremely versatile Johnson, which also seem to have been programmatically conceived. One striking example is the AT&T Building (see page 87) in New York, which counts today as an icon of post-modern architecture.

Charles Eames took a quite different route from Johnson in his steel-frame residential

# MIES VAN DER ROHE

One of the most successful architectural trends around 1910 was *Neoclassicism*, the stern monumentality of which worked as an opposing pole to the mobile flowing forms of *Art Nouveau*. Ludwig Mies van der Rohe, born in Aachen in 1886, was employed early on in the studio of Peter Behrens (see page 23), one of the leading Neoclassicists of his day, and so came into direct contact with the style; he was in fact placed in charge of the execution of Behrens's project for the German embassy in St. Petersburg (1911–12). As a result his first personal projects reveal an intense involvement with the classicist architecture of the 19th century. The mainspring of Mies's architectonic inspiration was the work of Karl Friedrich Schinkel. Schinkel had been responsible, among other things, for the celebrated Alte Museum in Berlin, but also for numerous villas for the Prussian royal family in the neighbourhood of the Residenz (royal palace). Mies took from them a fine sense of proportion, clear forms, and a close relationship with the surrounding countryside, and then integrated these qualities into his early villas, such as the Urbig house in Potsdam (1914–17). But his ideal projects, which were the Country House in Concrete (1923) as well as the Country House in Brick (1924), reveal not only his involvement

*Ludwig Mies van der Rohe with the "Barcelona" chair he designed in 1929*

with his great forebear Schinkel, but reflect in their ground plans the discussion going on at the time about the abstract art of Theo van Doesburg. Mies van der Rohe's *Classicism* was therefore a translation of classicist trends into contemporary architectural language, which culminated in his renown architectonic credo "less is more."

But it would be to misunderstand Mies to think that this motto would lead to an architectural puritanism. On the contrary, precious materials such as marble and gleaming high-grade steel were frequently his chosen materials, as for instance in the famous German pavilion for the 1929 international exhibition in Barcelona. The open plan of the pavilion, with its unexpected encounters – with, for instance, a sculpture by

*Classical elegance in black steel and glass: the Neue Nationalgalerie in the Berlin Kulturforum, constructed between 1965 and 1968*

Georg Kolbe – and its carefully studied delineation of interior space, revealed Mies van der Rohe's astonishing sense of the right dimensions and proportions, and give the visitor a unique sense of space.

The discrepancy between Mies's inclination for simple forms and his preference for costly materials – as exemplified in the Barcelona pavilion – caused the architect Hans Poelzig to frame his revealing bon mot: "We build simply, however much it costs."

Controversy also arose in these years over Mies van der Rohe's Villa Tugendhat, which he built in 1930 in Brünn, and which carried over the principle of an open ground plan, as developed in the Barcelona pavilion, to a residential building. This led to the question whether it would actually be possible to live in a house which broke so radically from the typical design for a luxurious private home.

Mies succeeded Walter Gropius and Hannes Meyer as head of the Bauhaus (see page 33) which was then under heavy pressure from the National Socialists. He moved it from Dessau to Berlin and there tried to save it, in vain. Most of the other projects which he attempted to launch after 1933 as an architect under the Third Reich also failed to take root. In 1938 he answered the call of the famous Armour Institute (later IIT) and went to Chicago. Here, in the 1940s, he created the new buildings in simple *rectilinear* forms for the Illinois Institute of Technology (IIT), whose steel frame construction, faced with brick or glass, became a model for other architects. Mies now succumbed to a desire which he had cherished for a long time, which was to construct a tall building. Whereas his sketches for a tall building on the Friedrichstrasse in Berlin (1921), a glass skyscraper (1922), and a tall office building in reinforced concrete (1923) never left the drawing board, he realized his dream of building a glass skyscraper with the twin towers on Lake Shore Drive in Chicago (1948–51) and the legendary Seagram Building in New York (1954–58), which became the model for a whole succession of skyscrapers of similar design.

*A gleaming icon of glazed high-rise architecture: the Seagram Building, realized by Ludwig Mies van der Rohe with Philip Johnson between 1954 and 1958*

However, Mies's classically elegant architecture, which was now totally dominated by glass and steel, had a late homecoming to Germany. His Neue Nationalgalerie in the Berlin Kulturforum, which he created in old age, forms a rationalist pole in opposition to the expressive architecture of Hans Scharoun's neighboring Philharmonie building.

The confrontation of the two buildings forms a dramatic finale to the trajectory of a generation of architects – that of the European avant-garde, whose influence stretched from the decline of *historicism* to the end of the 1960s.

The Berlin museum building is composed of two parts: a temple-like steel hall with an entirely glazed façade, and a large lower ground floor, in which the work of the classic modernists is displayed. In his handling of the tasks of building a "temple" and a "museum" Mies shows himself for the last time as the great classicist and follower of Schinkel. It was after all in his Altes Museum (situated not far from the Neue Nationalgalerie) with its front of ionic pillars, that the two tasks were successfully combined for the first time.

**Wallace Harrison, Max Abramovitz,**
***UN Building,*** New York, 1950

"We are planning a world architecture," said Le Corbusier, who as a member of the architectural commission contributed a large part of the preliminary design for the United Nations Headquarters, "and for this kind of work there is no other name … but discipline." So the most public site in one of the most important and cosmopolitan metropolises in the world was chosen for this most important of world building projects: the East River in New York. Le Corbusier sketched several outlines for the building. The low, level conference center and the upward-striving assembly hall were dominated by the administrative building, a slim, slab-shaped skyscraper. Innumerable critics interpreted this as an unwitting sign that world government had long ago been taken over by bureaucracy.

The building plans, produced by a major American architectural firm, Harrison & Abramovitz, emphasized the oneness of the nations still further. A homogenous gleaming curtain of green glass covers all 39 stories. The same, story-high window module is used 2,730 times. There was another sense, however, in which the UN administrative building represented world architecture: similar *curtain wall*-clad tall boxes are to be found everywhere on the face of the globe.

buildings, such as his Case Study House No. 8, built between 1945 and 1949, which arose out of a competition for the development of prototype houses, or the house which he erected in 1949 for himself and his wife Ray in Pacific Palisades, Santa Monica. Eames, who was also famous as a designer, used the same materials as Johnson – steel and glass – yet their almost contemporaneous buildings were fundamentally different. While Johnson's blazoned his belief in the dominant architectural trend of the time, Eames's fascinated by their reserved, almost fragile elegance. They had a characteristic truth to their materials: standard industrial components which could be ordered by catalog. The construction principles of this technicized house-building can be read from the façade, endowing what were, in the main, very simple materials with an aesthetic all their own.

The steel frames of his houses could be filled in various ways, most often with glass. The rectangular grid composed by the crossbars of the windows, and the sensitive way in which the houses were made to interact with the natural world around them without dominating it, revealed Eames's experience of traditional Japanese frame-buildings. The result was both filigree and balanced: masterpieces of aesthetic architecture.

### The new language of the skyscrapers

The skyscrapers designed by Mies van der Rohe ensured that the prestige office and administration buildings of big firms in these years used glass as their prime material. The

appearance of transparency and practicality conveyed by these buildings, their lightness and elegance, made them stand out dramatically among the *freestone*-clad, *eclectically* styled tall buildings dating from the turn of the century.

The core of all these skyscrapers was a supporting steel skeleton, on which the glassy façade was hung like a curtain. The standardized components of this curtain worked together with the exactly matched grid on which they were hung to create an impression of uninterrupted unity. The concepts of the "curtain wall," and the façade in the form of a grid quickly became synonymous with the architecture of commercial buildings in the 1950s and 1960s.

The glass wall was the solution architects had been seeking for a type of façade that would suit the constructional principle of the supporting skeleton. Instead of eclectic architecture whose pseudo-*Gothic* forms aped the massive appearance of a stone building, the glass wall provided a solution which carried over the lightness and variability of the supporting skeleton onto the façade.

In the last 20 years however, this exemplary honesty with materials has been counteracted by a renewed tendency to envelop skyscrapers in sheets of freestone in the place of the previous glass skin. This stone is intended to convey exactly that massive impression which was expressly avoided in the 1950s.

The glass façades of the 1950s ands 1960s demanded ambitious technical solutions from the architects in the interiors as well. Unlike traditional building in stone, glass gives no protection from heat or cold. The perfecting of air-conditioning, ventilation, and air-extraction techniques, as well as heat retaining double-glazing systems provided the conditions for the success of glass façades in tall buildings.

Even the project for the headquarters of the United Nations on the East River in New York, based on a design by Le Corbusier and carried out by Wallace Harrison and Max Abramovitz between 1947 and 1950 followed the trend. For the main building, which was the Secretariat of the UN, a tall slim glass wedge was the chosen style, with the side walls being without windows. The three buildings of the UN complex are so arranged as to constitute a well-proportioned and internally balanced ensemble of *rectilinear* forms. The differing heights of the three buildings for the Secretariat, the General Assembly, and the press, and the way in which they are graded in terms of space give them almost the quality of a three-dimensional abstract composition.

The theme of the steel or concrete skeleton with a glass curtain wall has remained modern, as is documented by the elegant glass buildings of the 1980s and 1990s by Jean Nouvel (illustrations pages 102–103) and by Norman Foster's skyscrapers (illustration page 80). The glassy cube, in various guises, is a leitmotif that runs through the whole architectural history of the 20th century, from the Bauhaus in Dessau, through Mies van der Rohe's Neue Nationalgalerie in Berlin to Jean Nouvel's Institut du Monde Arabe in Paris.

Once the glass wall had been discovered, it turned out to be a highly versatile way of facing a building, particularly a skyscraper. Architects have reacted to the changing tastes of clients over the last 40 years by exploiting the wide range of possibilities it offers: stressing the articulation of the glass wall in a particular grid, as in the Richard Daley Center in Chicago, built by Skidmore, Owings & Merill as well as C. F. Murphy in 1965, or by varying the ground plan, from the rectangular box through to the polygon, as created by Walter Gropius for the PanAm Building in 1963. All of these types of buildings, right through until the postmodern variants, are finally – leaving aside technical innovations in air-conditioning or ventilation – only variations on a theme which was established at the beginning of the century by the introduction of the new building materials – glass, steel, and concrete.

### Horizontal versus vertical

Glassy slabs in the style of Mies van der Rohe did not necessarily have to grow upwards. For the American car company General Motors (GM), Eero Saarinen, who was the son of the architect Eliel Saarinen, built research laboratories in the form of a long horizontal ribbon of glass. The building was part of a much larger installation for GM, including an assembly hall in the shape of an aluminum-covered glittering hemisphere.

Saarinen's formal language and use of materials was too technicist to be truly sober. At a time when the United States was carrying out experimental explosions with atomic bombs on the Bikini Atoll in Oceania without any particular precautions, and the competition between the United States and the Soviet Union to be the first into space was reaching its climax, architecture itself took on a distinctly futuristic aspect.

The centuries-old interaction between client and architect, which has outlasted every architectural epoch and fashion, came into play once again in the commission to build research laboratories for GM: buildings have both a functional and a prestige role to play, so it almost went without saying that the commission implied developing a design that would express the technical expertise and forward-looking attitude of the clients and their products.

## REACTIONS

### USA meets Europe

The most perfect variation on the theme of steel and glass must be the town hall created by Arne Jacobsen for Rødovre in Denmark (1954–56). Like Saarinen's GM complex the building did not develop upwards but horizontally. A strict grid articulated the three stories of the building. The separate segments were placed at right angles to each other following the same strict system. The administration block, which was both taller and longer, was linked by a glazed walkway to the lecture area lying behind, which was almost totally composed of large panes of glass. The extremely sober and yet highly elegant formal

Eero Saarinen, *General Motors Technical Center,* Warren, Michigan (USA), 1948–56

The administration building (foreground) of General Motors, with its *curtain wall* façade put together with prefabricated units, is comparable with the contemporary steel and glass buildings of Mies van der Rohe, and develops his style further in the imaginative use of materials (enameled metal plates sealed with neoprene strips). The building exhibits a colorful differentiation of shades in its materials, creating the impression of a layering of strata, given a rhythm by the vertical movement of the slender steel skeleton. Architectonically, both the research laboratories and the domed conference building (background), make a statement about the technical expertise associated with General Motors.

**Alison and Peter Smithson,**
***Hunstanton School,*** Norfolk,
Great Britain, 1949–53

"Water and electricity no longer come out of inexplicable holes in the wall, but through visible conduits. Hunstanton school doesn't just *look* as though it's made of glass, tiles, steel, and concrete, it *is* made of glass, tile, steel, and concrete." This statement by Alison and Peter Smithson was the first formulation of the philosophy of *Brutalism*, which was highly influential right into the 1970s, a "brutal" honesty in materials, construction and function.

language of the exterior was continued in the interior, as for example in the self-supporting stairs, which had gleaming steel rails and reflecting glass balustrades.

The challenge set by Mies van der Rohe's buildings to the younger generation of architects, to which Jacobsen was responding, was met – just as radically but in a formally quite different way – by Alison and Peter Smithson.

Their design for Hunstanton School in Norfolk, Great Britain (1949–53), refers back to Mies's concept of steel-frame buildings. But in contrast to Jacobsen's strictly axial layout, their building has an asymmetrical ground plan. Nor did they use only glass and steel: their steel frame construction was *faced with brick.* The decisive innovatory factor in their much-talked-about school building was that all conduits for water, electricity, and so on, and all supply shafts were clearly on view. This unconditional honesty about materials which showed everything and hid none of the technology of the building is, however, the point at which the Smithsons began to take leave of

Mies van der Rohe's carefully balanced and aesthetic architecture. It announced a new turn in 20th century architecture which was to be the mark of the 1960s and 1970s, the so-called "Brutalism."

## ARCHITECTURE AS SCULPTURE

### Spirals of art

Frank Lloyd Wright had been setting his mark on American and European architecture and exerting his influence over numerous younger architects for over half a century when he completed his most notable late work, the Solomon R. Guggenheim Museum (first sketch 1943), intended to offer public access to its patron's collection of modern painting.

Since the early 19th century a museum had become one of the most significant building commissions. Rulers and the aristocracy had, from the Middle Ages through to the 18th century, built up private art collections for their personal enjoyment and edification; then, around 1800, the middle classes discovered an interest in art. The transformation of the Louvre in Paris into a museum, and the building of Karl Friedrich Schinkel's Alte Museum in Berlin set a model for modern museum culture and were soon followed by many other buildings.

This then was the background to the instructions that Solomon Guggenheim gave to the 70-year-old Frank Lloyd Wright when commissioning him to build his museum in the up-and-coming art metropolis of New York, instructions that were as lapidary as they were difficult to follow: the new museum should be unlike any other. In fact the solution that Wright found was extremely unusual and totally unique.

**Arne Jacobsen,** *Town Hall at Rødovre,*
near Copenhagen (Denmark), 1954–56

Building doesn't come much more elegantly precise than this. Jacobsen's Rødovre town hall must be the most perfect variant on construction in glass and steel. It was also a sharp denial of the reigning building tradition of Denmark, with its tendency to use natural materials such as wood and brick, and the preference for lots of color. The building was also a new interpretation of the concept of a "town hall." Instead of hiding away the workings of the administration in the usual secret compartment, Jacobsen puts democracy on show in a fully glazed assembly hall for the local council.

Like an inverted cone with its point buried in the earth, the main body of the building rears up, a sculpture in its own right. To get to the pictures the visitor has to go up in a lift to the top; the route then leads the visitor gently downwards in broad spirals which can be divined from the exterior of the windowless cone. The ramp he follows encloses a bright, atrium-like interior court which runs through the center of the building, crowned with a shallow glass dome.

There has been much argument as to whether Wright's museum, the completion and opening of which he did not live to see, is a sufficiently museum-like setting for the pictures of the Guggenheim collection. But it is absolutely certain that Wright created a unique building which reminds one, with its utopian formal language, of the early architectural visions of the 20th century, and thus thoroughly corresponds with the abstract pictures housed therein.

## LE CORBUSIER

### The new community – the Unité d'habitation

Although the construction of the UN complex originated with a sketch by Le Corbusier, other architects were then brought in to carry out the detailed design of the building (see page 60). However, Le Corbusier, who was always the great planner and outrider of the avant-garde, also entered the public arena in Europe, with projects which served to confirm his

importance as the most important architect of the 20th century.

As early as the 1920s the general shortage of housing caused many architects to concentrate on the problem of building homes and *housing schemes*. In the foreground of their plans was the opening up of apartment design to provide more air and light and to rationalize building methods, but social needs were also met by the provision of communal facilities such as laundries and roof gardens in the housing schemes.

Le Corbusier himself engaged with the questions of collective living in his theories on town planning, presented in his book *La ville radieuse* of 1935.

His Unité d'habitation in Marseille (see illustration page 66), built between 1947 and 1952, was a complex designed to satisfy the most diverse needs of its inhabitants in a single building. The Unité had a unique infrastructure, including a hotel, a roof garden, a children's paddling pool, a nursery school, and a shopping center. It is not by chance that the architecture of the building as well as the structures on its roof are reminiscent of a giant ocean liner, the practical yet aesthetic forms of which had often occupied Le Corbusier in previous works. The Unité resembles a large ship at the edge of the harbor at Marseille, a ship which can supply all of its inhabitants' needs over an extended period with its shops and social arrangements, and in this way serves to exemplify Le Corbusier's ideas of collective living.

**Le Corbusier, *Notre-Dame-du-Haut,***
Ronchamp, Vosges (France), 1950–55

Walls several feet thick – in fact they are
double – in roughcast concrete bend to
enclose an inwards-turning meditative
space. The massive hung roof shaped like
mushroom cap, separated from the wall
by narrow glass inserts, is dramatically lit
and seems to hover. The variously shaped
and colored windows inset deeply into
the wall emphasize the successive
climaxes of the liturgy.
The pilgrimage chapel is a highly
expressive sculpture, which seems
at first sight to have nothing in common
with the rational apartment blocks that
Le Corbusier was building at the time.
Yet just as the Unité d'habitation gives
material form to a rational concept of a
place to live, so Ronchamp translates
the functional and emotional demands
of its religious purpose. In both cases
the requirement for the building is
rigorously fulfilled.

The 370 apartments in the Unité, which can
cover from one to several floors, are placed
in relationship to each other through a
complex grid of ground plans, which can be
divined from the articulation of the façades.
Unlike the somewhat monotonous grids of
the American skyscraper fronts, the façade of
the Unité is a work of graphic art. A glazed
gap in the facade indicates the presence of
the shopping street which is located inside the
Unité to serve the needs of the inhabitants.
The expressive roof landscape gives the
building, which stands on concrete supports,
an additional air of technicity.

### Sculptures in concrete

The Unité also struck a new note in its use
of materials. Raw concrete – *beton brut* –
without which a Le Corbusier building is
unthinkable, took on a more independent
quality in this one, standing on an equal
footing with other materials in the façade.

In all of Le Corbusier's late work we can
see a breaking free from the language of
Modernism which had become a worldwide
norm: it was still developing, and gave a significant impulse to the development of other
architects. In particular, his use of *beton brut*
was an important stimulus to architects such
as Kenzo Tange (see page 83) and Louis I.
Kahn, and found its embodiment in the
*Brutalism* (see page 69) of the 1960s.

This development in Le Corbusier's work
continued with the church of Notre-Dame-
du-Haut. This was erected between 1950 and
1955, and became one of the most significant
church buildings of the 20th century. There

was nothing here of the cool, clear materialism
of the glassy rectilinear skyscrapers he was also
building at this time. Instead of a standardized
or typified building, which could be erected
anywhere in the world given the appropriate
technology, Le Corbusier created at Ronchamp
a one-of-a-kind sculpture in concrete, whose
powerful visual effect can scarcely be encom-
passed in words.

The dominant feature of the building from
the outside is its roof, which projects far out
from the walls, and then dips in the middle
like the brim of a hat. The inner space has an
Expressionistic feel, with its irregularly set
windows and the curved forms of wall and
roof. If you permit yourself to respond to the
expressionistic formal language of Ronchamp,
become open to the way the lines and the light
are directed, and take in and understand this
architecture with your own eyes, then even this
gradual apprehension will become meditative
in a unique way which expresses the function
of the building as a sacral space.

## THE NEW CITY

### Le Corbusier's Chandigarh in India

At the end of his architectural career, Le
Corbusier was given the chance to dare to
realize an idea that had accompanied him all
his life: to turn his ideal of a new city into fact.
From 1951 till his death in 1965 he was occupied with the building of Chandigarh, which
had been founded as the administrative
capital of the new Indian state of Punjab.

India did in fact already have, in the 20th
century, considerable experience of the founding of new cities. The English architect Edwin
Lutyens had created the new capital New
Delhi for India when it was still ruled by Britain
under a viceroy. Le Corbusier understood how
to move from the impressive Classicism of
Lutyens buildings to a monumentality that did
not employ the Classicist language of forms.
He allowed himself to be inspired by Indian
architecture as well as the Indian way of
life, then mixed them with the specific formal
vocabulary of Modernism.

Le Corbusier realized the buildings of
Chandigarh with Jane Drew, Maxwell Fry, and
his longstanding collaborator, Pierre Jeanneret.
At the focal point of the of the city stand the
Administration Building, the High Court, and
the State Assembly Building. He again made

an expressive use of concrete, as he had in Ronchamp, and created sculptural roof landscapes in the style of the Unité.

But despite the quality of the individual buildings, it became clear that the project was doomed to failure. Planned as a symbol of the "New India," which gained its independence in 1947, Le Corbusier's work of genius was a work for the future, a vision of a city that was right for cars – in a world where most people went on foot because they could not afford any other means of transport. Even an architect of the caliber of Le Corbusier could not implant his elevated architectural vision in the Indian reality of Chandigarh.

## Architecture as the expression of a new world: Brasilia and Niemeyer's plans

When democracy set foot in Brazil in 1945, the breakthrough into a new era was also symbolized in architecture in a most extraordinary way. In the mid-1950s, the architect Oscar Niemeyer, who was a convinced communist, and the town planner Lúcio Costa were commissioned by President Juscelino Kubischek to plan a new capital city in the interior of that Latin American country: this was to be Brasilia.

The city was constructed between 1956 and 1963, for a population of 500,000, in a location chosen as a starting point for the opening up of the interior.

As an expression of progress and modernity it was conceived in the shape of an airplane, divided into three components – cockpit, fuselage, and wings – corresponding with city areas, and each of them with a particular function allotted to it: government, administration, residential.

The architectonic and functional center of the newly created city was the "Square of the Three Powers" (illustration page 66). Niemeyer's Chamber of Deputies was crowned with a saucer-shaped construction, and the Senate had a dome. Between the two there towered a pair of distinctive slab-shaped skyscrapers, which contained the offices of the administration. Both the monumentality and the axial quality of the buildings are characteristic of Niemeyer's architecture.

Highly praised at first, subsequently vilified, the visionary project actually fell victim to the reality of the country. The buildings are indeed strong, expressive visual creations, but the architect had not taken any particular account of the climatic conditions of the Brazilian interior. Much more serious turned out to be the magnetic effect which the airplane-shaped city center exerted on the people in the country that was around it. The city is now surrounded by a ring of more or less official slums, which has swollen the number of inhabitants to two million. This has had obvious fatal consequences for the overburdened civic infrastructure of Brasilia, which had originally been designed for a quarter of that number.

**Oscar Niemeyer and Lúcio Costa,**
*Cathedral,* Brasilia, 1956–63

In 1956, President Juscelino Kubitschek of Brazil commissioned the building of a new capital city in the Amazon forest 600 miles (1,000 kilometers) northeast of Rio de Janeiro. Lúcio Costa designed the general plan of the city and Oscar Niemeyer was responsible for the architecture.
Arranged in a circle, 21 supports curve inwards and widen to meet in a halo at the top, which projects an impressive ball of light downwards into the building, bathing it in gleaming colors.
Oscar Niemeyer's buildings for Brasilia, especially the congress building with its two concrete bowls (illustration page 66), the presidential palace "floating" in water, and the cathedral with its mighty concrete rays all have a fantastic yet grandiose quality which places them among the highest achievements of modern architecture.

# TOWN PLANNING IN THE 20TH CENTURY

## 1930–2000

The 20th century marked the transition from town architecture to town planning. The transition occurred as a result of the industrial revolution which took the traditional city beyond its limits, and gave birth to a new ideal: the modern city. The attempt to realize this ideal came to grief in the 1980s, leading to nostalgia for the traditional city. But at the end of the 20th century, the changing economic context brought the question of the city and the possibility of exerting an influence through planning, onto the agenda once more.

### The modernist city

Whereas the designs for garden cities and "Usonia" (see pages 40–41) took root in the country, the French architect and socialist Tony Garnier made detailed plans for a model of a modern industrial city. The project, which he presented in 1904 for a "Cité industrielle," had separate areas demarcated for different functions, such as living, working, relaxation, and transport. The traffic system had separate roads for vehicles and pedestrians, through-roads, and access-roads. Green spaces took up more than half of the city area. Set in the midst of these were loose groupings of simple free-standing apartment blocks, built of reinforced concrete using industrial techniques, and affording plenty of air and light.

Garnier did the conceptual preparatory work for the Modernist town-planners. Both his architectonic details and planning ideas became their basic principles. But it was the ambitious abstract projects of Le Corbusier which first gave these ideas ideological force and promoted their final breakthrough. In 1922 he worked out his plan for the "Ville contemporaine." Whereas Garnier's town was small, with buildings a maximum of three stories high, Le Corbusier wanted to provide homes for up to three million inhabitants massed into residential areas with buildings up to 60 stories high. His "Plan voisin" three years later placed his designs in a real location for the first time. He suggested replacing a part of the historic old city of Paris with 18 skyscrapers 650 feet (200 meters) high. The theoretical foundation of this signed manifesto was worked out by the fourth Congrès Internationaux d'Architecture Moderne (CIAM) and published in 1943 by Le Corbusier and the French CIAM group.

This "Charter of Athens" was the manifesto for the new city. Whereas the traditional city drew a boundary between itself and the country, divided up its activities between public and private zones of influence, differentiated between public streets, squares and parks, and private buildings, and separated town planning from architecture, the modernist city would be a single, open space for living that was organized by a central state planning authority. In place of the mixed-use road system open to all means of transport that was to be found in the traditional city, the modernist city would have a traffic system separated hierarchically according to function. The housing question was inseparable from the crisis in the old cities, and should no longer be left in the hands of private speculators, but instead dealt with by erecting whole areas of mass housing, all built to the same standard, and offering light, air, and sun for all.

The Charter of Athens became the guidebook for all new town planning and building worldwide in the decades that followed. Its emphasis on the new, found particular favor with the states founded after the Second World War. East Berlin's city center was one of many dedicated to the collective idea. Over the ruins on either side of the Frankfurter Allee, Edmund Collein, Werner Dutschke, and Josef Kaiser built the first socialist residential complex between 1959 and 1965. But the West built almost as many mass housing schemes of questionable value: right up until the mid-1970s, estates with tens of thousands of separate living units were put up as the old tenement areas were torn down. Centers that had developed over centuries were programmatically rebuilt in the name of making the cities accessible for cars, and motorways were driven through the heart of the old cities.

The chance to build a completely new city occurred only rarely, however. Between the years of 1951 and 1965 Le Corbusier was commissioned by Pandit Nehru to plan the state capital of Chandigarh, which was intended to be the symbol of modern India. Over a space of

*The bowl-shaped congress building, and behind it the skyscraper housing the government offices, on the Square of the three Powers in Brasilia by Oscar Niemeyer*

around 250 acres (100 hectares) he laid out a grid of through roads. In between these there were residential areas for 150,000 people, with all the 13 different castes of Indian society living separately from each other. The only area shared by all was the line of commercial establishments along the east-west axis, in the middle of which was the civic center. The state government was separated off in its own area to the north of the city.

Similar concepts inspired Brazil to built a new capital city 600 miles (1,000 kilometers) away from Rio de Janeiro on the high plateau of Planatina. The competition to plan the city was won by Lúcio Costa in 1957. Four years later Oscar Niemeyer had already erected the most important buildings, and Brasilia was inaugurated in 1961. Costa's plan was based on a very simple grid of

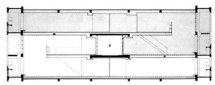

*The Unité d'habitation in Marseille by Le Corbusier (1952), and a cross-section through three floors showing two living units (page 64)*

four- to ten-lane motorways. The east-west axis is 1.4 miles (2.2 kilometers) long and 1150 feet (350 meters) wide, and along it lie all the buildings housing local government, sports, and the armed forces, and hotels and theaters. It culminates in the "Square of the Three Powers" with the 38-story government building, the bowl of the congress chamber, the dome of the senate, the law courts, the foreign ministry, and the cathedral (illustration page 65). At right-angles to this monumental axis runs the 8.7-mile (14-kilometer) long north-south axis, flanked by residential complexes with green areas around them, in which people live in slab-shaped buildings five or six stories high. The banks and the shopping center are located at the intersection of the two highways.

Brasilia is an exemplary demonstration of the failure of modern town planning. It was successful only insofar as it solved the housing problem. In all

*Alvaro Siza Vieira, "Bonjour Tristesse," the "critical reconstruction" of an apartment block in the run-up to the International Building Exhibition (IBA) in Berlin-Kreuzberg, 1982–83*

other ways it could not even live up to its own promises. Brasilia's road system does not permit you to cover a distance of a mile simply on foot, you have to go by car, taking a six-mile detour. The international town planning ideas realized here take no consideration of the site or of the traditions of the country. The functionally divided city, intersected by motorways, left nowhere for civic life to grow. It merely represents a collection of buildings, not a city. Despite the enormous open spaces, there is none that can be used by society. Because the plan accounted for every square inch of Brasilia, today three-quarters of the inhabitants live in satellite towns which have grown up without any plan at all. The main lesson that was learnt from Brasilia was that town planning efforts that impose the new instead of giving space to what has developed historically deny themselves from the outset any chance of sustained development.

## The renaissance of the city

So, theory looked again at the traditional city. In his book *L'Architettura della Città*, published in 1966, the Italian Aldo Rossi stressed that the form of the city, its ground plan, was valid for every era. Only the use that is made of it must be appropriate to each era. An example he gave was the Placa del Marcato in Lucca, the oval form of which is based on the Roman amphitheatre that stood on that spot. In the 1970s, the Dutchman Rem Koolhaas published several analyses of the metropolis of New York. In his book *Delirious New York* he celebrates the principle of mixed use. The skyscraper which accommodates offices and dwellings, as well as places of entertainment under the same roof, and which, as seen in the Rockefeller Center (illustration page 49) also creates a free space, is Koolhaas's prototype of the city building. Koolhaas's 1972 drawing "The City of the Captive Globe" shows how the most diverse architectonic manifestations can be put together into a unified city by means of a system of blocks. The work stresses the advantages of separating architecture and town planning.

In 1977 the "Charter of Machu Pichu" was drawn up. It was the antithesis of the Charter of Athens, and it demanded, amongst other things, the preservation of historic buildings, the continuity of the city ground plan, the integration of various uses, and the priority of public transport over individual transport.

Thereafter town planning concentrated more and more on the inner city. Between 1984 and 1987, the Internationale Bauausstellung (IBA, the International Building Exhibition), turned West Berlin into a showplace for town planning ideas. Under the slogan "careful city renewal," superannuated buildings were set in order and their ability to last into the future demonstrated in the shadow of the Wall. Under the slogan "critical reconstruction," the ground plan of the city that had been destroyed by the war and by modernist town planning was reconstituted with the most varied examples of contemporary architecture. The IBA was extremely successful in its basic project of regaining the inner city as a place to live. But so long as the project "city" was the preserve of the public authority alone and only council housing was put up, only the form of the city was created; its substance – civic life – was not.

Spain was more successful: in an extraordinary act of concerted effort between 1981 and 1993, innumerable squares were brought to life again in Barcelona, and all over the country schools, tramways, and cultural centers were constructed. At the end of Franco's dictatorship the collectivity, which had been long repressed, reasserted its rights over civic space.

## Today's situation

The individualization of society at the end of the 20th century has put a question mark once again over the idea of the city as a community project. The liberalization of the economy is undermining the planning monopoly of the town councils. These had already lost their active role in city development through the crisis in financing brought about by that liberalization, which had enhanced the role of private investors. When there is doubt that the city can be planned at all, aesthetic concepts step into the background.

In the mid-1990s the German Dieter Hoffmann-Axthelm reflected on the question of whether it

was still possible to plan under these conditions and to ensure a continuing development for the city. His *Anleitung für den Stadtumbau* (Guidelines for Rebuilding in the City), takes a position against large town-planning interventions: the basic structure for the city is already there in the historically given layout of the streets. Working upon a structure of small units offers the guarantee that all town-planning goals are achieved and that no part can be developed at another's cost. After the excessive weight of private enterprise in the 19th century and the dominance of the state in the 20th, the "third city" should be based upon cooperation.

His plea for small-scale cooperative development appears completely utopian in the face of larger changes in the cities. All over the world it is not the centers themselves that are developing, but the peripheries.

The regions of southeast Asia are expanding the most explosively. For example, the triangle of Hong Kong, Macao, and Canton is fusing into a mega-agglomeration with unimaginable speed. The number of inhabitants of Canton has doubled in only five years. Hong Kong's satellite city, Shenzen, has a population 115 times greater than 20 years ago. These quantum leaps are occurring within giant building projects . Macao is planning land reclamation which entails filling in an area of water 23 square miles (60 square kilometers) in size. Between Hong Kong and Canton half a dozen overspill cities are planned and whole bays are being filled in to gain valuable building land. Some 300,000 people will live in skyscrapers at least 40 stories high. This growth leads to an unbelievable concentration of population: there are 20 times more people on a single square yard in Hong Kong than in a big city in Europe. The resultant problems, for instance with the traffic, are reminiscent of the crisis in the European cities in the 19th century. History seems to be repeating itself.

Yet in face of the much greater speed and force of the problem it seems questionable to try to deal with it using town-planning methods that were developed over the past 100 years. The cities of southeast Asia have become the experimental terrain for a new model of the metropolis: the chaos city. This "city" is no longer constituted by the collectivity of its inhabitants which expresses itself in a unified type of building, but in the confrontation of conflicting interests, which takes advantage of an open but temporary spectrum of opportunities. In the permanent process of growth and change inherent in such a city, planning has no chance.

*Land reclamation projects in Hong Kong, circa 2000. Left in the picture, facing Lantau, the new airport as an island in the sea*

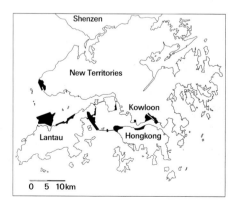

## "The Swinging Sixties"
# Vision and Reality
## 1960–1970

## SOCIALISM VERSUS CAPITALISM

### Let's make a revolution

To a blast of guitar music and bass rhythms from the Rolling Stones and the Beatles, and the sound of Jimi Hendrix's version of the American national anthem at the Woodstock festival, the youth of the world formed into a Protest Generation. Men let their hair grow longer and longer, and the multicolored batik T-shirt replaced the once obligatory, more formal shirt and tie.

University campuses from Berkeley to the Sorbonne developed into the intellectual spearheads of the protest. Their complaints initially were regarding unsatisfactory conditions of study, but their protest became increasingly political, turning against the traditional social values held by the Western world, and denouncing as a falsehood the network of structures – often democratic only in appearance – which made social privilege an everyday fact of life.

It was chiefly the situation in the United States that fueled the protests. The American civil rights leader Martin Luther King, following the example of Mahatma Gandhi, instigated peaceful protests demanding the implementation of equal rights for black Americans, who were still discriminated against, especially in

the South. But very soon the tide of protest turned against the role of the United States in Vietnam, where it was waging a barbaric proxy war on behalf of the pro-Western South against the communist-indoctrinated North.

In the Eastern bloc as well, reform movements were widespread. In revolt against daily repression and continually being told what to do and think, the citizens of Czechoslovakia demanded socialism with a human face. Freedom of expression was granted, whereupon the people demanded unrestricted democratization, provoking resistance by the party leaders of the "brother" countries. In August 1968, Warsaw Pact tanks crushed the hopes of the Prague Spring, bringing the world once more during the Cold War to the brink of an open military conflict.

During this time New York finally grew to the stature of the capital city of art, where Andy Warhol made screenprints of a Campbell's Soup tin, turning it into a work of art, and declared to the world that everyone could have their 15 minutes of fame in a world shaped by the presence of the media. Advertising, trademarks, stars, but also anonymous accident victims – Warhol's grids of multiple screenprints struck such a general chord that his series of Marilyn Monroe and Mao Zedong became real icons of the 1960s. The everyday became artistic reality for Andy Warhol, Robert

---

**1960**: A total of 17 states in Africa become independent: the end of colonial rule. The excess potential for nuclear destruction ("overkill") in the United States and the USSR results in an atomic stalemate. Ten-power disarmament conference begins in Geneva.

**1961**: On 13 August East Germany puts up the Wall between East and West Berlin. The contraceptive pill is developed and distributed. Death of the American film actor Gary Cooper.

**1962**: Cuba crisis: Khrushchev agrees to Kennedy's demand that he dismantle Russian rockets. First performance of Benjamin Britten's *War Requiem.* Suicide of Marilyn Monroe.

**1963**: US President J. F. Kennedy assassinated in Dallas on 22 November.

**1964**: Arafat takes over the leadership of al-Fatah (the Arab movement to drive the Israelis out of Palestine). International action at the time of the building of the Aswan dam in Egypt rescues the temple of Abu Simbel. In the cinemas is *A Hard Day's Night,* the British film

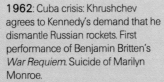

*A demonstrator holds up a bloodstained Czechoslovakian flag to a Soviet tank as it drives by: Prague 1968*

with and about the Beatles.

**1965**: Nobel Peace Prize awarded to the international children's aid organization UNICEF.

**1966**: In China, Mao's so-called "Cultural revolution" mobilizes the youth against (among other things) the inflexible Communist Party organization (ended 1969). In the West, beginnings of student unrest against the Vietnam War. Indira Gandhi becomes prime minister of India.

**1967**: Israel's six-day war against its Arab neighbors. Death of the socialist revolutionary leader Ernesto "Che" Guevara, who becomes an idol to revolutionary youth all over the world. First successful heart transplant in Cape Town. Herbert von Karajan sets up the first Salzburg Festival.

**1968**: Troops of the USSR, Poland, Bulgaria and East Germany invade Czechoslovakia to halt the path to reform. Assassination of the

*"That's one small step for a man, one giant leap for mankind": Neil Armstrong on the moon*

American civil rights leader Martin Luther King and of Senator Robert Kennedy. Starvation in Biafra, the civil-war plagued eastern region of Nigeria. The Club of Rome investigates the "Limits of Growth."

**1969**: US space mission Apollo 11: Neil Armstrong is the first man to walk on the moon. Pop festival at Woodstock (USA).

Rauschenberg, Tom Wesselmann, or Roy Lichtenstein, who made pictures like comic strips blown up to a very large format. Art became popular – "Pop Art."

In the 1960s socialist visions began to bloom all over the world, taking issue with the capitalist economy based upon private property and private ownership of the means of production, from a standpoint ranging from criticism to total rejection. Not only the new China of Mao Zedong, the Latin American revolutionaries Che Guevara and Fidel Castro, but also the theoretical acceptance of the social theories of Marx, Lenin or the Frankfurt School spread the idea of a socialist society resting upon equality, solidarity, and justice, which also in turn influenced both architecture and lifestyles.

## BRUTALISM

### The new openness

As early as the 1920s Rudolph Schindler had built a house for himself in America in which he tried to formulate new ways of collective living in the private sphere, reflected in the layout of the house. At the same time architects such as Gropius, working on housing schemes in Europe, were influenced by socialist views of society.

One of the important ideals which can be traced through the history of modern architecture in the 20th century is the attempt to lay bare the principles on which a building is

constructed, and from that the way it works. Load-bearing elements of a construction in *reinforced concrete* were revealed as such by not being covered with glass plates or *freestone*. The different function of the non-load-bearing parts of the façade could be stressed by the use of different material. The contrasts between materials would make the viewer draw conclusions about the role of different parts of the building. Behind that lay the concept of an honest architecture that did not hide its structures behind an interchangeable variety of façades. The American architect Louis I. Kahn (see page 71) formulated this principle very clearly when he postulated that for him, an architectonically designed space was one where you could see exactly how it was made.

Apart from Kahn and, among the younger generation, the Smithsons in England, it was once more Le Corbusier who most espoused this principle in his late work. It was to his use of *beton brut* (French, "brut" meaning "rough," "unfinished"), pure, naked concrete that we owe the idea of Brutalism: an architectonic direction which was founded on the ethical rather than aesthetic concept of a coherent style, and was to remain an important component of architectural forms of expression right through into the mid-1970s.

That Brutalism was an ethical rather than aesthetic concept can be seen from the fact that the idea of honest architecture which it promoted was not bound to the use of partic-

**Owen Luder Partnership, *Tricorn Centre*,** Portsmouth (UK), 1966

Brutal Brutalism: the Tricorn Centre includes offices, shops, restaurants, even apartments, and swallows up people and cars. Its only contact with the existing city is through the entrances via which visitors disembark into the surrounding streets. Docked in the center of the city of Portsmouth, the Tricorn complex is an autistic phenomenon. The brutal effect of the mega-complex is increased by the fact that the building is entirely made in concrete left rough from its formwork. Buildings such as the Tricorn Centre brought Brutalism and its favorite material into disrepute soon after the center was built. The recognition that the city is less in danger from materials and styles than from particular types of building, has not yet been fully acted upon. Centers such as the Tricorn go on being built.

ular materials. The principles of construction can just as easily be displayed when wood and brick are used as with steel and glass. However, under the influence of Le Corbusier it was the material most relevant for the time, *concrete*, which played the leading role in Brutalist building.

The most important thing was to show the logical principles behind the building. This applied by no means simply to the *façade* but also very much to the ground plan, which – once again in the ideal case – should be developed on the basis of the requirements that the users had for their building. Although the fundamental principles of Brutalism cast a great deal of light on the creation and reception of architecture, they were finally very seldom put into practice. They did after all not only presuppose an unconditional and equal agreement between the architect and his client, but also that one was able to break free of all modish trends – a virtually impossible undertaking, since no one can escape from the straightjacket imposed by the spirit of the time.

The supporters of Brutalism were very seldom able to translate their high theoretical ideals into buildings. What in fact arose were massive concrete forms which seemed to cut

themselves off consciously from the outside world, the antithesis of the glassy elegance of the skyscrapers with *curtain walls* or the expressive strength of an Eero Saarinen.

## EXPRESSION IN CONCRETE

### Curve instead of corner

Whereas before 1945 airplanes chiefly served military purposes and civil aviation was a much smaller affair, this situation changed dramatically after 1945. The times when pioneers of flight such as Louis Blériot or the Wright brothers just about managed to fly 300 feet (100 meters) were in the distant past, and the first crossing of the Atlantic by Charles Lindbergh was a faraway tale of flying history. In the place of the ocean liners, which had for a long time had the unique privilege of linking the continents, came the planes. The time it took to travel distances which had previously taken several days, now shrank to a few hours.

Civil aviation enjoyed a tremendous boom in the 1950s and 1960s. This boom is still going on today, and the number of flights per year, continues to rise. In a world in love with consumption, holidays and business, travel by plane quickly lost the image of an expensive luxury and became an affordable everyday matter for everybody. Gone were the days in which astonished children pointed up in the air, gazing with longing at the planes which circled majestically over their heads.

The increase in air travel was reflected in the building of newer, more modern, and above all bigger airports, which not only had to get passengers comfortably off on their travels, but also had to reflect the spirit of the age.

Whereas Eero Saarinen's research laboratories for General Motors (see page 61), created in the 1950s, had been a model of glass, soberly rectilinear construction, his style underwent a transformation at the end of the decade. In place of restful formal shapes, his work acquired a distinct expressivity. The Expressionism of the first half of the century (see page 24 et seq.) took on new life in his work, albeit in the form of quite different premises. Whereas the Expressionists of the Amsterdam School tended to use brick for their Gothic-influenced architecture, Saarinen's bold constructions would have been unthinkable without the versatility of reinforced concrete.

# LOUIS I. KAHN

Louis I. Kahn, born on the Estonian island of Ösel (today's Saarema) in 1901, is recognized as a master with light. His work is characterized by buildings that are basically geometric in form and to which their clarity imparts a majestic severity. His refined skill in directing light gives almost all his buildings an agreeable atmosphere and creates many surprising spatial effects. Kahn, who arrived in the United States in 1905, did not step into the international limelight until after the Second World War.

He had studied under Paul Cret at the University of Pennsylvania, where he received an academic education in the Beaux-Arts tradition, graduating in 1924; he did not carry out any projects outside the Pennsylvania area until he built the Yale University Art Gallery between 1951 and 1953. The Yale museum was articulated in two large cubes, which were divided by a cylindrical stairwell and a central service area. This arrangement reflects Kahn's architectonic principle regarding the functional placing of the "service" spaces and the areas which they

**Parliament building in Dhaka with presidential garden; rising up in the center of the buildings: the "crown" which lights the assembly chamber**

serve, a hierarchy underlining the mental clarity that can always be discerned in the substance of his architecture. Functional ground plans, simple constructions, and the aesthetically sophisticated deployment of both slits and wall-openings to allow light to enter, are the consistent thread that runs throughout all of his creative work. Yet the work as a whole remains extremely heterogeneous.

The Margaret Esherick House in Chestnut Hill, Pennsylvania (1959-61) is still in the tradition of *Neues Bauen*, and pays sensitive homage to the principle of open space with its combination of rough exposed concrete walls and large-paned glass façades. But projects such as the Kimbell Art Museum in Fort Worth, Texas (1966-72), with its round-arched roofs, are dominated by folkloric influences. Yet in both of these it is possible to discern a single, sensitive creative voice. Reacting to the Esherick House, where the transition between inside and outside is defined by the means of ventilation flaps – without negating the edge of the space – Robert Venturi, a pupil of Kahn's, wrote in his post-modern best-seller *Complexity and Contradiction in Architecture*: "It is not a particular style that makes the essence of an interior space, it is

what goes round it and the border between inner and outer." This agreed with Louis I. Kahn's conception according to which a building was primarily a shelter. He started his teaching at Yale in 1947, and never ceased to stress that every room was defined by its natural lighting as well as its construction, a formula with which he was able to unite technological and engineering factors with the sensual effect of a building's inner life.

Kahn's architectonic innovations lie in the use of prefabricated concrete parts, whose dimensions are determined by the radius of action of a builder's crane – "the extension of the human arm." His ideas on the direction of light as part of the structure of a room remain exemplary to this day. Since Louis I. Kahn did not go by hard-and-fast rules and principles, and every design began "from zero," he developed a host of typologies in his 50 years of architectural practice.

In business terms this way of working was constantly getting him into financial difficulties. Kahn lived for his work. In spite of an extremely full order-book, this very busy architect was always surprised when a client offered him a well-paid commission. Kahn would have undertaken for nothing tasks that led him further in his world of ideas. And he is said often to have thrown away all his plans just before the delivery date and start the work anew. When he died unexpectedly in 1974, his company was deeply in debt.

A key time in his life was a year-long stay in the American Academy in Rome, which enabled him to undertake trips to Greece, Egypt, and around Italy itself in the years 1950-51. Although he was already 50 years of age, studying the buildings of antiquity inspired him anew with the awe at their massive materials and heavy parts, which he had acquired from Cret, his Beaux Arts teacher: culture gained solidity by being rooted in the classics.

Using durable materials such as brick, *freestone*, and bare concrete, Louis I. Kahn created a monumentality situated on the border between architecture and sculpture. His synthesis of the two disciplines is most clearly expressed in the First Unitarian Church and School in Rochester, New York (1959-62), and is also clearly visible in the Salk Institute for Biological Studies in San Diego, California (1959-67). The façade of the church is distinguished by a heavily modulated, almost windowless surface. The building works like a massive *cube*, shaped by horizontal and vertical grooves. The windows disappear into vertical slits which give a visual rhythm to the façade. The brick walls in addition to the terra-cotta components strengthen the monumentality of the architecture. For his Salk Institute building

**Study building with pool: Salk Institute for Biological Studies in San Diego**

**Louis I. Kahn, about 1962**

Kahn once again created windowless cubes – this time in bare concrete – and grouped them round a courtyard. Openings in the walls are placed only where there is an unrestricted view on to the Pacific – so the space outside becomes a determining factor in how the space inside is experienced.

The design concepts of the many-layered wall, and the interplay of closed space and transparency were also operative in Kahn's most important work: the parliament building at Dhaka, Bangladesh (1962-83).

Eight appendages – cubes and "light-cylinders" – are arranged round an inner, cylindrical core. The concrete façade is articulated with grooves filled with white marble and pierced with semicircles, circles and triangles which produce fantastic light effects within. The parliamentary building resembles a citadel, and is crowned with a parabolic umbrella-shaped dome. Undoubtedly Kahn's last project, which was only finished after his death, and for which he was posthumous awarded the Aga Khan prize in 1989, belongs among the jewels of contemporary architecture.

# ALVAR AALTO

The Finnish architect Hugo Alvar Henrik Aalto was born in 1898, the son of a land surveyor. At only 23 he achieved an outstanding diploma at Helsinki polytechnic. This was the beginning of a career as the most famous architectural ambassador for his country in the 20th century. After his death in 1976, it was only a few months later that a 50-Finnmark note appeared, bearing his portrait and his most important late work, the Finlandia Hall in Helsinki.

In the midst of a wooded landscape: all the patients' rooms in the TB-Sanatorium Paimio face south

*Alvar Aalto during the time of the International Building Exhibition in Berlin, 1957*

His plans for both architecture as well as design had long since become major hits on the export market. The use of freely swooping curves, windowless brick walls, and rhythmic glassed façades are among Alvar Aalto's trademarks, placing him among the so-called "other Modernists" who did not confine themselves to white, unadorned *rectilinear forms*. A moderate who was both sensitive and close to nature, he remained all his life at a distance from "radical Modernism" but without his developing any trace of Historicism in his formal vocabulary.

Aalto's architecture, with innate feeling for materials and closeness to landscape, quickly awakened the respect of the European *Neues Bauen* movement. He was inherently a practical man who left only a few lapidary utterances about his understanding of architecture, but his work is considered as the first meaningful Scandinavian contribution to the international debate on architecture. Particularly notable is his synthesis of Finnish tradition (connecting elements in wood) with avant-garde functionalism (the visibility of the inner organizational structures). He created 20 buildings in foreign countries, among them a residential hall for students at the Massachusetts Institute of Technology in Cambridge, USA (1948), and a block of flats for the International Building Exhibition in Berlin in 1957. The Essen opera house was completed only after his death.

Aalto created four buildings that have become icons of modern architecture: the sanatorium in Paimio (1933), the Villa Mairea in Noormarkku (1939), and the community center in Säynätsalo (1952), all in Finland, as well as the 1935 town library in Viipuri (today Wiborg in Russia).

The sanatorium in Paimio in southwest Finland lies within a wooded landscape, and could only be built through joint financing by 50 communes. The guiding principle of the design, which was expressed in Aalto's submission for the competition in 1928, was to put a wide space between the tuberculosis patients and the rooms for the staff. This led to the ambitious scheme of creating a long and narrow building for the patients' rooms, which was a novelty in hospital design. All the rooms face south, to let in as much sunlight as possible. Because of the length of time the patients spent in bed, the ceilings were in dark shades and the lighting was indirect. The building is laid out asymmetrically, with several wings, and seems to draw up the landscape into itself. It is a classic example of modern architecture in which light, air, and sun form the parameters of the design, and served as a model for many other hospitals.

The introduction of light is also a defining element in the town library at Viipuri. The ceiling of the main reading room has circular openings from which light falls onto the interior. Arranged around a large open staircase is a U-shaped reading table, lit from above, from where it is also possible to see the book-issue desk. This library brought the *International Style* to Northern Europe.

The architecture of the Villa Mairea is also an ingenious combination of international Modernism with the vernacular building tradition. The client, who was president of a Finnish wood business, asked his architect to build a house in the middle of a landscape of pine trees, where the rim of the forest formed the edge of a site opening to the southwest. The façade is made of vertical wooden elements, enclosing organically shaped structural parts. The interior, organized on the principle of "flowing space," is especially noteworthy. In his standard work, *Space, Time, and Architecture*, Sigfried Giedion describes the impression it creates thus: "It is architectural chamber music, demanding the closest attention in order to understand how motifs and intentions are carried out, and in particular to recognize fully how the space is handled, and the extraordinary use of materials." The large windows permit the interpenetration of inner and outer space. The forest seems almost to penetrate the house, finding an echo in the slender wooden pillars. In the Villa Mairea, Alvar Aalto created a spatial continuum entirely in the spirit of Modernism, and it is unfortunate that he never put his ideas on paper, since it is almost impossible to deduce his theoretical position about architecture from his buildings alone.

*The stepped composition of the community center at Säynätsalo*

Although completed only in fragmentary form, his general plan of the center of Säynäsalo, 185 miles (300 kilometers) north of Helsinki, is one of his most important town-planning projects. The only part that was finished is the community center, which is characterized by its stepped construction. Aalto planned for two different levels within the whole and topped the composition with a slanted roof – a striking characteristic in his work – and let grass grow on the steps: a touch intended to link the building with nature.

Alongside his work as a member of CIAM, Aalto also made a name as a designer and a furniture maker. To this day, Artek, of which he was one of the co-founders, produces his strikingly designed chairs in bent plywood. The steel tubing furniture, which he had designed for the sanatorium in Paimio, reflects his connection with Bauhaus design (see page 33) – although he neither learned nor taught there. Alvar Aalto was an architect who preferred building to engaging with the theory of his discipline: "With every building I write ten volumes of philosophy."

*International Style and Finnish building tradition: the Villa Mairea in Noormarkku*

Saarinen had experimented several times with flying roofs held up by steel, as can be seen for instance in the ice hockey stadium at Yale University, Connecticut. But his best-known work in this style was to be the terminal for the airline company TWA, which he built on what used to be Idlewild Airport in New York, but today bears the name of the murdered American president John F. Kennedy. Used hundreds of times as a backdrop for feature films, the futuristic building was soon known all over the world.

Like a bird gently gliding through the air on outstretched wings, the arched concrete roof of the terminal shelters the passengers who commence their journey here. The dynamic volumes of the roof flow over the gently curving Y-supports, whose concentrated strength appears to push the roof upwards. Everything flows and glides in and out in the TWA terminal, now convex, now concave, while great glass spaces open up to let the light stream into the interior. With all its modernity and the futuristic ambience that strikes us today as so characteristic of the taste of the early 1960s, the building still radiates a beauty and harmony that very few of the steel and glass cubes of the period are able to convey. Saarinen's TWA terminal is a unique sculptural building, and, in its abstract representation of a bird, an example of *architecture parlante* in the best sense.

At almost the same time (1958–62) Saarinen was confronted with the task of building for an airport yet again, but this time it was not a single departures terminal, but the whole airport: Dulles Airport in Washington DC. Once again he designed a swooping roof for the high main hall, concave this time. However, in contrast to the TWA building, this one has a certain monumental quality arising from the regularly placed supports which are wider at the bottom, a quality that is not dissipated by the wide areas of glass, and which is indeed intended to express the importance of this airport that serves the American capital.

Reinforced concrete appeared to be adaptable and supple in the extreme, and the airy mobile-looking roofs of the 1950s and 1960s would not have been possible without it. However, such structures are only as durable as the materials and construction methods which architects and engineers bring to bear

on them. The potentially limited life of such roofs was made apparent by the frightening and totally unexpected collapse of the Berlin Congress Hall roof in 1980, when one person was actually killed by the falling debris. It had been designed in 1957 by Hugh Stubbins, Werner Düttmann, and Franz Mocken for the International Building Exhibition, and was seen as a sign of German-American unity. It had quickly become a Berlin landmark, referred to by the locals with affectionate irony as "the pregnant oyster" because of its unusual shape. After lengthy discussions, a decision was finally taken to rebuild it with an improved and, it is hoped, safer roof in celebration of the 750th anniversary of Berlin.

## A space for music in organic forms

It was back in the 1920s that Hans Scharoun, an architect practicing mainly in Berlin, formulated his principle of not working from a definition of what the façades would be, but by developing a building on the basis of the ground plan. This system, which he evolved chiefly in the course of designing private houses, was intended to create a harmonious intermingling of the various functional areas of a house, from everyday life, through work, to sleep. Unlike Mies van der Rohe, whose Neue Nationalgalerie (New National Gallery) was to appear later within sight of Scharoun's Berliner Philharmonie (Berlin Philharmonics) and which is both elegant and slightly constrained in its rectangularity, Scharoun deployed organically growing forms, whose rounded or sharply pointed shapes stood in striking contrast to many houses produced by the *Neues Bauen*

*Eero Saarinen,* **TWA Terminal,**
J. F. Kennedy Airport, New York, 1956–62

The roof spreads over the heads of visitors and passengers like the wings of a bird about to take flight. Underneath everything is open, everything flows. The traveler can see his airplane as he drives up in his taxi to the entrance. Held up by only a few Y-shaped supports, the prestressed concrete construction makes an optimal use of the plastic possibilities of the medium. The way in which Saarinen translates the symbolic meaning required of the building places the TWA terminal among the most impressive examples of expressive-organic building.

**Hans Scharoun,** *Philharmonie,*
Berlin, 1960–63

Three five-sided volumes turned towards each other under a tent-like concrete bowl determine the shape of the Berlin Philharmonic's concert hall. The geometry is so complex that a new cross-section had to be drawn every 20 inches (50 centimeters) in order to build the hall, which is as complex as the music performed there. Man and music are at the center of this entirely novel construction, with the stage forming the ideal focal point surrounded by banks of seats. All 2,200 members of the audience are in contact with each other through connecting aisles and through the management of space and the acoustics, which are equally good from every seat. All this combines to make the Philharmonie, the design for which goes back to Scharoun's *Expressionist* People's House of 1920, the aesthetic and conceptual summit of organic architecture.

movement at the time. His forms were, however, never an end in themselves, but were designed to give the owners of his houses a living environment that suited their needs as accurately as possible.

The crowning glory of this organic style of building was the Berlin Philharmonics (1960–63), which towers up expressively on the edge of the Tiergarten (the zoo). It was originally planned for another site, where it was to be the hub of a cultural center including a library, museums, and a place for visitors to stay, but so far it has remained the only part to be built. (In the context of the rebuilding of Berlin as a capital city, the debate about rebuilding it at the end of the 1990s has flared up anew and with even more passion than before.) While Scharoun pointedly did not make any grandiose architectural gestures in the entrance and foyer, in the concert hall itself the building opens up in all its beauty. The blocks of seats are juxtaposed to each other like a terraced southern landscape, affording equally good acoustics

and an uninterrupted view from any seat in the pillarless hall. A corresponding democratic element in this layout is that you can get from any seat to another in the auditorium without using the exterior corridors.

## Sailing architecture

Seldom in recent decades has any building become such a definitive and universal landmark, even a national symbol, as the Sydney Opera House, designed by the Danish architect Jørn Utzon. In point of fact, Utzon's powerful design, first outlined in 1956, provoked considerable controversy in Australia, which dragged out the building time until 1974. It is hardly surprising that the design, which is so full of movement, found an important supporter in Eero Saarinen when it was submitted for the international competition, and his influence as one of the judges helped Utzon to get the prize. Utzon himself drew his inspiration from many and various architectonic sources. The *classicist* Modernism of someone such as Gunnar Asplund influenced him as much as the organic buildings of Alvar Aalto. There was also the fact that Utzon had gathered experience for a while in the office of Frank Lloyd Wright.

The Sydney Opera House stands on a tongue of land extending far out into the harbor. Its nearness to the water and harbor is reflected in the extraordinary structure of crowding shell shapes that give it its memorable character. The brilliant white shells awaken associations of wind-blown sails and the ebb and flow of sea waves.

## Olympic pioneers

The Berlin Philharmonics and the Sydney Opera House are united by more than their exciting architecture, which in itself has become symbolic of their cities. Both of them are assembly buildings that have to receive large crowds of people. Since Max Berg built the Breslau Jahrhunderthalle between 1910 and 1913 (see page 21), halls with self-supporting roofs which could be realized without the need for view-obstructing pillars had become an important theme in architecture.

As we have seen from the work of Saarinen, in around 1960 there was a great deal of experimentation with new multiple tent-shaped constructions, particularly roofs. This produced especially attractive architectonic solutions for the problem of building a hall, which left the purely functional demands of that building project far behind. Numerous roofed arenas for competitive swimming, ice hockey, or basketball were produced, including those for the Olympic Games, where a multitude of spectators was offered not only a dry place to sit, but also an unrestricted view.

Among the pioneers of sports arenas and halls in Europe was the Italian engineer Pier Luigi Nervi, whose elegant reinforced concrete stadium in Florence (1930-35) is one of the icons of modern architecture. It was in the course of building airplane hangars that Nervi evolved a principle for constructing roofs out of intersecting precast concrete beams, making it possible to span enormous spaces. This technical principle had many applications beyond airplane hangars. Between 1956 and 1957 Nervi constructed the Palazzetto dello Sport, which was followed by its big brother, the Palazzo dello Sport for the Rome Olympics of 1960. Under the 300-foot (100-meter) wide dome of the Palazzo, 16,000 spectators could be accommodated. The principle of intersecting concrete beams underlying the construction of the dome led additionally to its decoration with an elegant and charming lozenge pattern.

Only four years later Kenzo Tange (see page 83), together with Uichi Inoue and Yoshikatsu Tsuboi, created a possibly even more inspired arena, full of ingenious touches, for the Olympic Games in Tokyo in 1964. The core of Tange's tent-like building was a steel rope that spanned two supports carrying the membrane-like skin of the roof. This roof construction was supported at the edges by a *reinforced concrete* frame. The aim of this so-called "natural structure," with its especially light materials and its woven network of supports, was to be able to span a space offering room for more than 16,000 spectators. The design of the Olympic Arena in Tokyo was a model for the tent-like Olympic buildings in Munich in 1972 (illustration page 81), and Tange was working at this time on similar solutions with Richard Buckminster Fuller and Frei Otto. It was the largest interior space with a roof unsupported by pillars that had been built at that time. But it was more than that; it was also perfectly constructed, a masterwork of *architectural engineering*, offering an aesthetic spectacle of particular charm, a charm arising from the interpenetration of the concave volumes of the roof skin and the wide-branching concrete supports at the side. It is also more than a further variation on the theme of sculptural architecture as already brought to masterly perfection by Saarinen. The powerful architecture of Tange's Olympic Arena develops an almost musical rhythm, which seizes the viewer's attention and directs it along the arched skin of the roof, up to the crown, then leads it gently all over the broad architecture of the hall. If the viewer allows himself to be absorbed by the movement of the architecture and follows its lines with his gaze, he will begin to feel in himself the gentle sway which is the essence of Tange's building.

**Jørn Utzon, *Opera House,*** Sydney, 1956-74

Looking like wind-filled sails, 12 white cement shells up to nearly 200 feet (60 meters) high stand on a deck of natural stone at the tip of a tongue of land extending into Sydney harbor, irrational and without any direct function but to arouse emotion. Yet they have become the symbol not just for Sidney but for the whole the fifth continent. They stand in two rows on top of the "experience zone": the concert hall, opera theatre, stage theatre, two foyers and main restaurant. The horizontally layered building underneath contains several stories of servicing departments for all the "experiences" presented above. Utzon's 1956 design for the Opera House, which won him the international competition and the contract to build it, places this Danish architect in the organic tradition of Wright, Scharoun, Asplund and Aalto.

Pier Luigi Nervi, *Palazzo del Lavoro,*
Turin, 1961

Pillars and roof are one in the Palazzo del
Lavoro. The radiating beams branch out
into the quadrilateral roof covering. Pier
Luigi Nervi, an engineer, equated good
construction and good design. Whereas
his exemplars Robert Maillart and Eugène
Freyssinet still worked with steel, Nervi
created a daring supporting structure in
reinforced concrete, whose plasticity,
proportion and rhythm endowed it with
aesthetic effect.

Carlo Scarpa, *Rebuilding of the Castel
Vecchio,* Verona, 1956–64

A steel upright supports a *Gothic*
travertine relief: Modernism meets History.
Carl Scarpa's rebuilding of the Castel
Vecchio, which had been rebuilt many
times over the centuries, brought an
exemplary solution to one of architecture's
hardest tasks: how to approach existing
buildings. Everything old that had
survived was restored, everything new
was shaped in appropriate modern
materials and forms. By contrasting and
layering different historical periods,
Scarpa made every epoch visible: history
could be experienced.

## APPROACHES TO HISTORY

### Tradition and Modernism together:
### foregrounding an aesthetic

One of the most difficult architectural tasks is
dealing with historic buildings. There is often a
conflict between the priorities of the owner,
who may put function or grandeur first, and
those of the conservationists, who will want all
the historic remains preserved as completely
as possible. With war-damaged buildings a
decision is relatively easy to reach: either you
make the new building an exact 1:1 copy of
the old, as for instance in post-1945 Warsaw
– or you look for a different, modern, architectonic solution to replace the building that was
destroyed. The result is always a new building:
in the first case in a *historicist* garb, in the
second case in a contemporary one.

But how do you deal with existing historical
buildings that have been changed and rebuilt
many times over the centuries, so that every
epoch has left behind a different layer? Should
one opt for a specific period, such as the
Gothic or the Baroque and carry out all necessary rebuilding or restoration in that *style*, as
was frequently done in the 19th century? Or
should one decide to leave all the historical
layers on view, and add contemporary changes
in a style appropriate to the times?

This last course was the one adopted by
the Venetian architect Carlo Scarpa in what is
perhaps his most important work, the restoration between 1956 and 1964 of the Castel
Vecchio, which is now used as a museum, in
the northern Italian city of Verona. Taking
deliberate cognizance of the mixture of styles
already present there, Scarpa attempted with

a combination of sensitivity and willingness to
experiment, to bring back a considered cultural
unity to the building, which would take the
demands of modern art into account. The result
is a grandiose total artwork, in which the historical strata from individual periods, and indeed
the restorations of previous periods, blend with
Scarpa's open architecture to form a completely
new interpretation of the building. Scarpa made
a clear distinction between modern building
materials, such as concrete, steel, and glass,
and historic materials, so that the various
different facing materials are juxtaposed,
creating an entirely original charm.

Scarpa, who first became famous for
exhibition architecture, used architecture in the
Castel Vecchio as a means of putting both the
building and its exhibition pieces on display.
The result is architecture as *mise-en-scène,*
which directs the visitors' gaze as well as the
route they follow, and uses surprising and
shocking contrasts of materials and colors to
put the historic exhibition pieces – sculptures
as well as paintings – into a new and totally
unexpected light.

## THE GLASS OFFICE

### Transparency as a sign of corporate identity

It is not only in the area of museum building
that new and excellent solutions have been
found to answer traditional needs. At the end
of the 1960s, some office buildings demonstrated similar outcomes.

A special place must be awarded to the
work of Kevin Roche and John Dinkeloo. As
early as 1961, they created an open type of
architecture, laid out around a garden, in the
Oakland Museum in California (completed
1968). During the same period, they repeated
in a skyscraper the theme of the garden inte-
grating nature with a building. For the headquarters of the Ford Foundation, instead of
monotonous offices all branching off from a
central corridor, or great rooms divided off by
partitions, Roche and Dinkeloo created a giant
winter garden extending over twelve floors,
with the glazed fronts of floor after floor of
offices opening onto it.

The idea of the glazed greenhouse, which
had figured in the earliest stages of architecture in glass, now became linked to the theme
of the modern office. In this way, employees
were given the feeling of working in a healthy,

natural environment, a measure which not only improved the working atmosphere, but also fostered the corporate identity that still figures to this day among the most important motivating and productivity-enhancing factors in business.

For the headquarters of the College Life Insurance Company of America, Roche and Dinkeloo designed (between 1967 and 1971) three identical *pyramid-like* volumes on a quadrilateral ground plan. These futuristic buildings embodied a steel and glass construction on two sides, which was backed by two concrete planes. The staggered siting of the three buildings was intended to allow the accommodation of a potential extension to the complex which was planned for a later date. This could be added on, in the same style, without necessarily creating an over-large and monotonous complex.

The dislike of hierarchy and monumentality, and the demand for democracy that characterized the generation of 1968 also found expression in architecture. The concept of open architecture expressing an open society is the defining feature of the headquarters of the Centraal Beheer insurance company in Apeldoorn, in the Netherlands, built by Herman Hertzberger, Jan Antonin Lucas, and Hendrik Eduard Niemeijer between 1970 and 1972. The building can be extended in all directions, and consists of single interlocking square blocks in which open space and work space intermingle. Like a city within a city, offices and small shops are placed next to each other, and there are views from all the terrace-like projections. Even the offices take up the note of individuality, in that they are very sparsely furnished, giving the users room to complete them in their own style.

**Kevin Roche, John Dinkeloo, *Office buildings for the Ford Foundation,*** New York, 1963–68

No more cells: in this building all the offices open on to an enormous winter garden accessible to 12 stories. Nature and the city, the individual and the community, appear to have been reconciled. Kevin Roche and John Dinkeloo's building for the Ford Foundation is not just a totally new kind of office block. The construction became the prototype for countless buildings with glazed atria for all possible uses. But unlike the ubiquitous malls, commercial headquarters and hotels built on this model, the Ford Foundation building does not retreat into an inner world. Two façades of the 13-story square building open full on to the city.

# HIGH-TECH ARCHITECTURE

## Victory of Technology

On 21 July 1969, Neil Armstrong became the first man to walk on the moon. "That's one small step for a man, one giant leap for mankind," the American astronaut of the Apollo 11 mission told fascinated viewers, watching live as he leapt from the ladder of the space capsule to the surface of the moon.

The conquest of the moon was the culmination of 10 years of continuous competition between the superpowers (the United States and the USSR) for supremacy in space. For a long time – at least since 12 April 1961, when the Soviet cosmonaut Yuri Gagarin became the first man to go into orbit in space – it looked as though the Soviets would be the first to put a man on the moon. But eventually it was the Americans who won, thanks to immense technical and economic resources, overweening ambition, and a fair portion of luck.

Millions of enthralled television viewers on Earth followed the moon landing for hours, in spite of the uncertain black and white pictures, the crackling and rustling sound, and the almost unrecognizably distorted voices of the astronauts.

The moon landing was a triumph of technology, which planned and realized a high-tech fairytale with military precision. Less than six months later, Apollo 12 took off for the next moonshot. The future had begun. Soon the launching pads at Cape Canaveral in Florida and the Apollo mission control at NASA in Houston, Texas, became familiar sights. Bare scaffolds and ramps, piping and lifts, innumerable video screens, telephones, and headphones gave viewers a direct impression of the equipment necessary to bring to fruition a task of the magnitude of space flight.

## Architectural promise – speaking architecture

High-tech constructions, for example the launching pads and the mission control center, became a much more frequent everyday sight. The constructions that architects wrote into their designs became ever bolder. In the wake of *Brutalism* as practiced by the Smithsons in England, exposed pipes, wiring, and ventilation ducts became the trademarks of high-tech aesthetics.

The quintessence of 1970s architecture and its love of technology was the Centre National d'Art et de Culture Georges Pompidou in Paris, called the Centre Pompidou for short, the appearance of which alarmed quite a few of those who first saw it, and indeed continues to do so. It was built between 1971 and 1977 in the Place Beaubourg in the heart of the French capital, and gave the impetus to the "grands projets" with which President Mitterrand also sought to immortalize himself in the cityscape, such as the controversial Bastille opera house built by the Canadian Carlos Ott (opened 1989), or the new building for the Bibliothèque Nationale François Mitterrand (National library) by Dominique Perrault (opened 1996). The Centre Pompidou

The future becomes the present

# High-tech and Post-Modernism

## 1970–1980

---

**1969**: Georges Pompidou becomes president of France.

**1970**: Intensification of the "Troubles" – the conflict between Protestants and Catholics in Northern Ireland. Care for the environment is the issue of the day.

**1971**: Death of the jazz musician and trumpeter Louis Armstrong.

**1972**: Murderous attack by Arab terrorists on the Israeli Olympic team in Munich. Signing of the SALT I Agreement for the limitation of strategic weapons between the USA and the Soviet Union. Re-election of President Nixon.

**1973**: The Watergate affair clouds Nixon's electoral victory. Military coup in Chile brings about the fall of President Salvador Allende and the installing of a military regime under General Augusto Pinochet.

Worldwide petroleum crisis. The Arab states use oil for the first time as a political weapon. The first volume of Aleksandr Solzhenitsyn's description of the Soviet prison camps (*The Gulag Archipelago*) is published, and he is deprived of his Soviet citizenship the following year. Death of the painter Pablo Picasso.

**1974**: The German Federal Chancellor, Willy Brandt, resigns as a result of the Guillaume Chancellery espionage affair.

**1975**: End of the war in Vietnam which had begun in 1963. Death of General Franco in Madrid, followed by the building of a parliamentary democracy. Nobel Prize for economics awarded to Milton Friedman. Microsoft Corporation founded by Bill Gates. First showing of the US film *One Flew Over the Cuckoo's Nest*, with Jack Nicholson.

**Scene from the film *Star Wars* by George Lucas, with Carrie Fisher as Princess Leia and the robot R2-D2**

**1976**: Death of Mao Zedong. Jimmy Carter becomes president of the United States. A chemical accident in the Italian town of Seveso pollutes the environment with dioxin,

causing a severe reaction to chlorine. The 13-year-old violinist Anne-Sophie Mutter begins her career. Disco music from the films of John Travolta becomes popular.

**1977**: Abduction of the head of the German employers' association H.-M. Schleyer in Cologne by terrorists of the Red Army Faction. First showing of the American science-fiction film *Star Wars* by George Lucas.

**1978**: Cardinal Karol Wojtyla of Crakow becomes Pope John Paul II.

**1979**: Nobel Peace Prize awarded to the Catholic nun Mother Teresa. After the flight of the Shah, the Ayatollah Khomeini returns to Iran from 15 years in exile to lead the Islamic revolution.

**1980**: Iraqi invasion of Iranian territory begins first Gulf War.

is a thoroughly Pop Art object, a museum with universal popular appeal, the sparkling peak of an architectural style wittily exposing to view what would normally be hidden inside.

The architects of the Centre Pompidou, Richard (now Lord) Rogers, who is British, and the Italian Renzo Piano, made little effort to adapt the building to its historic neighborhood. It was a new palace of culture intended for an almost limitless range of uses and included a space for visiting exhibitions and a library, as well as the collection of the Musée de l'Art Moderne. The makers' "carefree" treatment of the historic built environment was much the same as was going on elsewhere in Paris in the 1970s, where only minor importance was accorded to the architectural heritage. Not long before, Les Halles, the old market building near the center of Paris, had been razed to the ground, despite considerable protests, thus eliminating an important element of 19th-century Paris.

Rogers and Piano's building was permeated with the spirit of the time. With its megastructure (550 feet (166 meters) long, 210 feet (66 meters) wide, 140 feet (42 meters) high) it dominated the originally important smaller-scaled city structure surrounding it with astounding arrogance.

Even today, in its now slightly dated futuristic dress, it conveys the impression of one great building site. It did not have a traditional *façade* but a complex web of interwoven steel tubes exterior to the glazed walls. So that whole of the interior space – some 160 by 480 feet (50 by 150 meters), part of which would have been occupied by escalators – can be released for exhibitions, the escalators are on the outside, carrying visitors in plexiglass-covered tubes up the west façade to the actual exhibition spaces as if through a time-travel apparatus. Brilliantly colored ventilation shafts remind one more of a ship than a museum, though these are yet another quotation from 20th-century architecture, in that they are reminders of the quotations from ship's architecture first introduced by Le Corbusier. Everything is openly on display – supply cables, shafts, and tubes – and metal fire escapes scale the heights of the building: a colorful, cheerful mixture of everything, creating, in a way only possible in Paris, a building whose unique charm lies in being utterly open.

**Richard Rogers, Renzo Piano, Centre**
***National d'Art et de Culture Georges***
***Pompidou,*** Paris, 1971–77

Open and visible ventilation ducts wind through the façade like brilliantly colored entrails. A plexiglas tube pumps visitors through the steel lattice work. The Centre Pompidou is literally a culture machine, as unique as it is un-elitist, drawing people in because it is such a contradiction to its stony environment. The "walls" are so glassy and set so far back that the barriers between city and house, between inner and outer, between art and person, dissolve. The load-bearing elements and means of access are on the outside, so that the whole of each of the six floors, 50 by 150 meters (160 by 480 feet) in area, can be used – as a national museum for modern art, media center, cinema complex, and assembly hall. The Centre Pompidou perfectly expresses the philosophy of high-tech architecture for the first time. A building should function like a catalyst. It is a shell in which technical services are provided and processes are stimulated, but do not become set.

**Norman Foster Associates, Ove Arup and Partner, *Hong Kong and Shanghai Bank*,** Hong Kong, 1979–86

Normally a tall building should be a powerful symbol externally, but inside have as many useful surfaces as possible; according to this way of thinking, the technology that services the building is of secondary importance, hidden in minimal interior space. The British high-tech architect Norman Foster approached this particular project in a quite different way: the primary elements of his Hong Kong and Shanghai Bank are two groups of four steel frames that project, clearly visible, 600 feet (180 meters) into the air. Each one of them has all its means of access grouped at a single point on its exterior. Between them 47 floors, each 105 feet (33 meters) wide are suspended like bridges. The central space remains open, creating an atrium as high as the towers, which directs light by means of giant electronically steered mirrors into the depths of the building. The technology dominates the building.

The playful brightness of the building is complemented in exemplary manner by the sculptural fountains in the Place Igor Stravinsky, commissioned by the Paris city council and executed between 1982 and 1983 by Jean Tinguely and Niki de Saint Phalle. Inside the giant bowl of the fountain there is a total of 16 individual sculptures – rotating hearts and bright red mouths, water-spurting fantasy figures and musical clefs, as well as turning cogwheels and flywheels. These are intended not only to awaken associations with the work of the great composer Stravinsky, but also to make the square at the side of the Centre Pompidou into a favorite place for people to rest, which, unlike many deserted inner city squares, it has become. The romantic playfulness of Tinguely and Saint Phalle's fountain sculptures as well as the colorful technical language of forms of Rogers and Piano's Centre Pompidou convey a carefree feeling which is very seldom achieved in 20th-century combinations of sculpture and architecture.

Not long after the completion of the Centre Pompidou, Richard Rogers completed the headquarters of Lloyds in London (1979–86) a building that flirted with its own technicism, with curves and gleaming metal parts more reminiscent of a car factory than an insurance company. But in the Lloyds building, the gleaming steel architecture with its giant ventilation tubes descending a distance of 10 stories, strikes a menacing note which is markedly absent from the Centre Pompidou.

Rogers continued putting into practice his ideals of making technology aesthetic right into the 1990s, as for instance in the headquarters of the British commercial television Channel 4 (1995). The architecture of the Channel 4 building looks as technical as the workings of a modern television station has to be. You cross a glass and steel bridge to enter the reception area, whose concave façade is entirely glazed. The canopy over the bridge hangs on a construction of red supports and gleaming steel cables, placed for decorative effect in front of the glass façade. Glazed lifts travel up and down the outside of the building, which also has oversized ventilation shafts – Rogers' trademark.

High-tech forms and a prestigious image go together here in a synthesis which is as impressive as it is of high quality, and prove that the principles of Rogers's truth to construction methods are still capable of producing a pleasing visual effect 20 years later than the Centre Pompidou, and remain as appropriate to their time as ever.

### Technical sobriety – Norman Foster

Norman Foster is another leading British representative of the architectural style, who has raised the technology of buildings to a stylistic trademark. The curved building which houses the Willis, Faber & Dumas insurance company in Ipswich (1970–75) clearly displays its structural framework, covered only by a protective sheet of glass. In the Hong Kong and Shanghai Bank also, the load-bearing columns from

**Günter Behnisch, Frei Otto,** *Olympic Stadium,* Munich, 1968–72

Freed from the burden of the past, cheerful, and modern: this is how Germany wanted to present itself at the Olympic Games of 1972. Working with the landscape architect Wolfgang Leonhardt, Günter Behnisch planned the area of Munich designated for the games, which had once been part of an airport, as an open park. The sports arenas are loosely divided. Partly set into the ground, they are in close relationship to the artificially raised landscape. They are roofed by a plexiglas canopy hung on slanting steel masts, a completely new system explored here for the first time by Frei Otto. Their soft forms seem to grow out of gentle hills. The illusion was perfect. But this insubstantial construction needed concrete foundations going down as deep as 130 feet (40 meters). The modification of the terrain required the moving of millions of cubic feet of earth.

which the whole construction of the tall building is suspended are not hidden by the traditional *curtain wall*; rather, Foster has made the monumental suspension system the actual theme of his building.

It was precisely because of his soberly technical architectural language, articulated in a form free of historical connections, that an architect like Norman Foster was destined to be put in charge of the rebuilding of the Berlin Reichstag, the new seat of the German Bundestag (parliament), which he effected between 1995 and 1999. As in earlier buildings, Foster's architecture achieves its form primarily through the materials used and the emphasis on the principles of its construction. Hidden behind its 19th-century façade, the building has a completely new inner life all in glass whose aim is transparency; it is crowned by a *dome*, also glass. It may be that, in terms of preserving a historic monument, violence has been done to the older building and its equally historic transformations in the 1950s, but Foster's high-tech architecture does convey a distinctly progressive view of the world, which is doubtless the one desired by those who commissioned him.

## A tent for sport

It is already some years since Kenzo Tange's Olympic arena in Tokyo (illustration page 83) deployed construction and materials to produce a unique high-tech adventure with a breathtaking aesthetic effect. Günter Behnisch and Frei Otto took this idea of an airy tent roof combining weather-protection and maximum transparency and used it for the Munich Olympic stadium in 1972. Its complex roof, constructed of plexiglass plates fitted together, covered large areas of the sports stadium, which held 70,000 people.

Tent constructions of the type developed by Frei Otto had previously been considered suitable only for temporary buildings due to the problem of durability. Otto had made comparable constructions for the National Garden Show in Cologne in 1957, and the German Pavilion at the world exhibition in Montreal in 1967.

A special requirement of the Munich Olympics area was that it should fulfill various functions. It had to be a contemporary sports ground, but it also had to be capable of acting as a park where the people of the Bavarian capital could relax, and it needed to be only a few minutes' tram ride from the city center.

In terms of architecture, a special effort was made to produce a noticeable contrast to the architecture of the stadium that was built in Berlin in the Nazi period for the first Olympic games ever to take place on German soil in 1936. Instead of the *freestone* slabs and *classicist* forms which Werner March was forced to add to his modern concrete construction at the demand of Albert Speer and Hitler, the new Munich Olympic stadium was airy, gently curved, and open. In this way its message to the world community was quite different from its predecessor's; the image of West Germany which it communicated was modern, progressive, dynamic.

**SITE, *BEST* Supermarket,** Towson, Maryland (USA), 1978

The supermarkets produced for the BEST chain by the group of architects calling themselves SITE, Sculpture in the Environment, are entirely original sculptural buildings in places where you would least expect them: suburbs and industrial estates. The element of surprise has become the trademark of the supermarkets and their architects. Unexpected changes – such as a wall set at an angle and sitting diagonally – disturbed and provoked the jaded perceptions of the visitor. But behind this disruption of traditional expectations of how the façades of buildings should look, there was less a criticism of a society that had strayed from the right path, than an attempt, to use architecture to change such a banal and ritualized process as shopping into an all-day happening in an ever more homogenized consumer society.

## DE-ARCHITECTURE

### Advertising and consumption

Thousands of impressions and images crowd in on everyone daily. The visual signals that thrust themselves upon us from our surroundings every day become ever stronger: from the traffic sign to the billboard, to the television advertising spot. There is no visit to the cinema that is not accompanied by a glimpse of the big wide world preceding the actual film experience. Well-made advertising has even become a form of entertainment itself, in the French film compilation of the best commercials of the year in Cannes. Since Andy Warhol's serial pictures of soup cans brought advertising into art, the aspirations of advertising to become art have heightened.

But all this has only one aim: to attract notice at any price, and to stand out from the competition – starting best of all at the point of sale. This was the line adopted by the American supermarket chain BEST, who had their stores designed by the group of architects going under the name of SITE (Sculpture in the Environment).

In the 1970s, SITE deliberately set out to shock and astonish with their store designs. Monotonous, characterless supermarkets, all built from the same design, had been springing up like mushrooms everywhere. Considering that there were quite enough of such boring stereotypes around, SITE opted for humor, and took the line of making their buildings both surprising and confusing for shoppers. Instead of the usual smooth and flawless façades, customers suddenly found themselves confronted by walls that were

apparently crumbling and on the point of collapse, indeed heaps of bricks appeared to have formed beneath them already. In one case there was a wood growing behind the entrance to a supermarket, looking as though it was about to split the architecture apart, and reoccupy its old terrain. Of course all this was an illusion, a trick with the unexpected, intended to make shopping a dramatic experience for the customers. SITE were gambling on the idea that the shock would also force them to recognize that the supposed danger was only a sham, intended to confuse, but finally also to amuse and entertain them.

The SITE architects themselves christened their buildings "De-architecture," thus taking up a critical position against the functionalist boredom of other stores. However dramatic the façade of a BEST building might be – behind it there was just another supermarket.

## POST-MODERNISM

### The return to style

The critique of functionalism inherent in SITE's sculptural buildings was not the preserve of the SITE architects alone. Elsewhere, clear doubts were being expressed as to whether the architectural concepts of Modernism, which had dominated the history of building for so long and had in the meantime become entirely standard, were the only way to salvation. In particular the premise upon which residential building is based, that it should produce an appropriate social context for the inhabitants, was acknowledged to have been scantily observed in reality. The buildings upon which Modernism was founded had both quality and a spirit of adventure; whereas the apartment blocks now going up were getting ever drearier, without any sense of a standard – slums in a standard box format.

From its inception in the late 19th century, Modernism had striven to banish traditional forms of building and decoration from architecture. *Pillars* and *gables* were replaced with *rectilinear* boxes with flat roofs. Constructed of reinforced concrete and glass, they were entirely without ornament, except for their gleaming white or glazed façades. But under the surface of modern architecture, which covered an astonishingly wide spectrum from Saarinen's richly curved Expressionism to the severe grid-shaped buildings of the old masters of the Bauhaus,

# KENZO TANGE

Beside the elevated tracks of the Tokaido Express in Tokyo, there stands on an angularly shaped piece of ground measuring only 225 square yards (189 square meters), a towering cylinder just 26 feet (8 meters) across. This houses lifts and service rooms; the all-glass offices are attached to the sides. From the tower 14 floors jut out, constructed out of *reinforced concrete* prefabricated parts. It is the headquarters of Shizuoka – a press and radio company. At first sight – although only at first sight – it appears to be an extremely effective piece of advertising. In addition to this, it is one of the key buildings of Kenzo Tange.

Tange was born in 1913 in Osaka, and his work combines traditional Japanese thought on building with international Modernism. He is considered to be the leading proponent of Structuralism, on the basis of his theories about building and the city, which he evolved while

*Kenzo Tange, circa 1965*

Tange proposed to hang the motorways for the new city 130 feet (40 meters) up in the air over the old city and the bay. The ground would be kept completely open, a single "open space." The traffic could not possibly disrupt people's private lives.

The starting point of the urban net was to be a

that will replace the present city center, and will spread step by step over the whole bay of Tokyo. Along this line communication can take place in a minimum of time. There is no simpler or swifter possibility."

row of access towers from 480 to 640 feet (150 to 200 meters) high and 640 feet (200 meters) apart. These would at once be branches of the city traffic system and atria for the buildings, providing vertical access, installations, water pipes, and electrical cables. Platforms where people would live and work would be suspended between the towers. Whereas the framework would be a rigid, unalterable structure, the platforms would be adaptable to all kinds of functions, to suit the changing demands of the users.

Such plans were far from infrequent at the end of the 1950s. But whereas in Brasilia, for instance, somewhat old-fashioned, slab-shaped skyscrapers co-exist with a modern transport system, Tange was able to translate his schema of functions into a coherent city plan, worked out in the smallest architectonic detail. He is an architect who never views town planning and architecture separately from each other.

Tange's ideas have influenced urbanists all over the world, notably Herman Hertzberger and the Structuralists in Holland. In later works, Tange adapts the form of his buildings to the post-modern spirit of the time, yet he remains true to his intentions. His last big project, Tokyo town hall (1986–91) looks at first sight like a skyscraper cathedral. Yet here too the complex is laid out around a citizens' forum, has ramps running through it, and is poised over a motorway that is itself elevated on stilts.

He was building on stilts 40 years previously in his first designs, for the Peace Center in Hiroshima (1949–56) and his own home in

Tokyo (1951–53). The large room which forms the upper story of his house has no fixed functions. It can be divided into three with sliding doors, according to the needs of the inhabitants.

The house reveals the second great source of the architect's inspiration: traditional modes of construction. At the 1959 CIAM congress in Otterlo, Tange compared the role of tradition with that of a "catalyst, that provokes and promotes a reaction, but is no longer recognizable in the end result." So Tange did not simply adopt the forms of traditional Japanese houses, but also the way they are built: with a wooden skeleton. He constructed the administration building for the district prefecture of Takamatsu (1955–58) in reinforced concrete, a material whose stability is similar to that of wood. It is visually quite similar to a project for an office building in reinforced concrete that Mies van der Rohe produced in 1922. But whereas Mies as a European had to reinvent visible construction, Tange needed only to follow Japanese tradition.

*The roof membrane of the Olympic hall hangs on a cable anchored to two concrete masts. This method of support is borrowed from the traditional roofs of Japanese temples.*

In the mid-1950s, Tange wrote a book that celebrated the Ise temple as the prototype of Japanese architecture. In 1964 he reinterpreted the soaring shape of the temple's roofs, which had developed originally from tents, for the two Olympic arenas in Tokyo. A cable is stretched in a parabolic curve between two masts, and upon it hangs a steel net which supports the roof skin. The sacral effect of the inner space in the temple is thus transferred to a building which in today's context has an equally religious character.

*New town hall, Tokyo*

working as professor at the University of Tokyo between 1946 and 1972.

The most radical plan for a city ever devised was the plan for Tokyo presented by Kenzo Tange in 1959, which presupposed a city structure based not on the buildings of the city, but on its infrastructure. Its aim was to point the way for an orderly growth of the city to a metropolis of ten million. "Cities of this size will be needed to fulfill the functions that are essential to the life of a modern society." The most important idea is at the beginning: it is the future function, not the present form, that should be the starting point for town planning. For Tange, the main function of the city was communication. And, at the end of the 1950s, communication meant movement. So the first part of the plan for Tokyo was the plan for transport.

Tange's conviction was that the city as it was, with its buildings, streets, and squares, did not offer sufficient room for the ever-increasing movement occurring within it. Therefore the city must develop "new structures for new mobility." "We propose an axis for the city

*Shizuoka press and radio company*

Gropius and Mies van der Rohe, new currents began moving as early as the beginning of the 1960s – new currents that took a renewed interest in historical forms of building for decoration and *ornamentation*. Some people were no longer willing to follow the rigorous concepts of Bauhaus Functionalism, which they looked down on as boring.

In the vanguard of the movement were the early buildings of the American architect Robert Venturi, whose publications *Complexity and Contradiction in Architecture* (1966) and *Learning from Las Vegas* (1972) created the foundations for post-modern architectural theory. Both publications show the breadth of

**Robert Venturi, *Vanna Venturi House,***
Chestnut Hill, Philadelphia (USA),
1962–64

The house which Robert Venturi designed for his mother is a new formulation of the Prairie House, with central chimney and harmoniously developed interior spaces, embodying enclosure and transparency at the same time. The façade, according to Venturi, is a "symbolic picture" of a house, looking back to the revolutionary architecture of the 18th century. As one of the first Post-Modern buildings, the house has become a classic.

Venturi's frame of reference that takes in both the tradition and culture of the everyday. On one hand he espouses the internally fractured mannerism of Roman post-Renaissance culture: on the other, he posits architecture as an advertising medium – the principle of the "decorated shed."

Both sides are already on show in the house for Venturi's mother, Vanna. It is an inventory of the petit bourgeois, American suburban house that never really came into contact with the developments of Modernism, if you disallow Frank Lloyd Wright's Prairie Houses (see page 16). The façade expresses meaning without reference to the building as a whole, which is effectively a denial of the principles proposed by Functionalism. And his use of architectonic *noble orders* in the context of a suburban house is a deliberate flouting of these principles.

With its severe, broken pediment, the house follows the principle of "asymmetric symmetry,"

that is recognizable not only in the articulation of the windows, but also in the flat chimney, which turns out to be the back wall of the attic bedroom. The strict cubic quality of the main front, the *flattened arch* over the entrance, the *Diocletian windows* at the back, reveal Venturi as a connoisseur of revolutionary architecture of the type proposed by Ledoux in his houses at the Salines de Chaux (1776). The broken pediment is an element of mannerist architecture, used here as a light shaft for the rooms in the sides of the roof. The "black box" doorway is pure form – a cube – the actual door lies at a right-angle to the front, on the right.

Venturi wanted to show that even in the age of *Brutalism* it was still possible to build poetically. The façade is consciously modeled on the rationalist architecture typical of the 18th century. It is an attempt to win back the "art of building" after the age of Modernism. But the Vanna Venturi house is equally an expression of its own time. It is the first call to post-Modernism, uniting a modernist shaping of space with the idea of the "symbolic image" of a house in the façade. That the "quotation" is broken, is integral to Venturi's approach, which can become directly ironic. Other buildings, apart from villas, have been treated in the same way. In 1960–63 Venturi built the Guild-House, a home for elderly people in Philadelphia, where similar elements were inserted, to give what was a dreary block a new dignity.

Venturi, a pupil of Louis Kahn, whom he admired greatly, thus effected the transition from that which came "after Modernism" to a new variety in architecture, which has today already become classic.

Venturi was even more occupied with architectural theory than with the expression of it in buildings. His purpose was to bring back into the collective memory the architectural canons that had proved valid for many centuries. This canon, with its models such as the principles of using the *orders* of columns, symmetry in building, and so on, had been considered conclusive since Vitruvius and Palladio. Anyone who understood it knew what context of meaning was attached to a particular form, for example the *column* or the broken pediment.

The assumed relationship of prestige and ornamentation had been questioned by the

Modernists in the 1920s, who chose to place the functionality of their buildings in the foreground instead.

From this point of view Venturi's architecture was certainly not modern, but rather on the conservative side. But even when he turns to historical forms, Venturi's buildings are unthinkable without classical Modernism, since they are defined by criticism of it. Venturi's idea was not to refer back to pre-Modernist styles, but to propose an alternative to its dreary and low-quality offshoots. His architecture was therefore a first attempt at going beyond Modernism, the first impetus towards Post-Modernism.

## The pleasure in quotation

Venturi was certainly not the only one to show himself open to the *styles* of the past in his buildings. Charles Moore is another of the founding fathers of Post-Modernism, even though at first sight his buildings do not look as though they are peddling the ornaments of bygone eras.

In the case of his own house in Orinda, which is built in wood and appears both restrained and compact, from the exterior the spirit of the building only becomes clear when one observes how it has been conceived. The core of the house consists of two forms resembling baldachins resting on pillars, around which Moore has arranged all the other parts of the building. In this way, the whole forms a rectangle.

Baldachins are canopies resting on pillars, which are erected over holy places. Since the late *Antiquity*, baldachins have been one of the particular *noble orders* of architecture, particularly sacral architecture. It would be inconceivable for any fairly large church of the medieval or baroque period not to have baldachins providing a roof to the altar.

Moore transported an object with a deep sacral meaning in architecture into a place without any sacral meaning – his own home. The ironic break, the intellectual pleasure of playing with a quotation from history, these are the ideas which clarify the use of the baldachin in the interior of the house. If the use of the larger of the two baldachins in the central living area is still at the limits of the acceptable, the use of the second one to provide a roof to the bathtub definitively tips over into the ironic. Moore's passion for playing with historic

architectural forms, putting them in a context where they are out of place, can be found in other areas of the Orinda house. For instance, instead of normal windows and doors, there are sliding doors of a type found in stables.

A house with quotations from vernacular architecture and baldachins which belong in sacral places not only gives free play to many associations, it also says a great deal about the ironic cast of mind of its architect, especially when the house is his own.

Moore's post-modern delight in quotation and in *architecture parlante* is much more clearly visible in what must be his best known project, the Piazza d'Italia in New Orleans, built between 1974 and 1978, commissioned by those of its inhabitants who were of Italian origin. At their wish, the square and its fountain are created on the basis of a stylized outline of Italy, as a boot. The piazza is laid out in concentric circles, at the heart of which lies Sicily, washed by the waters of not the

**Charles Moore, *Piazza d'Italia*, New Orleans, Louisiana (USA) 1978**

Buildings can and must speak. They require freedom of speech. They can say wise, nice, powerful, and also stupid things. They must make connections with the past and awaken memories. This attitude made Charles Moore the most self-satisfied storyteller of Post-Modernism. For his Piazza d'Italia, Moore transported theater sets depicting Italian geography and architectural history to New Orleans. He copied *friezes* to make sprinklers. He covered *pillars* with steel. Those with architectural training may well be entertained by the irony with which elements from Roman *Antiquity* and the *Renaissance* are mounted. The uninitiated may be more inclined to smile at the expense. The completely circular piazza, carved out of the middle of a shopping center, is far from being the center of social life that its Italian forebears were. But even this polemic against Functionalism is intentional.

**Ricardo Bofill, *Apartment Complex Walden Seven*, Barcelona, 1975**

The tall apartment block has always been a problematic architectural type. The Spanish architect Ricardo Bofill tried to counter the danger of anonymity by his articulation of the building. It was not a success. The many walkways, bridges, and arcades crossing the five inner courtyards around which the 16-story cluster of buildings in Barcelona are grouped, only serve to make it appear threateningly labyrinthine. The exterior zones are sacrificed to an impractical ground plan. Later housing projects of Bofill's rely upon gigantic, antique-style columns, likewise without success. Behind the *fluted* cylindrical forms lurk exiguous recesses and dark winding staircases. The formalist project becomes too obvious. Post-Modernism brings itself into disrepute.

Mediterranean but the fountain. Behind is a monumental construction of columns, brilliantly colored and full of noble materials, which brings together a unique collection of quotations from the formal language of Antiquity, a confluence of the concentrated architectural power of the Roman Empire and the Italian *Renaissance*.

It seems as though Moore is constantly giving his public a knowing wink, as much as to ask whether they have really got all the abstruse little architectonic references gathered into his Piazza d'Italia. And one does indeed require a certain grounding in architectural history and forms in order to get the joke. Once more Post-Modernism shows itself to be primarily an intellectual movement.

Moore transforms a Doric *frieze* into a sprinkler for his fountain, the *capitals* of the columns are illuminated, and he even gives himself a prominent place in the joke by making in his own likeness two faces spewing out water. The result of this is joyful, humorous architecture, but functional it is not.

## The end of Modernism?

In the mid-1970s everything seemed architecturally possible, including things definitely not permissible before: from columns to flat roofs, brightly colored air extraction ducts to expensive marble facing placed next to ventilation shafts. Suddenly everything could be mixed and matched.

The movement which had begun in the early 1960s as more of a quiet protest against the excessively powerful *functionalist* trend in Modernism, had by the 1970s become a raging storm: a dramatic reversion to the *styles* of the past, which polarized not only architects but the whole of society and carried on working right into the 1980s. It was the first architectural Biennale, held in Venice in 1980 at the instigation of Paolo Portoghesi, that brought American and European architecture face to face, and finally established Post-Modernism in Europe.

The most resounding comeback was made by the *column*, an important formal element of Western architecture since the time of the ancient Greeks. The most powerful champion of the column was Ricardo Bofill, but he did not use it at all as the architects of *Antiquity* intended. They thought in terms of the *orders of columns* which prescribed the interrelationship of supporting and supported elements

as firmly as the decoration of columns and frieze. Instead of chiseling the columns out of fine marble as the ancients had done, Bofill and his fellow practitioners at his Taller de Arquitectura office pre-cast them in concrete. He used the gigantic *fluted* columns or monumental *triumphal arches* to articulate the façades of his apartment blocks, as in for example Les Espaces d'Abraxas at Marne-la-Vallée near Paris or at the Temples du Lac at Saint-Quentin-en-Yvelines, in order to invest buildings that had no sacral meaning with a monumental air.

Bofill's buildings are too dramatic. His orders of columns which extend up ten stories do not terminate with any *entablature* as ancient *temples* would have to have done, and memories spring to mind of Albert Speer's gigantomania in Germany or the Stalinist *wedding-cake* style of the 1950s.

Post-Modernism gradually lost the ironic note that had been introduced by Moore and others. In its place came a dogmatic architecture which used the classical quotation in any old way as long as it was expensive. The playful variety of forms which James Stirling and Michael Wilford deployed in the new Stuttgart Staatsgalerie (1977–84, illustrated on page 96) was now the exception, and in Bofill's buildings with their grand gestures, it was altogether absent. Instead, he built apartment ghettos in *classicizing* dress that only offered a very limited alternative to standardized Modernist housing estates.

With classicism so much in favor, it is hardly surprising that at the end of the 1970s Albert Speer, who had been Hitler's architect, enjoyed an unexpected return to favor. His work was republished in folio format and enjoyed a highly uncritical reception.

Architecture was threatening to degenerate into a ragbag of quotations, from which anyone could pick exactly what he liked, package it, and present it in a new context, completely freed of any historical relationship to the current architectural form. A hundred years of modern architectural development seemed in danger of culminating in an infectious *eclecticism*. If Charles Moore could bring Italy to New Orleans for the Piazza d'Italia, why should Arata Isozaki not, quite straightforwardly, quote Michelangelo's Roman Piazza del Campidoglio in the Tsukuba head office in Japan (1980–83)?

The circle closed in the area of skyscraper construction as well; people cold-shouldered the metropolitan elegance of a Mies van der Rohe, suddenly reverting to the cumbrous shapes of *Art Deco* that had first appeared in the 1920s and 1930s in the work of Raymond Hood and William van Alen, but were now tricked out with a *classicist* repertoire that had become nothing more than a fashion.

The versatile Philip Johnson left a lasting mark on Post-Modernism with the American Telephone and Telegraph (AT&T) Building. Clad in pink granite, the building towers up into the skies, emphasizing its vertical lines through the articulation of its windows, for all the world, as if in direct opposition to the horizontal strip windows of Modernism. The monumental broken pediment that crowns the building, trumpets far and wide from whose mind this building sprang. And the entrance in *triumphal arch* mode, which openly and proudly spans several stories, underlines the relationship between the building and its owner. In just the same way as the skyscrapers of the 1920s, the AT&T Building manifests prosperity and growth in architectural form. It is no longer *functionalism* and transparency which are crucial in tall buildings, but prestige.

The play with traditional forms reached its climax with the Humana Building found in Louisville, Kentucky (1982–86), designed by the American architect Michael Graves. A distinguishing feature of the building was its striking pastel coloration, with slabs of pink granite and greenish glass. It was also notable for the fact that Graves tried to break through the traditional *rectilinear* shape of tall buildings and structure its volumes differently. However, viewed in relief, the resultant building is far from satisfactory. Apart from the multiplicity of classical quotations – the loggia, tempietto, and belvedere – there is the overhanging part of the façade, which is partially held up by metal supports and makes the building too much of a hodge-podge to live up to its pretensions to grandeur.

**Philip Johnson, *American Telephone and Telegraph (AT&T) Building*,** New York, 1982

A *base* shaped like a *triumphal arch*, a shaft of vertical strip windows, the whole crowned by a broken *pediment.* Philip Johnson has dug deep into Post-Modernism's grab-bag of quotations. Dividing the building into the classic three parts, base, middle, and roof, he makes it as plain as possible for a modernist that he interprets a tall building as a tall house. But Johnson does not only use the divisions of Antiquity; Brunelleschi's colonnade in the 15th-century Pazzi chapel in Florence was an important source for the entrance, and the relationship between the pediment and an 18th-century Chippendale bureau was immediately noted. In a time when exciting skyscrapers had been replaced by unexciting tall boxes in steel and glass, the AT&T Building initiated a decisive change of direction for this type of building.

Building in the global village

# Crossing boundaries

1980–1990

## CULTURES OF EXPERIENCE AND CONSUMPTION

### The times before the change: austerity in the East, prosperity in the West

The movement that began in the early 1980s in Poland as a vociferous protest by workers of the Lenin shipyards in Gdansk, organized by the Solidarity trade union under Lech Walesa, climaxed on 9 November 1989 with the fall of the Berlin Wall. Between these two events lay a decade in which the world began to change in a way that was barely perceptible to the individual, but at the end was perceived to have taken a totally new direction.

Under Mikhail Gorbachev, leader of the then all-powerful Communist Party, the Soviet Union began to emerge from a period of stagnation under Brezhnev into the era of glasnost ("openness") and perestroika ("transformation"). After 80 years of dictatorship, the communist system in Russia was economically at rock-bottom. Determined reform from within led the way out of stagnation, and the radical reform of society was introduced. Democratization, judicial reform, and de-Stalinization were pillars of the reform movement. After years of oppression and imprisonment, Andrei Sakharov, the physicist, Nobel laureate, and outspoken critic of the Soviet system, became a moral authority. Others, such as the winner of the Nobel Prize for literature, Aleksandr Solzhenitsyn, who had been deprived of his

citizenship for his critical attitude, returned to their homeland after many years of involuntary exile. The states that had become part of the Soviet bloc at the end of the Second World War and were members of the Warsaw Pact, were dispersed on the break-up of the USSR. They began the change to more or less democratic countries, a laborious process which has not yet come to an end in the 1990s.

The world order still seemed quite clear and unambiguous at the beginning of the 1980s: over here was West and over there was East – good here, bad there. Then, over-night, that all collapsed. The Cold War that had held the world in its icy grip since 1945 melted away, leaving behind a political and cultural vacuum.

While the Poles in the 1980s lived under the threat of martial law, East Germany struggled to manage scarcity, and the Rumanians starved under their dictator Ceausescu, in Western Europe and North America a euphoric culture of celebration set in.

Wherever there was a historic anniversary, it was celebrated with a bang. In the mid-1980s, the "European City of Culture" system began, with one city each year being selected for the role. The festive luxury of Charles Moore's and Michael Graves' late 1970s architecture found its echo in the deliberately sumptuous tone of the 1980s. Lulled by the sense of security produced by extraordinary prosperity, societies financed almost limitless

**1981**: Lech Walesa becomes chairman of the Polish trade union Solidarity, which is now officially permitted. Murder of the Egyptian president Anwar el-Sadat, who had initiated the peace process with Israel in 1977. Sensational success of the first performance in London of Andrew Lloyd Webber's musical *Cats*.

**1982**: Falklands War between Argentina and the UK. Helmut Kohl becomes German Chancellor. Umberto Eco's novel *The Name of the Rose* published.

**1983**: US President Reagan initiates research into the Strategic Defense Initiative, a defense shield in outer space against enemy rocket attacks ("Star Wars"). Highly criticized, it is halted in 1993. The organism responsible for the viral infection AIDS is discovered.

**1984**: The Indian prime minister Indira Gandhi is murdered by the Sikhs of her bodyguard. Nobel Peace

Prize awarded to Bishop Desmond Tutu in South Africa for his peaceful struggle against apartheid. Milos Forman's film about Mozart, *Amadeus*, receives eight Oscars.

**1985**: Mikhail Gorbachev becomes general secretary of the Communist Party of the Soviet Union (and head of state in 1990), and introduces

perestroika. The American pop singer Madonna also enjoys great success as a film actress.

**1986**: After a serious fire in a reactor in the nuclear power plant at Chernobyl in the Ukraine, all inhabitants for 18.5 miles (30 km) around are evacuated. Death of the French feminist Simone de Beauvoir, life-long companion of Jean Paul Sartre.

**1987**: Signing by Gorbachev and Reagan in Washington of the agreement banning all medium-range nuclear missiles. Beginning of the Palestinian *intifada* (uprising) in the Israeli-occupied territories. The Montreal Protocol is signed by 24 countries which undertake to cut their use of CFCs by half by 1999, to

**After the opening of the frontiers of East Germany to the West, on the night of 9–10 November, 1989, Berliners from both sides of the city stormed the Wall at the Brandenburg Gate.**

reduce damage to the ozone layer over Antarctica.

**1988**: Benazir Bhutto becomes the first woman to be elected prime minister of an Islamic country, Pakistan. Worldwide tributes to Nelson Mandela, in prison for 25 years for his opposition to apartheid, and demands for his release. Historic center of Lisbon destroyed by fire.

**1989**: Bloody suppression of a prodemocracy demonstration in Tiananmen Square, Beijing, followed by a wave of oppression, arrests, and executions. Change in East Germany and fall of Berlin Wall on 9 November leads to democratization and free elections in other Eastern bloc countries. Ayatollah Khomeini imposes a fatwa passing a death sentence on Salman Rushdie, his novel *The Satanic Verses* (1988) is seen as blasphemous. Environmental catastrophe off the coast of Alaska, a damaged tanker spills 40,000 tonnes (190 million liters) of crude oil.

consumption, with reassuring results in terms of employment figures. In the West, the real social problem seemed to be what to do with ever-increasing leisure.

Post-Modernism soon lost its luster, but the tendency to build palatial banks and tall office buildings at the greatest possible expense stayed on, not only in the expanding economies of southeast Asia from Bangkok to Jakarta, but also in the old world, from Paris to Frankfurt to Chicago.

Although the *columns* and *pediments* of Post-Modernism went out after a few years, new directions in architecture had begun, the hold of classical Modernism had been broken, and the horizon had opened up for different concepts in architecture.

## The museum experience: facilities become an event

No category of building is more indicative of the culture of celebration and experience that broke out in the 1980s than the museums, which went up in countries and cities everywhere. The museum had established itself as a middle-class temple of culture in Europe at the beginning of the 19th century, and at the end of the 20th century it was, in terms of architecture, still accorded a central role in not only the transmission of art and culture, but also of the pleasure of enjoying art. While the price of works by painters such as Van Gogh, the Impressionists, or Picasso shot up to astronomical heights, an exhibition culture of a type not known before developed in the new

temples of art. Hundreds of thousands of visitors were attracted to gigantic exhibition events such as "Spirit of the age" or "A new spirit in painting." Art was "in," and afforded museums a lucrative trade in products such as catalogs, posters, and postcards. Architects also now began to realize that they had a chance to make museums something other than the grandiose but ultimately empty shells for works of art that they had previously been. Museum buildings became works of art in themselves, and reflected the artistic ambitions of architects and those responsible for commissioning them.

This had already been the case with Frank Lloyd Wright's ambitious Guggenheim Museum (illustration page 63) in the 1950s, and with Rogers and Piano's Centre Pompidou (illustration page 79) in the 1970s. Despite their differences, the museums have much in common: they have a welcoming atmosphere and create a sense of being the beacon of the age, which continues to attract huge numbers of people to visit them.

## Past – present – future

To get an idea of the poles between which museum architecture was fluctuating at the end of the 1970s one needs only to look at two American buildings. On the one hand there is the extension to the National Gallery of Arts in Washington DC, designed by leoh Ming Pei and finished in 1978. Its unusual trapezoidal shape, which consists of two triangles pressed together, conditioned by the available terrain, in conjunction with its surface covering of marble, gives it a striking but timelessly classic appearance. The Getty Museum in Malibu, California (1973), on the other hand, is one of the earliest examples of a Post-Modern architectural concept applied to the task of building a museum. In point of fact the building leaves one with highly mixed feelings, as instead of the inspired modern architecture such as that delivered by Wright, Rogers and Piano or Pei, what arose in Malibu was a copy of the no longer extant Villa dei Papyri in Herculaneum, Italy, whose original site was thousands of miles away.

Not only are copies of lost buildings of the past used for museums, but also the structural fabric of real historic buildings. With the discovery of the particular charm that emanates from disused industrial and transport buildings, museum building acquired a whole new arena. The best example of an old railway station being put to a new use is the museum at the Quai d'Orsay in Paris (rebuilt by the architects Gae Aulenti and Italo Rota), which since 1986 has housed the most precious collections of Impressionist art in France.

The 1980s saw the creation of a complete mile of museums in Frankfurt, which stretch along the Main. There is the Museum für Kunsthandwerk (Applied Art), which was built between 1979 and 1985 by one of the most prominent of the 20th-century American museum architects, Richard Meier, with his characteristically purist white façades, as well as the Deutsche Architektur-Museum (Geman Architecture Museum), created between 1979 and 1984 by Oswald Mathias Ungers, and others, gathering several outstanding examples of modern museum architecture in one small area.

### Building artistically for art

It can easily happen that the ambitions of the architect, to create a museum that is also seen as a work of art, clash with the wishes of the artists, who want only a simple shell in which they can display their pictures appropriately. This was certainly the case with the Abteiberg Municipal Museum, which was planned and realized by Hans Hollein between 1972 and 1982 in Mönchengladbach.

Hollein's building was the prelude to a unique wave of enthusiasm for creating museums which was to sweep Germany in the years that followed. From the beginning,

Hollein's building divided critics and visitors to the museum into two camps – ardent supporters and vehement detractors.

Instead of creating one single building, Hollein created a museum landscape in several parts, which fitted together more or less organically. This procedure resulted in a visual plethora of different forms, housing not only the town's own collection but also traveling exhibitions, libraries, and rooms for events and lectures, as well as cafés. This total concept was by no means a new one for a museum. But Hollein found a way of allocating to each function its own area, each one an architectonic unit standing out individually in the terraced museum landscape.

Corresponding to the varied uses of the different museum areas, different materials were employed in a hierarchy of values depending on the part of the building that was involved, from *brick* (a relatively cheap material) for the terraced landscape to *hewn stone slabs* (a grander option) for entrance steps. Metal, glass and plastic were also used. The language of forms in which the parts of the building are expressed is a reminder that Hollein's architecture appeared in the age of Post-Modernism, as for instance the way in which an entirely secular place, the entrance hall, is endowed with the dignity of a temple.

### Playing with traditional models

Post-modern! That is the first thought that comes into the head of anyone who is looking at the Neue Württemburgische Staatsgalerie (1977–84, illustration page 96), built by James Stirling and Michael Wilford. Although the central rotunda of the Staatsgalerie reminds one of Karl Friedrich Schinkel's Altes Museum, which was itself borrowed from the Pantheon in Rome, it is in fact much more than a collection of classicist quotations.

Whereas Hollein's museum cannot avoid a certain brittleness despite its ambitious formal choices, Stirling and Wilford have placed the element of playfulness more to the fore. The warm brown tones of the hewn stone slabs, with which the façades are faced, contrast with the brightly painted metal elements in the canopy and the entrance, whose rounded and mobile forms are a deliberate contrast to the rigidity of the stone.

There is a remote reminder in such elements of Stirling's roots in English *Brutalism*.

Playfulness is a strong element elsewhere in the Staatsgalerie: as for instance the Tuscan *columns* half sunk in the floor, or the blocks of *hewn stone* which seem to have fallen out of the façade, and remind one of the romantic ruins of the 18th and early 19th centuries.

But it was not only in Germany that new museums reached new heights of architectonic ambition. One of the most disputed projects of the 1980s was the extensive rebuilding at the Louvre in Paris. A wing of what had once been a French royal palace, once used by the finance ministry, had to be removed prior to a drastic reorganization of the priceless contents of the Louvre, which was to include the provision of underground access to the collections.

On the square in front of the Louvre there is now a glass *pyramid* by the New York architect Leoh Ming Pei, shaped like those of ancient Egypt, which gives an intimation of the massive rebuilding that necessitated these major incursions into the historic substance of so important a complex as the Louvre. The glassy elegance of the construction, often glowingly described as "super-" or "ultramodern," is in conscious contrast to the *baroque* weightiness of the Louvre.

## DECONSTRUCTION

### New ways to reality

When standing at various spots in Stirling's Neue Staatsgalerie you suddenly get a flash of that desire to unsettle the viewer, also to be found in the work of the SITE architects, and which consists of making an odd use of structural elements of the building. One example of this is the play with the "romantic ruins" idea, or there is the massive double T-beam, which holds up the canopy and ends in nothing, whereas you would have expected it from a constructional point of view to rest on another beam. Whereas SITE and Stirling use this effect sparingly, the American Frank O. Gehry made it the crux of his style. He began developing it from the end of the 1970s, but it was only in the mid-1980s that he broke through on to the world stage.

As architects often do, he used his own home to demonstrate the powers of innovation that he promised to deploy in all his building. This house, which he built in 1978 in Santa Monica, California, was certainly a very strange piece of architecture, which did not in any way fit the model proposed by the modernists, with their strict, rational, white

**Ieoh Ming Pei,** *Louvre, Entrance Pyramid,* Paris, 1983–88

Dramatic change was called for, but also continuity. The Louvre was to become a modern museum, the 800-year-old palace of kings was to become a house of the people. And yet the building had to remain what it was: a monument to the glory of France. And so the quiet Chinese-American architect Ieoh Ming Pei accepted the axial *baroque* layout and chose the form of a *pyramid,* which had been the geometrical symbol of grandeur since the time of the ancient Egyptians. But how could he rededicate a monument of kings, designed to keep the people at a distance, to become a symbol of democracy? Pei chose to make the pyramid in glass. The visitor passes through it into ancillary rooms below ground, and from there into one of the most important museums in the world.

**Behnisch and Partner, *Hysolar Research Building*, Stuttgart, 1987**

Steel girders shooting out of the building, distorted stories, a roof that looks as though the wind was about to lift it off: a mixture of materials ranging from corrugated iron through to wood, steel, glass and concrete, and what is presumably intended to be the greatest contradiction of all: this chaotic building serves for research into solar installations – an exact science. But: the world of natural sciences is not so securely based at the end of the 20th century as it once used to be. Open contradictions come closer to reality than simple explanations, which is why Günter Behnisch, the best-known representative of Deconstructivism in Germany, chooses to make contradictory truths perceptible. Deconstructed constructions exist to make boundaries tangible, but not to deny the force of gravity. In point of fact, because this building does in fact remain standing, it makes the laws of gravity clearer. The open clashes of Deconstructivism emphasize both the individuality of each phenomenon and its dependence on the whole. For Behnisch, Deconstructivism is an image of the individualized society: democracy in a building.

*cubes*. However, Gehry's buildings did not fit the model that was being propagated so successfully by the post-modernists either, with their borrowings from both *Antiquity* and *Renaissance*.

The strange impression created by the building starts with the steps that lead to the entrance: these are squares of concrete with the appearance that they have been pushed together at an angle, and thus form a kind of *podium* supporting the two small wooden platforms in front of the wooden entrance door. Over the entrance area towers a strange cage of wire mesh, while to the side of the unspectacular entrance door there is a sort of corrugated construction with a noticeable lack of right-angles and an expressive corner window at the end.

Everything that was required for a sensible construction, with an unambiguous allocation of supporting and non-supporting parts, seemed to have been dissolved into what appeared to be a chaotic mishmash of cheap building materials that did not appear to belong together in any way at all. Gehry's house was a targeted, vehement architectonic provocation, a combination of aesthetic impossibilities that entirely disrupted habitual ways of seeing. This vehement early work was the prototype of Gehry's subsequent buildings. Its elements do not belong to any

traditional construction, but work together almost as though they had been taken apart and shuffled, and then reassembled in a new, and apparently haphazard, way. The sober functionality of Construction has turned into Deconstruction.

## Construction – deconstruction

The buildings of the deconstructivists of the 1980s and 1990s are inconceivable without both the influence of the Modernists of the 1920s, and the art of the Russian Constructivists (see page 34 et seq.). Their utopian architectural visions, which in fact seldom got off the drawing board, were taken up by a vanguard of young architects and turned into buildings.

Also in Gehry's projects, as well as those of other architects such as Peter Eisenman, there is a decided "building-site" quality and an undogmatic use of building materials evincing an urgent search for a new direction in architecture.

Modernism was recognized to have frozen into a tradition, but instead of overcoming it by turning back – as the post-Modernists were doing so successfully at the time – the deconstructivists engaged with architectural history in a different way. They tried, by means of unusual alienation effects, to deprive architecture of its assumed perfection: "disturbed perfection" was consequently one of the formal imperatives of

deconstructivist architecture. At the same time their partially fragmented, partially expressive buildings gave architectonic expression to the lack of direction society had, and to the almost impossible attempt to make holistic sense of the innumerable parts of the reality that make up the Global Village.

The Deconstructivists first received international recognition through the exhibition "Deconstructivist Architecture," which was organized by Philip Johnson and Mark Wigley in 1988 in the Museum of Modern Art. It displayed work by Gehry, and also buildings and projects by Peter Eisenman, COOP Himmelblau, and Bernhard Tschumi. From then on it was only a matter of time before Deconstructivism would rise to become a worldwide stylistic movement, and conquer both the design studios as well as the architectural schools.

The breaking down of functions and forms into their component parts (de-construction), the inclusion of these parts into larger structures – whether of society or the city – and their analysis, found expression not only in the work of architects, but also in the writings of the French philosopher Jacques Derrida – the pioneer of Deconstructivism – who even did concrete work with Bernard Tschumi and Peter Eisenman among others in the Parc la Villette in Paris.

## From LA to the world: Frank O. Gehry

With the building of the California Aerospace Museum, which Gehry completed in 1984, Deconstructivism in the United States was ready to make its public debut. Slanting walls, a variety of materials, and interpenetrating volumes made the building into a sculpture. A Lockheed F104 Starfighter, which seems to swoop over the main entrance, gives the building its universally accessible tone as well as announcing very plainly that this is an aerospace museum. But it does more. The fighter gives the façade of the museum a dynamic element, which is echoed in Gehry's unusual diagonal positioning of the volumes of the building. Yet, despite the surprising way in which the parts of the building cut across each other, and the suddenly opening angles of vision and the slanted walls, Gehry's Aerospace Museum has already lost much of the fresh unconcern and the conscious negation of convention inherent in his home in Santa Monica. Compared with his own house, the museum works like a dog on a leash. The surprising use of materials such as corrugated iron and wire mesh, the deliberately project-like and provisional air that had given Gehry's house almost the feeling of a building site, has given way to something more closed, more strictly subordinated to the functional needs of the museum.

**Thomas Spiegelhalter,** *Ökohaus,*
Breisach, 1989–91

It immediately reminds you of Frank O.
Gehry's house in Santa Monica or Günter
Behnisch's Hysolar research institute in
Stuttgart, but neither playful nor
Deconstructivist goals are involved. The
barrel roof is also a reservoir for rainwater.
The collector for water heating is also a
sunshade, the solar panels, besides
creating electricity, mark the entrance. An
autonomous house, which does not need
to use electricity from the national grid or
any more water than is freely supplied by
nature. The other installations fit
seamlessly into the Deconstructivist
language of forms. It is not clear whether
it really is ecologically sound to use as
many technical resources as are involved
here to make an environmentally friendly
building. What is clear is that
consideration of ecological problems will
be a major demand on architecture in the
21st century.

In the last two decades Gehry has risen to become one of the most sought-after architects in the world, and examples of his buildings can be seen scattered all over the globe. In Weil am Rhein he created the Vitra Design Museum, in Prague he produced a commercial building that looks similar to a dancing couple (illustration page 101), and in 1997 he completed the Guggenheim Museum in Bilbao, which has the silhouette of a stranded whale.

## RATIONALIST TRADITION IN ITALY

### With cool hearts

In contrast to the occasionally over-emphatic fireworks of Post-Modernism and the very serious playfulness of Deconstructivism, there is the Rationalist tradition. Naturally, it too has not remained untouched by the revolutionary whirlwind that swept its way through architecture in the 1970s and 1980s. However, the rationalists have used that revolution in their own way, while still retaining a firm hold on their strict concepts of the building and the city, which are rooted in both cultural and regional tradition.

It is not surprising that it is first and foremost Italian architects who have stayed within a tradition, such as that founded by Terragni

for instance. It was characteristic of the Italian rationalists of the 1920s and 1930s, unlike their German colleagues who had proselytized for the *Neues Bauen* not least for ideological reasons, that they saw no contradiction in the creative interaction and cross-fertilization of Modernism and tradition. So it was that rationalism became a traditional strand in 20th-century Italian architecture, which, despite the partiality the fascists had for monumental building, has continued unbroken to this day.

Since the 1960s one of the most prominent representatives of this architectural direction has been Aldo Rossi, whose buildings have been appreciated throughout the world for many years. His work has both a strict as well as a monumental quality, with decorative as well as playful elements. In this way, his finest buildings almost seem to provide the sensation of being surrounded by the atmosphere of a southern piazza on a warm and balmy market day.

In 1969, Rossi began the design of the Gallaratese apartment building and arcade in Milan, which was eventually completed in 1973. His radically pared-down façade consists of seemingly endless rows of monotonous concrete discs with uniform square openings. In 1971 he and Gianni Braghieri won the national competition for the cemetery of San Cataldo in Modena, which they had started building in 1980. The shadows of the empty, glassless windows of the charnel house that are cast by the hard southern light, conjure up the melancholy of the painter de Chirico.

The interpenetration of playful and monumental elements in Rossi's work can be seen clearly when one compares the rebuilding and enlargement of the Hotel Duca in Milan (1988–9) with the apartment buildings which Rossi designed for the IBA, the Internationale Bauausstellung (Building Exhibition) in Berlin in 1987. The clear articulation of the façade in the lower part of the Hotel Duca, using vertical strips faced with ashlar masonry emphasized by intervening areas of glass, is repeated in the upper part of the building. But the façade here is a unified red, pierced with smaller windows instead of hewn stone and glass, which counters the vertical direction of the building. As a consequence, the upper stories appear to rest with noticeable weight on the pilasters, thus giving them the appearance of *columns*.

Rossi used only a few inspired devices to give great formal variety to the façade of the hotel, whereas for the Berlin residential complex he was much more expansive. Here, too, we find a play on different building materials such as glass and *brick*. And we can also observe how Rossi gives a balance to the façade by putting in a horizontal band of differently colored clinker, which contrasts with the vertical emphasis provided by the towers housing the stairwells, which are slightly set back from the building line. These stairwells are also crowned by *pitched roofs*, a type very typical of Berlin, so bringing in a playful element.

Despite the different materials and the emphatic color, the basic forms of Rossi's buildings are strictly *rectilinear*. They also have the additional feature of fitting the historic proportions of the urban space, as well as using indigenous elements such as the *pitched roof*, which not only breaks up the contours of the building, but can be understood as a quotation. This does not, however, have any *historicist* connotations, and is nothing like a copy of the kind that can be found in Moore or Bofill's buildings, but instead entirely maintains the independence of the content.

**Aldo Rossi,** *Apartment Buildings,* *Kochstrasse,* International Building Exhibition, Berlin, 1987 (above), *Hotel Duca,* Milan, 1988–91 (left)

Two cities, two building tasks – yet clearly the same forms: the main body of the building faces the street, articulated into base, middle, and roof, a heavy façade, grid windows. The buildings in Berlin and Milan are a translation of the thesis which the Italian architect Aldo Rossi formulated as early as 1966 in his book *L'Architettura della Città.* According to this, the city is composed of a universally valid order of building types, so there is no necessity for each age to invent a new architecture; all that is required is to interpret the traditional canon rationally in the light of current requirements. Eleven years later Rossi made the following analogy between architecture and town planning: "A building is a reproduction of the sites of a city. In these terms each corridor is a street, each inner courtyard a square. In my designs for dwellings I relate to the basic types of living space, which have evolved in the course of a long process of urban architectural development."

### Syntheses of past and present

One of the basic tasks of the IBA Berlin, for which Rossi realized his project, was the restoration of the city in the wake of the damage caused by the Second World War (see pages 66–67). This problem was in no way specific to Berlin. In the 1980s there was a generally greater awareness of the problems of dealing with the historic material around the site of a projected building, as well as the ground plan of the city itself – one of the certain benefits of Post-Modernism being that it reawakened interest in historical building styles. But architects such as Rossi also reflected in their theorizing on the historical meaning of cities and the possibility of a further functional development.

# SIR JAMES STIRLING

"Master of styles," was the heading that the *Deutsche Bauzeitschrift* gave to its obituary of the British architect James Stirling (1926–92). But he was much more than the creator of the useless columns and split pediments which tend to be dismissed today as jokes. As the leading protagonist of Post-Modernism, he prepared the ground for the paradigm-change in 20th-century architecture. His buildings are polemics against an ossified Modernism. The theories which he developed with Kevin Lynch and Charles Moore when he was Professor at Yale University led to a reconsideration of values that had been neglected by Modernism: the relationship to history and the

*Sir James Stirling, circa 1980*

surroundings of a building, as well as the power of architecture to make an emotional statement.

The re-evaluation began with quotations from the icons of architectural history. Between 1959 and 1963, long before the term Post-Modernism was coined, Stirling and James Gowan designed the Institute of Engineering at Leicester University. The overall shape of the tower-like part of the building, with its cantilevered lecture theater, seems a downright copy of the picture, much reproduced at that time, of the Rusakov workers' club designed by the Russian Constructivist Konstantin Melnikov in Moscow in 1928 (illustration page 35). The pillars with a capital in the shape of a truncated cone that turned up for the first time in the Olivetti building in Milton Keynes, England, in 1971, and which became the trademark of the firm which Sir James Stirling and Michael Wilford founded the same year, can be read as a greatly simplified quotation from the mushroom-shaped pillars created by Frank Lloyd Wright in 1939 for the Johnson Wax Company headquarters in Racine, Wisconsin (illustration page 16).

Stirling's Staatsgalerie in Stuttgart (1977–84) is an assemblage of historical quotations. The polychrome masonry echoes the medieval church

buildings of Pisa, and the sequence of rooms corresponds to a *neo-Baroque* suite. Stirling assembles a *Deconstructivist* covered entrance, *Gothic* pointed arches, vaguely antique pillared walks, and Bauhaus details around the ruin-like reference to Schinkel's rotunda in the Altes Museum in Berlin, making a varied and colorful collage. In his plan for the Berlin Wissenschaftszentrum (Scientific Center) Sir James also assembled together a whole repertoire of archetypes from architectural history: a cruciform basilica, a Greek stoa, a medieval campanile, and an antique theater.

Distinct from many of the modish hangers-on of Post-Modernism, Stirling never used other styles for their own sake. The exteriors of the Wissenschaftszentrum, so full of architectural "significance," are completely filled with identical utilitarian offices. The basilica of the Wissenschaftszentrum actually houses nothing but toilets and the caretaker's lodging. The real message of the pale blue and pink striped building is pure polemic against the paradigm of Modernism: the unity of form and function.

In his 1985 extension to the Tate Gallery in London, Stirling criticized another ideal of modernism: the showing of the construction. The façade displays a grid of masonry and plastered surfaces, which has nothing to do with the *reinforced concrete construction* inside. Whereas the galleries inside concentrate on displaying the works of J. M. W. Turner in natural light, the outside tries to fit in with the buildings around, a not unreasonable idea always neglected by self-obsessed Modernists. At the same time, the strong colors and spectacular entrance of the Clore Wing attract an attention from the public which would never have been achieved by the pictures alone. This entertainment value is an ideal which Modernism always rejected.

Stirling was fond of relating a key experience of his, which was that when he was a student he visited Palladio's Villa Rotonda. The plaster was falling off the pillars. Something that was pretending to be marble turned out to be "only" brick. But did that alter the architectonic quality of the building?

This latter was what Stirling always cared about most, as can be seen from his last building, the Braun factory in Melsungen, completed in 1992, for which the Stirling and Wilford partnership also engaged the services of the young Berlin architects Walter Nägeli and Renzo Vallebuona. The mighty building is in fact made up of a large number of highly independent volumes which fit precisely into the winding

*Colorful variety: the Clore Wing of the Tate Gallery in London (left). The curved administration building of the Braun AG works in Melsungen (right) responds to the topography of the surrounding hills.*

valley of the Pfieffewiesen. The complex displays not only the way the plastics manufactured there are made, but also the manner in which the building itself is constructed. For example, the concrete wall of the covered car park which extends along the back of the site, is draped with a mesh of formwork, in such a way that even in its completed state the fluid character of the raw material remains recognizable.

To be sure there are quotations from architectural history in Melsungen, but they are never there for themselves, but to create architectural

*As if constructed for the performance of Greek theater: the rotunda in the interior court of the Neue Württembergische Staatsgalerie (New Württenberg National Gallery) in Stuttgart is the summit of Stirling's connotation-rich collage architecture.*

qualities. The production shed may be reminiscent of Peter Behrens's epoch-making AEG-Maschinenfabrik in Berlin, but one's impressions are dominated by the wonderful view offered by the curved construction opening on to the landscape. The upturned truncated cones which support the administrative building are certainly a reminder of Le Corbusier, but above all they point to the off-center distribution of forces. You could list innumerable precedents for the colorful slanting window jambs, but their main effect is to give the light which reaches the desks of the office workers an inspirational fluidity. Have more spatial qualities ever been wrested out of a building task normally treated as workaday?

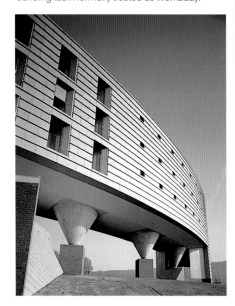

Carlo Scarpa's museum buildings of the 1960s had pointed the way, impressively, to a means of synthesizing old and new (see illustration page 76). But 20 years had passed since then, and the forms and demands of architecture had indeed changed.in that time. However, despite these changes, the fundamental question had remained the same: should one simply copy the old, or create something new in an environment laden with history?

The city of Venice offers a particular example in this area. The city on the water is a masterpiece of town planning, and its most important monuments are the responsibility of an energetic department dedicated to the conservation of historic monuments. One of the very few new building projects carried out in Venice in the 1980s was a housing development by Vittorio Gregotti, which was undertaken in the Canareggio area. Several factors had to be taken into account in this project, from the position of the site and the existing buildings, which would be a factor in determining both the size and proportions of any new building constructed upon it, to the specific historical development of residential buildings in Venice. For example, there is a typical Venetian tradition of maintaining the separateness of the private and public domains of a building, which makes it imperative that each apartment has an individual entrance, and is not – as is customary elsewhere – served by a communal staircase.

Gregotti's buildings, despite their reserved aspect, not only complied with all of these specifications, but furthermore employed both a rational and modern language of forms that did not insinuate itself into the historic environment, but instead showed much respect for it. Using *pitched roofs*, wooden loggias, and sash windows, Gregotti adopted Venetian architectural elements, but simultaneously lent them a contemporary appearance. He resisted the temptation to endow his apartments with a spurious nobility through the use of incrustations, *Gothic-influenced* arched windows, or other motifs from Venetian grand houses, and also that of utilising *deconstructive*, alienating effects to make the building more noticeable or meaningful in a way in which would run counter to its simple function as a residential building.

## THE TESSIN SCHOOL

### Architectural landscape with mountains

The rationalist architecture of individuals such as Aldo Rossi or Vittorio Gregotti, and their attempts to bring together traditional and contemporary elements, fell on particularly fruitful soil in the Italian-speaking Swiss canton of Tessin. Since time immemorial the mild climate and beautiful scenery around the Swiss northern shore of Lake Maggiore and around Lake Lugano had made this region a favorite area for the villas of the well-to-do. Since the Second World War in particular, the unique landscape of Tessin was being over-populated with poor-quality modernist type buildings of an utterly standard kind, which has led since the end of the 1960s to vehement protest by architects. Parallel to the crisis in classical Modernism in the 1960s and 1970s, this area produced its own architectonic direction: the Tessin school, which has been responsible for numerous public and private buildings of recent years. They put architecture that was monumental in place of

*Mario Botta,* Single-Family House, Vacallo (Switzerland), 1986–89

The side of this three-cornered building that faces the street is closed. The façade facing the valley is open; its two arches interconnect, and there is a semi-circular terrace in front. Like all Botto's buildings, the villa at Vacallo combines almost sacral inner rooms with a confident position in the landscape. Botta, who worked with Le Corbusier and Louis I. Kahn in his youth, obtains this effect with clear, timelessly geometric forms. The result is both dignified and subtle, due to the use of *brick*. While the building seen as a whole is thoroughly monumental, since each individual brick is only the size that the bricklayer can take in his hand, the human dimension is not lost. Because brick also provides visual evidence of the genesis and weathering of a house, and since it has been used from *Antiquity* right up till the time of Rationalism, Botta's buildings also acquire a historical dimension.

vernacular building but also took account of the nature of the landscape and the individual needs of the user.

One of the leading representatives of the Tessin school is Mario Botta, an architect who is himself from southern Switzerland, who early in his career had not only worked in the office of Louis I. Kahn, but also with the most influential European architect of the century, the Swiss-born Le Corbusier. In Botta's early work in particular, such as his buildings resting on pilotis, and in his use of concrete, the influence of both his mentors is clear.

It is possibly in the area of the single-family house that Botta achieves his best work, continuously finding new, surprising, and spectacular solutions, despite the fact that in formal terms he generally confines himself to the use of basic geometric shapes such as the circle, the rectangle, and the square. That this never results in a standard box in the

**Arata Isozaki,** *Ochanomizu Building,* 1984–87

The gleaming blue *cube* of the new Ochanomizu building by Isozaki rears up in willful contrast to the historic complex of buildings that surround it in central Tokyo. Besides offices, the building contains a large public hall and a room for chamber music. The façade of the tall building, with its severely carved square windows framed in a lighter color, and the monumental *colonnade-like* openings on the top floor, emphasize the independence of the new building and also make a connection to the historical buildings, whose autonomy remains preserved.

classic Modernist style derives from Botta's sensitive combination of these basic geometric forms, as well as upon the deliberate contrast between open and closed wall surfaces. A further characteristic of Botta's buildings is the colorful use of materials in the façades (usually red or yellow *brick*) which, together with variations in the brickwork, produces highly original results.

His round buildings, extremely reminiscent of imagined ideal buildings, are an intense reflection of themes that have occupied traditional architectural theory since *Antiquity*. The concrete results of this intelligent yet sensual process of creation are convincing, for no façade of Botta's is ever boring, and the

element of monumentality is both powerful and yet of a human scale. His formal means are many, and yet he applies them sparingly. Botta avoids all excess, anything overladen in his façades thus concentrates the effect of the means deployed.

One of Botta's most delightful family houses is that in Vacallo (see page 97). The triangular building has a beautifully structured brick façade at the back, which completely shuts it off from its surroundings. On the side facing the valley, however, the building opens out arrestingly with two intersecting arches. In front of the double arch is a gently rounded terrace, which takes up the theme of the arch and extends it into the landscape around.

## JAPAN

### Architecture as meditation

In their buildings of the 1980s, Botta with his Tessin country houses, and Gregotti with his small residential block in Canareggio in Venice, interwove historical and contemporary aspects in a thoughtful way, and came upon architectural solutions of the highest quality.

The Japanese architect Tadao Ando follows a very similar path in his buildings. He too relates consciously to the principles of a traditional architecture, the Japanese house, which both in size and form had to satisfy completely different requirements from its European or American counterparts.

And yet Ando's buildings do not at first sight work at all like the product of a mind sympathetic to cultural and historical tradition, but on the contrary seem to many viewers to be alarmingly modern. The cause for this lies not least in Ando's favorite building material, *concrete,* which scarcely any other 20th-century architect, even Le Corbusier, knew how to use so perfectly.

With their strict proportions, their studied use of light to enhance the sense of space, and the downright ascetic use of materials, Ando's buildings seem to relate concretely to Mies van der Rohe's dictum "less is more." But by comparison with Ando's buildings, Mies van der Rohe's appear almost luxuriously appointed; their expensive squared stone, their costly polished marble, and fine steel look like deliberate ostentation. Ando uses no such materials, only a combination of concrete and glass bricks, and yet with these he is

**Tadao Ando, *Kidosaki House*,**
Tokyo, 1982–86

This triple-occupancy house is relatively
large by Japanese standards, and
combines private and communal livings
areas. It is isolated by concrete walls from
the surroundings streets, and access is via
a rounded wall which leads straight to the
heart of the two-story house: a 40-feet
(12-meter) cube. As usual with Ando, the
choice of forms and materials is extremely
restrained, and at first sight the
architecture looks severe. But if you go
along with it, you begin to feel how this
restraint ennobles the form and the
materials. Perception of the particular
attributes of the surfaces is sharpened.
As in an abstract picture, nuances of
color and effects of light unite to offer a
unique experience of space. The large-
paned window areas set up a relationship
with the exterior with its delicate
arrangement of plants, intensifying further
the spatial experience.

able to create spatial effects which – as in
the case of the glass brick Ishihara House
with its shimmering light – have an almost
mystical atmosphere.

The extremely limited range of concrete
finishes deployed by Ando and the rough
surfaces of the walls give a very particular
appearance to his buildings, as for instance
the Koshino House in Ashiya, Hyogo, which
was built in two stages: from 1979 to 1981,
and from 1983 to 1984. Here it becomes
evident that Ando's architecture is not only
rooted in traditional Japanese house building,
but also has been strongly influenced by
Modernist architecture. While the layout of
the site retains the quality of an abstract
composition, the design of the interior has an
almost classical, but clearly monumental tone.
In a world flooded with color and noise,
Ando's buildings have a calming effect. Once
you have become attuned to the language of
his materials, his well-proportioned façades,
and inner spaces, you will be rewarded with a
feeling of meditative repose.

Neither the amusing Deconstructivist
leaning walls of Frank O. Gehry, nor the small-
sectioned town houses of Aldo Rossi can
command such attention as Ando's buildings,
which at first seem so spare and reserved, but
in reality are so expressive.

**Tadao Ando, *Glass Brick House
(Ishihara House)*,** Tokyo, 1977–78

The building is divided off from the world
around it by thick concrete walls, and so
creates an autonomous realm for its
inhabitants. The glass brick walls create a
luminous spatial effect within, which
reacts to every change in the light.

**Tadao Ando, *Koshino House*,** Ashiya,
Hyogo, 1979–81 and 1983–84

The parallel rectangular shapes in bare
concrete – embedded in the landscape
of a national park – are a masterly
achievement in the handling of archaic
spatial form. Ando found an aesthetic
means of overcoming the rough materials
through the use of lighting slits and large
openings in the walls. The second
building, also facing away from the road
and erected two years after the first, is
partially below ground, so that the internal
spaces have to be lit from above.
The Koshino house – an exclusive private
home – brings together Modernist formal
language and the beauty of the Japanese
landscape. It stands on a spot that seems
to have been made for it where the
ground falls away to the rear, affording
unexpected views.

Architecture for the
millennium

# A forward
# glance

1990–2000

## CONTEMPORARY BUT ETERNAL

### Change as precondition

With the fall of the Berlin Wall in 1989, the old conflicts between the superpowers of this century seemed finally to have been buried. One almost had the impression that it would now be possible to relax and enjoy the unexpected peace for which we had longed for such a long time.

But if the polarization of the world into East and West is a thing of the past, the apparently boundless optimism and the happy sense of a new start of the early 1990s have died away. They have given way to a new uncertainty, fed by the fact that the old clichés of Good and Evil do not have the familiar meaning in the new world order that once they had.

Signficantly, the cruel civil war in the former Yugoslavia has shown just how fragile the scarcely constituted new world order really is. And in many places in the world, be it in Africa or southeast Asia, it is far from clear how the next few years will turn out. Finally, the number of war zones has not decreased since the end of the East-West conflict; they are simply arising in different places.

So the 1990s have presented a particular challenge, especially in view of the new millennium. Pressing social problems and numerous ethnic conflicts are demanding swift resolution, and the tried and tested economic and social structures of the economically advanced countries have to adapt to rapidly changing global circumstances. With their completely new and, for many people, surprising challenges, the 1990s are not the hoped-for decade of repose but a decade of change and new directions.

### Buildings of today for the world of tomorrow

It is as hard for us to see what, in a hundred years, will be feted as the events of the 20th century, as it is for us to know, from our contemporary point of view, which will be the architectural works celebrated as masterpieces in years to come. Such an evaluation requires a critical distance which we perforce cannot have.

Without such a distance there is the danger that what appears to be the most important of today's trends in architecture will turn out to be a false trail, a short-lived fashion born of the spirit of the times, which in 50 years will seem scarcely worth a mention. No one knows which way our path is leading – and the same is true of architecture.

Despite the inevitable obstacles to determine which contemporary masterworks will last, it is possible to point to trends in operation now. Certain tendencies of the 1980s, such as the Deconstructivism of someone like Frank O. Gehry, or the Rationalism of an Aldo Rossi are continuing today, and developing in response to the changing demands of architecture.

**1990**: On 3 October Germany is reunified after a division lasting 45 years; the first elections since the war to cover the whole country are held.

**1991**: In the Gulf War, US-led troops secure the withdrawal of Iraqi occupying forces from Kuwait. Signing of the Maastricht Treaty regarding economic and monetary union and the common foreign and defense policy of Europe.

**1992**: UN Conference on Environment and Development – the Earth summit – held in Rio. UN aid flights and peace-keeping force alleviate conditions in Sarajevo. Number of HIV sufferers worldwide estimated at 10 million.

**1993**: Power struggle in Moscow; Yeltsin dissolves parliament. Peace accord between Israel and the PLO. Bill Clinton takes office as the 42nd president of the USA. The term "European Union" replaces "European Community" as

Maastricht Treaty takes effect. A human embryo is cloned for the first time; the experiment calls forth worldwide horror.

**1994**: Nelson Mandela elected the first black president of South Africa; end of the apartheid state. Hollywood takes on the German past in its own way: Stephen Spielberg's *Schindler's List* comes to the cinemas. Opening of the Eurotunnel under the English Channel.

**1995**: Jacques Chirac succeeds François Mitterrand, president of France for 14 years. Turkey continues to make war on the Kurds, harassing them beyond the borders of the country. "Multimedia" is the word of the year. Christo and Jeanne-Claude wrap the Reichstag building in Berlin.

**1996**: Refugees suffer terrible hardship in central Africa. After civil war in Rwanda and Burundi, conflict spreads to eastern Zaire. First parliamentary elections in Bosnia

under the strictest security precautions. The "mad cow disease" BSE leads to a ban on the export of beef and cattle from the UK.

**1997**: The UK returns Hong Kong to China. Civil war in Albania. Bloody end to siege of the Tupac Amaru rebels who had held hostages in the Japanese embassy in Lima, Peru. The New Labour leader Tony Blair becomes prime minister of Great Britain. NATO-Russia summit in Paris: ex-Warsaw Pact countries can now join NATO. The comet Hale-Bopp can be seen from the Earth with the naked eye. The fashion designer Gianni Versace is shot dead. Princess Diana and her companion

*Young techno-fans at the "Love Parade" in Berlin in 1995*

Dodi al Fayed are killed in a car accident in Paris. Mother Teresa dies at the age of 87. Earthquake damage in Italy, including partial destruction of celebrated frescos by Giotto and Cimabue in Assisi.

**1998**: President Suharto of Indonesia steps down after 30 years following strong demonstrations against him. "The Voice," Frank Sinatra, dies in Los Angeles. 10th Techno-Festival, "Love Parade" in Berlin.

If one examines the basic questions relating to the future development of society, one will also find some answers about the future form of architecture. One lesson that has finally been learned from the history of architecture in the 19th and 20th centuries is that society and architecture affect each other. Any architecture that exists only for itself, which just aims to please, without taking on the social and cultural needs of its users, is less likely than ever to be financed, nor will it be able to win a place for itself in the long term.

## ARCHITECTURE IN THE VIRTUAL AGE

### The power of images

Residential buildings and office blocks, factories and museums: these will continue to be the most important tasks of architecture. But the pressure of rising costs on a world scale will not be without effect on what they will look like, and how they will come into being.

It is almost inevitable that cost-considerations will make rationalization increasingy important in architectural, as well as other, undertakings. Standardization and mass-reproduction − leading themes of 20th century architecture − continue to cover everything from the total plan to the single window. Only a few architects and clients will be able to construct buildings of quality under these restricting conditions. Even under the most

advantageous of circumstances, standardized "average" architecture will continue to leave a large mark on the appearance of our cities. The architectonic highlight, the outstanding design and the end product with quality in every detail, will almost inevitably step more and more into the background.

A decisive role in this rationalization is being played by the invention of the computer, without which our daily lives would be almost as unthinkable as having neither telephone nor car. Although the computer as architect is still science fiction, many areas of the architect's work have for a long time been carried out by computer-supported design programs, and the statics of a building project as well as the logistics of the building site are calculated with the help of the "computer colleague."

In large-scale projects, virtual tours of projected prototype buildings are replacing the tedious job of studying models and scale-drawings. In a matter of moments a computer can take viewers on a tour through courtyards and office buildings, across whole city areas that are still at the planning stage, through any number of interior rooms that have yet to be installed. In the shortest possible time the architecture of tomorrow grows before the eyes of the beholder, and seduces the interested layman by the power of the image.

*High-tech architecture*, which is the most appropriate translation into concrete reality of such a planning principle, and which has in

**Jean Nouvel, *Galeries Lafayette*,**
Berlin, 1993–96

The building becomes immaterial.
Everything comprehensible disappears
behind polished high-grade steel and
other ungraspable materials. Four neon
tubes and a mirror dissolve the ceilings
into a "frozen sky." The expansive
construction of diagonal supports is lost
behind the iridescent shell of the double-
layered glass façade. Inside the Galeries
Lafayette, the German branch of the
French department store, a double glass
cone makes gravity seem to disappear, as
holograms and mirrors turn it into a
kaleidoscope. Glass is not used here as it
was in the glass palaces of bygone years,
as a transparent medium through which
to see the truth: it produces multiple
images of visitors to the store; a virtual
public is created.
But here begin the contradictions –
because the business that this building
serves has material interests. People's
perceptions go beyond what they can see.
The optical effects here, however, create a
blind spot for all their other senses.

fact been around since the 1970s in the buildings of Norman Foster or Richard Rogers, will
play a leading role in the next decades on the
global architectural stage. In spite of all the criticism that the worldwide reach of the Internet
has evoked, and all the fears it brings to the
surface, there is a tenacious fascination about
what is now already possible.

## Poetry in glass

It was Joseph Paxton's Crystal Palace of 1851
(illustration page 7) which started the extraordinarily successful progress of glass in architectural history. From Bruno Taut's Glass House
(illustration page 19) to Mies van der Rohe's
Neue Berliner Nationalgalerie (illustration page
59), from the villa to the commercial building:
the versatility of the glass façade has covered
so many applications, and the material has yet
to lose its charm.

The French architect, Jean Nouvel, has
added a new, almost poetic facet to the already
rich contemporary repertoire of architecture in
glass. He first received international recognition
with his Institut du Monde Arabe (IMA) in
Paris (1981–87), is on the banks of the Seine,
and which is, according to Nouvel's own
estimation, an "absolutely modern building."

The IMA arose as one of the "grands
projets" initiated by President Mitterrand in
Paris in the 80s. Because of its colonial past,
especially in the 19th and 20th centuries,
France still has close links with Arab culture.

The IMA became a unique showplace for that
culture in Paris, with a museum, rooms for
special exhibitions, a library, documentation
center, lecture hall, and restaurant, adding to
the repertoire of modern museum-building in
the 1980s. The particular merit of Nouvel's
building is the way that it links traditional
Arab elements, as for instance a pillared hall
reminiscent of a mosque, with glassy *high-
tech architecture.*

The balanced stratification of glass elements
gives the building an exciting aesthetic tension
even from the outside. The sightlines that open
up again and again through the glassy transparency of the building are complicated by the
superimposition of intervening constructional
elements. Despite the elegance of its form and
materials, the general effect of the building,
with its interrupted and reflected light, is one
of rich variety.

The design of the southern façade of the
IMA is particularly attractive. Nouvel has taken
various geometric forms in common use in
Arabian architecture, and put them in a
modern sun-shield consisting of 27,000 lenses
that expand or contract according to the light.
This shield is installed in the glass façade and
serves not only as a mundane protection
against the sun, but opens up the possibility
of a fascinating play with light and shade in
the interior. The geometric grid shape of the
sun-shield has a further function, in that its
inflexible language of form bespeaks the

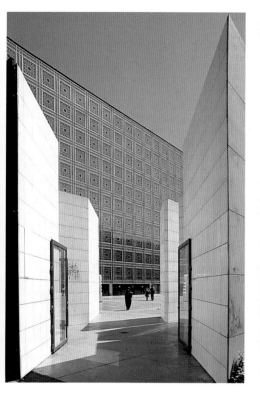

affiliation of the building to two cultures: Arab and European, which are synthesized within it.

Another example of Nouvel's expertise in dealing with the immaterial building material that is glass, is provided by the Galeries Lafayette in Berlin (1993–96), one of the few architecturally ambitious commercial buildings to have been erected in the 1990s on the Friedrichstrasse in the course of the rebuilding of central Berlin after reunification.

The core of the commercial building is the department store that gives it its name, the Berlin branch of the famous Parisian store Galeries Lafayette. It is a fact that in the consumerist culture of the West, the building of a department store is a particular challenge. What kind of attractions can be employed to tempt demanding customers? How can architecture rise to the challenge? One solution was given by SITE in the 1970s (illustration page 82): making buildings that turned a daily shop at the supermarket into a semi-dramatic experience.

Nouvel takes another route. He goes for big-city architecture, characterized by elegance and light, glass and transparency. The heart of the building consists of two glass cones whose bases meet at the ground floor, the one thus tapering upward, the other seeming to bore into the ground.

The impression created by this glass cone is overwhelming, a spectacular aesthetic coup, a new interpretation of the interior courtyard, which is such an important element in the architectural history of the department store. And of course, in a place dominated by glass, there is also the obligatory glass lift.

Even on the outside, Nouvel continues the conceit with the curving glass skin of the façade, which glides round the corner defying the cohorts of granite- and limestone-faced blocks all around it. Nouvel handles the roof zone in a playful manner, in that he deploys neither a pure *flat roof* nor a traditional tiled *pitched roof*, but develops his own particular architectural language by creating a roof whose sloping sides are made of glass.

## High-tech expression

Engineers have always been among the innovative and driving forces of architecture. But whereas at the end of the 19th century people, when confronted with the Eiffel Tower and the first skyscrapers in Chicago, were still arguing as to whether the works of the engineers could be considered as belonging to "real" architecture, this argument has long been decided. Without both the functional and aesthetic contribution of the engineer, the history of 20th-century architecture would be inconceivable.

But engineering and modern art can join hands beyond the confines of building as such, as for instance in the constructions and sculptures of Santiago Calatrava, a Spaniard living in Switzerland, whose work is also to be seen in the Museum of Modern Art.

**Jean Nouvel with Gilbert Lézenès and Pierre Soria, *Institut du Monde Arabe*,** south façade (left) and stairwell (right), Paris, 1981–87

At first sight the south façade looks like an Arabian lattice-work screen, intricately pierced. In fact, it consists of thousands and thousands of motor-driven blinds, large and small. They vary the penetration of light into the building according to the strength of the sunlight, and unfold a play with light and shade with meditative power. The Institut du Monde Arabe becomes a viewing apparatus focused on Arab culture. The spiritual, symbolic world of the Orient is united with the rationally directed world of the West. High-tech elements, which were included in the 1970s for their own sake, are at last used here in the service of overall artistic goals.

**Santiago Calatrava, *Pasarela de Uribitarte*,** footbridge over the river Nerbio, Bilbao, 1993

Even the approach to Calatrava's footbridge signals an experience to come. The bridge takes off from two elegant, sweeping ramps. But the high point of the sculptural construction is the parabola from which it is suspended. Everything in this building is in tension, seems to be in latent movement – there is nothing stiff even about the bridge itself over the river: it is gently curved. Calatrava's language of forms, reminiscent of organic archetypes, emphasizes this sensual note still more. The architect has understood how to present the apparently everyday act of crossing from one shore to the other as an experience. The bold sickle shape of his bridges is in the tradition of the great Spanish constructors Antoni Gaudí and Eduardo Torroja y Miret, and also the Frenchman Gustave Eiffel (see page 8).

Curving, dynamic forms, whose expressivity is a distant reminder of Eero Saarinen's TWA Terminal in New York (illustration page 73), are a running theme of Calatrava's work. Filigree concrete supports like ribs span his spaces, giving them an extremely lively character that is full of movement, as for instance in his exhibition building on the Spanish island of Tenerife, one of the Canary Islands (1992–95).

Analogies with living things almost force themselves upon you when you see Calatrava's expressive architecture: the backbone of a fish with the bones all slanting away at an angle from it, or the arched comb on the back of a prehistoric animal. A notable example of this is the Alameda bus station in Valencia that Calatrava built between 1991 and 1995, which is on several levels, dominated by a towering arch held up by filigree supports. The same motif recurs in much of the detailed working-out of his designs for bridges.

## An arrow into the future

Dynamism – that is the first impression given by the Vitra fire-station realized at Weil am Rhein in 1993 by the London-based Iraqi architect Zaha Hadid. It was a choice site. Here the grandfather of *Deconstructivism*, Frank O. Gehry had built the Vitra Design Museum, and woven an innovative element into European architecture. And here on the upper Rhine, the British-born Nicolas Grimshaw had also been active, designing the Vitra furniture factory.

Hadid's building plunges like an arrow into the landscape. The jutting concrete canopy of the complex rests on a little forest of astonishingly thin, straight, and sloping pillars, with a dramatic, expressive gesture that lends the building, for all its mundane purpose, the atmosphere of a monument. Slanted walls, walls that cut across each other, and volumes stacked on top of each other give the building expressive strength of an original and restless kind. From a bird's eye view, the building looks like a paper airplane, elegant and aerodynamic

**Zaha Hadid, *Vitra Fire Station*,** Weil am Rehin, 1993

Leaning blades of bare concrete cut across each other. A gigantic sheet of glass turns the fire-station into a display cabinet. The dramatically pointed slab of concrete which makes up the front canopy seems to float. The leaning steel rods which support it defy the logic of construction.
Now working in England, the Iraqi *deconstructivist* Zaha Hadid has been strongly influenced by Russian *Constructivism*. There could scarcely be a better expression of the essence of the project. Tension is the daily experience of the fire service, and tension is the keynote of this building, housing the fire fighting department of a furniture factory. The eccentricity of this sculptural building has something monumental about it, and its functionality appears incidental. And indeed the fire station has lost its original function; it has become a sculptural museum piece itself in the noted architecture park in Weil am Rhein.

at once, but with its markedly sloping walls it also invokes memories of a ship. Open and closed parts alternate and adjust themselves to a traditional canon of forms. This is architecture driven by an immense outlay of constructive and creative power whose individuality is such that, like the work of Santiago Calatrava, the whole building is consciously raised to the level of a sculpture. The building is as bewildering in its formal structure of interlocking planes, as it is heterogeneous in its deployment of materials, from aluminum and smooth concrete through to the sealed sheet of glass and the strip windows.

The building served as a pillar-less concrete shed for the fire engines of the Vitra furniture factory, but it also housed canteen and sanitary areas and a fitness room. Today it has lost its original function and is an important part of the architecture park at Weil am Rhein, where it serves as an exhibition area for the Vitra collection of chairs, and can also be used for special events.

Hadid's fire station was given much praise, and euphoric comparisons were drawn with the architectural visions of the Russian *Constructivists* of the 1920s, and the spatial effects of Mies van der Rohe's Barcelona pavilion. One should remain level-headed in the face of such excitement. Hadid did produce a strongly expressive fire station, which takes on the avant-garde with its quotations and contemporary forms of expression. Whether her building is in fact more than a milestone of *Deconstructivism*, a modish treasure in an unexpected part of the city, remains to be seen.

## THE AESTHETICS OF SIMPLICITY

### Reduction instead of expression

The contrast could not be greater between the neo-Expressionist/Deconstructivist buildings and projects of Zaha Hadid or Frank O. Gehry, which for all their artistic intensity are sometimes a little overwrought, and the work of the two Basel architects Jacques Herzog and Pierre de Meuron, who attracted worldwide attention when they were contracted to construct the new Tate Gallery in the old Bankside power station in London. The two architects were once the pupils of the rationalist Aldo Rossi, but their work is also clearly different from his.

**Jacques Herzog and Pierre de Meuron,** *Stone House,* Tavole, Liguria, 1988

"Less is more" was the opinion of Mies van der Rohe as early as the 1920s. Today, the architects favoring a "new simplicity" have come to see in it the riches of asceticism. Like Mies, the Swiss architects Jacques Herzog and Pierre de Meuron work with clear square shapes and simple spatial geometry. But their materials are more various and used with a greater variety and with greater impact on the senses; they make a point of them. Building materials become raw materials. In the Goetz Collection building (illustrated below) there is a combination of bare concrete, unworked plywood, and frosted glass. In the Tavole house (left) dry stone walls made of local chalk blocks that look like slate are used to fill the load-bearing modern concrete skeleton. The house, which stands alone in a hilly landscape with crumbling stone terraces for olive trees and vines, bespeaks radical abstraction and a new seriousness in architecture.

As early as the Stone House, which they built in Tavole in Liguria between 1982 and 1988, the two had evolved their simple but aesthetic basic concept. The house is a plain *rectilinear* block, with a *pergola*-like structure in front of it, constructed of a clearly visible concrete frame, with an *infill* of dry-stone walls. The constructional simplicity of the building is accompanied by an enormous aesthetic charm, which arises from a synthesis of materials having such different properties. The building is given its liveliness by the contrasting visual effect of the very different surface structures. In addition to this, the two

**Jacques Herzog and Pierre de Meuron,** *Goetz Collection,* Munich-Oberföhring, 1993

**Jo Coenen, *Nederlands Architectuurinstitut,* Rotterdam, 1993–95**

The telescoped and intersecting volumes of Coenen's Architektuurinstitut in Rotterdam, which includes other, smaller architectural institutions, offer an example of contemporary architecture that is full of visual tension and plays consciously with the various stylistic resources of 20th-century Modernism. The main building of the institute rises up in front of a long archive building, which screens off the area in an extended arc. It is oversailed by a monumental *pergola*-like construction, resting on menacingly pointed steel pillars. Within this dynamic construction, which is as functionless as it is impressive, the almost fully glazed rectilinear exhibition area is contained. By evening light in particular, this area appears to turn inside out, reflected in the surrounding water.

types of material stand for different periods of architectural history – concrete is the load-bearing material of Modernism, whereas the unworked stones of the dry-stone walls represent a tradition that extends back hundreds of years.

This seriousness in the use of form and materials, directed towards the specific function of the building in its location, is a leitmotif of the work of Herzog and de Meuron. In a quite different form, but with related aesthetic effect, we find this leitmotif again in the building constructed in 1993 to house the Kunstsammlung Goetz (Goetz Art Collection) in Munich-Oberfohring.

Once again the body of the building is a strict, diagonally placed *rectilinear block.* As in the Stone House in Tavole, the materials surprise: concrete, wood, and frosted glass. The color effect produced is unique, very delicate, and reserved, which gives the building a kind of airiness close to gaiety, despite its introverted appearance.

Above the fully glazed ground floor, which houses both a library and a hall, and is distinguished by the slightly greenish shimmer that it derives from the frosted glass, there are the three exhibition rooms themselves. They consist of a double frame of pinewood that is filled with beechwood panels. Even in the use of these woods you can see the architects' delicate sense of differentiation. The lightness of the color effects produced by the smooth, almost whitish beechwood elements are contrasted with the somewhat darker frames

in pinewood, which gave a more structured and raw effect through the presence of knots. This rectangular wooden construction is sandwiched between two ribbons of frosted glass. They serve to light the exhibition rooms inside, while completing the harmonious symmetry of the building on the outside.

In this Munich Exhibition Building Herzog and de Meuron achieved the task of creating a very reserved style of architecture which seems to subordinate itself to the artworks being exhibited, while remaining an extremely artistic piece of architecture – an effect created with the most economic means, by the surprising and extraordinarily attractive use of materials.

The extension and rebuilding work done on the Swiss Unfallversicherungsanstalt (accident insurance office) in Basel, by Herzog and de Meuron in 1995, is similar in terms of basic structure, and in the diagonal placement of the building. Especially noteworthy in this project is the remarkable way in which they have dealt with the old part of the building; it was simply packed into a glazed façade that was constructed out of variously treated glass panels. In this way the old building continues to be visible from the exterior, and remains largely unaltered.

However, this procedure does additionally have the effect of establishing a deliberately disturbing new layer over the building by the use of the various types of glass, which are of varying degrees of transparency, and have only a vague relationship to the articulation of the

old façade lying behind them. Reflections and insights, distortions in the structured panes, and the shadows cast by the sun-blinds and by the supporting framework result in a very pleasing intellectual game between the historic and contemporary elements of the building, molding them into a new whole.

Similarly, the typical seriousness of Herzog and de Meuron is also to be found in the rebuilding and extension that they carried out for the Swiss accident insurance institution. Notably, it stands out in a sharp contrast to the playfully ironic expressivity of many of their contemporaries.

## Practical but without severity

The formal agitation of many a Deconstructivist architectural fantasy is as far from the work of the Portuguese architect Alvaro Siza as it is from that of Herzog and de Meuron. That does not mean that he, or they, cannot produce exciting buildings! The best example of Siza's ability to produce modern architecture that is both thought-provoking and exciting is the row of white *rectilinear* structures, which he erected on a sloping location in the west of his hometown of Porto, and which together constitute the faculty of architecture. Built between 1986 and 1995, the buildings stand in a park surrounded by greenery, in relative isolation and repose.

The four rectilinear volumes, which are clearly indebted to the classic Modernist tradition, look very much alike at first sight, but turn out on closer inspection, as with the service area lying behind them, to be very different from each other.

In spite of the use of standard building parts, the variety of form is astonishing. Tall rectangular windows and horizontal window strips give the façades "faces," which are additionally accented by inset and projecting areas, half-roofs set back into the building to provide sun protection, and roofs which project out over terraces. Galleries and large glazed zones in the campus-like area between the buildings give the faculty – which contrasts strongly with its rather closed exterior aspect – an open and airy character.

The students of the architecture faculty in Porto are thus given a rich supply of possible forms for architecture just by looking at the buildings of their university. There is a danger with such a variety of architectural languages that a lack of coherence will ensue, but a master such as Alvaro Siza knows how to avoid this. The individual parts of his scheme fit together harmoniously, and form a loose, but organically coherent whole, which is beautiful, but still offers space for all the necessary institutions, from the workshops to the lecture hall, the exhibition room, the offices, and the obligatory cafeteria.

The functionalism of Siza's architecture does not result in monotony. In fact, its apparent severity turns out, on close consideration, to be a clarity of form and content, which has given Siza his deserved position as one of the most important architects of contemporary times.

**Dani Karavan, *Memorial to Walter Benjamin*, Port-Bou (Spain), 1994**

On 26 September 1940, the philosopher and writer Walter Benjamin put an end to his flight from the Nazi regime, and to his life, at Port-Bou. In memory of this event, the Israeli artist Dani Karavan designed a monument drawing on some of the conventions used in land art.
In accordance with the course of Benjamin's life and the title of one of his main works (*Passagen*), the work is composed of three paths, each signifying a different point. The third and last of the paths consists of a sloping tunnel blasted out of the rock, whose walls are clad in rusting steel. It is ended abruptly by a sheet of glass, beyond which roars the sea. The only way out is the hopeless abyss.
Rich in connotations, extremely economic in its means, the monument at Port-Bou could be a pointer to the development of architecture in the next millennium.

## SCULPTURE AND ARCHITECTURE

### The new aesthetic of history

One of the most controversial artists of the late 1980s and 1990s is Daniel Libeskind (Berlin, Los Angeles). It is surprising that his work excites so much passionate argument, since he can look back on only a small corpus of finished work.

His radical language of form and the great intellectual intensity of his engagement with the historical and political context of his buildings attract many people, but it is possible that they also frighten off many others, including potential clients.

One of the few buildings so far realized by Libeskind, who has been the winner of several architectural competitions, chiefly in Germany, is the Jewish Museum – or rather the Jewish department of the Berlin Museum – which was opened in January 1999. Its only relationship to the well-known museum buildings of the 1980s and 1990s is that it is indeed a museum. It does not wallow joyfully in quotations as does the *post-modern* Staatsgalerie in Stuttgart by James Stirling and Michael Wilford (illustration page 96), nor has it the noble elegance of Jean Nouvel's Institut du Monde Arabe in Paris (illustration page 103).

Libeskind's museum is intended to present the history of Jewish life in Berlin. Libeskind has himself characterized the building as a metaphorical symbol, as a museum built around a void, a void which signifies the loss of Jewish lives in the Holocaust.

Like Zaha Hadid's Vitra fire station in Weil am Rhein, the Jewish Museum, which is linked underground to the old *baroque* museum building, reminds one of an arrow or a zigzagging streak of lightening. This has a deeper meaning with Libeskind, in that you can see it as a deconstructed Star of David, relating to the places that were once the centers of Jewish life in Berlin.

The goal which Daniel Libeskind is trying to reach is high, as is the intellectual construct from which he is working. His theme is a difficult and unwieldy one, and his architecture is accordingly gauche, going forward and back, with empty corners and high concrete walls, which deliberately exclude visitors and people who come to look, and takes on the character of a complicated architectonic sculpture.

In spite of, or rather because of, this complexity, it may be supposed that Daniel Libeskind's Jewish Museum – radical, uniquely and intensively involved with its historic location – will in future count as one of the most important museum buildings, not only of the 1990s, but of the century.

### Reactions – physically enshrined memory

If the 1980s, with their great museum complexes, look in retrospect like an uproarious decade of celebration culture, the 1990s can be most properly described as a decade of more reflective memorial culture.

This involvement with history and the memory of both people and events has become one of the central themes of the decade, with monuments, exhibitions, and memorials. The reasons for this are – as always – multifarious. Without doubt, the approaching end of three time-spans – the decade, the century, and the millennium – is playing an important role in the process of reflection – on what has been as well as on what is yet to come. But also the shadows of significant anniversaries, such as the fiftieth anniversary of the end of the Second World War, have left their mark.

It is certainly not by chance that much recent architecture can also be interpreted as monumental sculpture. This is especially true of the work of Daniel Libeskind, whose complex language of forms links his works to the history of the location for which they were planned, in a deeply thought-out way. But in the same way as architecture has entered into a dialogue with sculpture, numerous contemporary sculptures reveal clear links with architecture. In many cases it seems as though the barrier between architecture and sculpture is on the point of breaking down.

One of the most impressive and perhaps thought-provoking memorials to express its message by architectonic means is the "Commemorative Passages" for Walter Benjamin, created by the Israeli artist Dani Karavan in 1994 on the border between France and Spain at the little Spanish coastal town of Port-Bou.

The Jewish philosopher and writer Walter Benjamin, who was a native of Berlin, came here in 1940 while fleeing from the Nazi reign of terror, and in deepest despair took his own life. Dani Karavan has depicted this with great sensitivity and visual skill in the architecture of his memorial. Between two rusty red, steel walls each 77 feet (2.35 meters) high, a very narrow stairway consisting of 87 steps, also made of steel, leads down a slope from the burial ground of the sleepy little frontier port. The top steps are roofed over, those below are open to the sky. The stairs lead nowhere. At the bottom there is nothing but the pounding sea, an abyss of hopelessness that Benjamin himself may have felt when he realized his flight was leading nowhere.

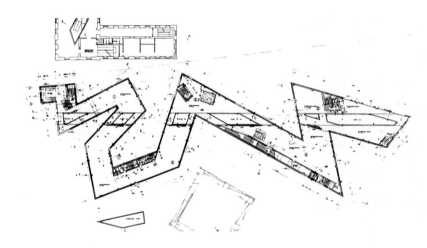

The engagement with history, especially the Nazi regime that had in effect flouted all moral law between 1933 and 1945, is also one of the main preoccupations of a German artist living in Paris, Jochen Gerz. In his works, which demand the participation of the viewer even more than Karavan's memorial, he also continually draws upon traditional architectonic means.

One of his most important projects is the 1993 memorial on the Schlossplatz in Saarbrücken, where the names of all the Jewish cemeteries existing in Germany before the Second World War are engraved on the underside of 2,146 paving stones. Another monument, called *Die Bremer Befragung* (the Bremen questionnaire), inaugurated in 1995, sticks out like a viewing platform from a bridge over the river Weser. An engraved plaque challenges the passers-by to imagine what their own memorial and its theme would be. His involvement with architectonic

**Daniel Libeskind, *Jewish Museum*,** Berlin, 1989–98

The Jewish Museum is the first design that Libeskind, the most intellectual of the *Deconstructivists* has been able to build. Its outline represents a part of the Star of David. Through this lifeline, rich in detours, runs a straight band of emptiness, signifying the loss of Jewish culture through the Holocaust. Every one of the windows, cut with the precision of a paper pattern into the zinc façade, makes a mental connection to the real places where this life was once lived.
Here although Daniel Libeskind's designs consist only of lines, they produce impressive architecture. And even though the complex academic references will be impenetrable to the uninitiated visitor, the forceful impact of the architecture on the senses delivers the message of the building.

## ARCHITECTURE IN THE 21ST CENTURY

### Handling resources responsibly

Architecture, if it aims to be good architecture, has been experimental since Antiquity. Each experiment breaks new ground, and seeks an answer to problems relevant to its day. Paxton's Crystal Palace made of glass, Eiffel's tower constructed out of iron, and François Hennebique's early reinforced concrete constructions: all were architectural experiments whose consequences reverberated into the 20th century.

One of the most important problems facing humanity at the end of the 20th century is the fact that the ecological dimensions of our world have shifted dramatically. Architecture must discover viable solutions for the new demands that this poses. For the way in which we handle natural resources will dictate our future. And this does not only mean taking a responsible attitude to non-renewable fuels, the use of which is causing ever greater pollution and environmental destruction. It is becoming ever more clear that things we take for granted such as drinking water, which we in the northern countries think we have more than enough of, have to be handled sparingly and responsibly, and be treated as what they are: a precious necessity for life.

The answers that architecture has brought to the numerous ecological demands and challenges are many and various. They begin with down to earth measures such as putting in insulation walls which – unlike ordinary wood and stone walls – retain large amounts of energy for use in the house which would otherwise get lost in the air outside. Thus the expenditure of heat is lessened, which, apart from protecting natural resources, also brings a financial saving to the owner or the tenant, who needs to spend less on oil or other fuel.

Arranging the ground plan of the house to suit the natural disposition of light and sun is another measure that can significantly reduce the consumption of energy. Solar radiation in particular can be utilized: solar panels collect the radiation which is used for heating the house and the water. Sunlight can also be used to generate electricity via photovoltaic cells, and thus will take over a considerable part of the provision of light in a house.

**Nicolas Grimshaw, *Editorial offices and printing works of the Western Morning News*,** Plymouth, 1993

High-tech designs, which at first were chiefly a way of displaying innovative construction details, today fulfill all the demands of architecture – a development to which Nicolas Grimshaw has been a major contributor. In his building for the *Western Morning News*, the editorial offices and the printing works are accommodated under the same roof, providing optimal working conditions. The building has the internal and external transparency to be expected from a media enterprise. Located on a hill in Plymouth, the building is a landmark with its distinctive shape like the prow of a ship, and its tusk-like steel supports holding up the all-glass façade. It creates a connection with the history of this maritime city while also symbolizing its economic rebirth as a center of service industries.

form is at its most concrete in the monument against fascism that he realized with his wife, Esther Shalev-Gerz, in Hamburg (1986–93). This consists of a 40-feet (12-meter) high square post that is covered in lead, which was gradually sunk into the ground. The people who passed by it over the years were invited to scratch their opinion of fascism onto the soft surface of the lead before the pillar was entirely sunk into the ground, and their inscriptions preserved there.

Just as Libeskind evokes an engagement with history in his architecture through its appeal to the senses, Karavan and Gerz challenge spectators of their architectonic sculptures to engage with their theme. Only by being drawn into the work can spectators be able to achieve an understanding of it. Contemporary artists and sculptors have taken up a position of intense involvement with historical events and people, which points the way to a future direction for both of these art forms.

**Alessandro Mendini, *Museum*,**
Groningen (Netherlands), 1995

Situated on a canal basin, and accessible only via a footbridge, the *Deconstructivist* museum island of Groningen bristles with shrill, bright buildings leaning this way and that in a hubbub of different materials and forms. Looking at first sight more like an overgrown piece of furniture than a building, the museum houses art of all periods collected in Groningen. The list of artists who worked on this ambitious project reads like a "Who's Who" of Deconstructivism, including Mendini from Italy, Philippe Starck from France, and the Austrian COOP Himmelblau architectural practice. So it is not surprising that in among all the diagonals and curves in steel, artificial stone, wood, and concrete, right-angles are in short supply. The Groningen Museum's most significant counterpart is the Guggenheim-Museum in Bilbao (opened 1998) by Frank O. Gehry.

Numerous experimental buildings have sprung up of late, trumpeting their purpose with names such as eco-house, or low-energy or energy-saving house, which have a tendency to confuse rather than enlighten the majority of visitors. But all the ecological requirements that such a house has to fulfill – often at enormous expense for those who commission it – need not be detrimental to its architectural impact. This is perfectly demonstrated by the house in Breisach (illustration page 94) created by Thomas Spiegelhalter of Freiburg, who specializes in sculptural architecture. His *Deconstructivist* and technical language of forms is coupled in an exemplary manner with ecological functions.

The porch is made up of solar panels that provide the hot-water supply, and an L-shaped wind and sun shield gives the building formal dynamism while also housing the photovoltaic module of the house. The barrels on the roof, which emphasize the pronounced technicity of the building's appearance, serve as rainwater collectors.

The building embodies a unique synthesis of up-to-the-minute patterns of use, and an absolutely contemporary language of form that points the way into the new millennium. The architect's responsibility for the future of the environment cannot be overestimated. But this responsibility is also a challenge which will lead to new, exciting architectonic answers in the 21st century.

**Richard Meier, *John Paul Getty Center*,**
Los Angeles, 1992–97

A "new acropolis" was what the John Paul Getty Foundation asked the New York architect Richard Meier to build, in order to display its famous collections of Greek and Roman antiquities, European painting, drawing, and sculpture from the Renaissance, baroque, and classical periods, as well as applied art and photography. The Getty Center consists of six main buildings clearly separate from each other. Nonetheless they can be appreciated as a cohesive complex. Because of the restrained nature of the architecture there is no conflict between the works of art being exhibited and the building. Meier, who was making a name for himself throughout the world for his typical white-tiled façades turned for this, his biggest project to date, to Italian travertine, which glows pinkish in the California sun. In order to achieve a unified color for the façades, all the stone had to be cut from the same quarry.

# GLOSSARY OF TERMS

The words in *italics* in the main text are explained in this glossary. Those italicized here are further elucidated elsewhere in the glossary or in the names index.

**abstraction** Tendency in modern art starting about 1850 to simplify forms when representing a naturalistic model in a work of art, especially in painting. The culmination of this tendency is in painting without a subject – abstract painting – as for example in the period around 1910 with the works of *Piet Mondrian* or *Kasimir Malevich*.

**academic** The nature of the education, conforming to traditional values, formerly offered by art schools. Is generally used pejoratively to refer to conservative art in contrast to innovative movements such as *Impressionism, Expressionism* and the *Secession.*

**Amsterdam School** Influential Dutch *Expressionist* architectural movement, whose chief representatives, *Johann Melchior van der Mey, Michel de Klerk,* and *Pieter Kramer,* constructed strongly expressive buildings in brick.

**antiquity** Generic term describing the two high periods of early European culture: Greek antiquity (at its apogee in the 5th and 4th centuries BC) and Roman antiquity (1st and 2nd centuries AD).

**arcade** A range of *arches* carried on piers or *columns,* either free-standing or attached to a wall.

**arch** Any upwardly curved element which forms a link between two vertical elements. Extremely varied types of arches have existed since the time of Ancient Rome. The use of different types of arch characterizes specific epochs of architectural history (semicircular arch: *Romanesque, Renaissance*; pointed arch: *Gothic*). Flattened arches are also frequently to be found; these consist of a segment of a semicircular arch. The functional purpose of an arch is to distribute a down force (e.g., the weight of a vaulted roof) into several supports.

**architectural engineering** Building of a kind which since the days of *Antiquity* could only be carried out with special technical knowledge. In the 19th century this was represented mainly by stations, bridges, and also buildings entirely of *iron,* such as the Eiffel Tower. The 20th century has seen architectural engineering carried to new heights, especially in sports stadia. (See *Pier Luigi Nervi* and *Frei Otto*).

**architecture parlante** French term meaning "speaking architecture," describing buildings where the form gives an indication as to their use, as for instance in the case of *Fritz Höger's* Chile House, which was built for a shipping company.

**Art Déco** A style in art in the 20s and 30s, whose name derives from the "Exposition internationale des arts décoratifs et industriels modernes" (Paris, 1925). One of its distinguishing marks is rounded corners.

**Art Nouveau** Generic term for a movement which had many variants: "Art Nouveau" in France, "Modern Style" in England, "Jugendstil" in Germany, "Stile liberty" in Italy, "Modernismo" in Spain. With its flat-looking *ornamentation* displaying a wealth of vegetal curves, it was the complete opposite to *academic* art.

**Arts and Crafts Movement** Influential movement in the area of applied art, originating in England in the middle of the 19th century under the leadership of *William Morris, Philip Webb* and *John Ruskin.* They were in favor of a return to the craft tradition of the Middle Ages and were against industrial mass production.

**attic** (specialist sense) An erection above the cornice, hiding the beginning of the roof. Often used to give emphasis to a centrally projecting volume.

**axis (line of sight)** A straight line from the eye to the object of sight. Buildings and gardens are generally laid out *symmetrically* on either side of a line of sight, which enhances their effect. Window axes are imaginary lines running from back to front or from side to side of a building.

**baroque** (Portuguese "barocco" – small stone, unevenly shaped pearl) This idea, derived from the art of the jeweler, was used in a derogatory sense (meaning bizarre or bulbous) by the classicists about the previous era. The terms cover art and culture of the 17th and 18th centuries in Europe. It was very different in the various countries. Generally starting from the formal canon of *antiquity,* the baroque developed colorful and opulent decorations, sometimes made of *stucco,* which created a particularly magnificent impression. It was disliked by the classicists of the 18th and early 19th centuries on the grounds that it was overladen. It was brought to life again from about 1860 in the *neo-Baroque.*

**base** Bottom section of a building or sculpture (see *pedestal*).

**belvedere** (Italian: beautiful view) Originally the description of, among other things, a pavilion (usually in a garden), which can be used to admire a view.

**border** *Ornamental* decorative panel at the edge of a fabric. Also used in connection with walls.

**brick** See also *clinker.* Block made of clay in various colors (usually red or yellow) baked till it is hard. Bricks that have been submitted to a great heat are called clinker, and were much used in expressionist architecture.

**Brücke, Die** A group of artists from Dresden, founded in 1905 and including among others Karl Schmidt Rottluff, Erich Heckel, Otto Müller, Max Pechstein and Ludwig Kirchner. Their strongly expressive and highly colorful works, influenced by *Gothic* models and primitive art, founded the German *Expressionist* movement in painting.

**Brutalism** Idea introduced by *Le Corbusier* originally relating to the use of unfinished, bare concrete, and taken up by the *Smithsons* and others in Great Britain. Brutalism stands for architecture that is truthful about its materials, and where nothing is covered up, so that functional relationships are directly visible.

**capital** The top of a column, a form deriving from the architecture of Antiquity. It differs in shape according to which *order* it belongs to (Doric, Ionic, Corinthian or Composite).

**cast iron art** An art form found in the decorative arts and architecture, especially in 19th century Prussia (*Schinkel,* Memorial on the Kreuzberg, Berlin 1818–21) which was attributed a high degree of national importance.

**cement** Waterproof building material made of a mixture of burnt lime and clay. An important ingredient of *concrete.*

**ceramic tiles** Tiles made of fired clay, for the most part glazed and colored (see *faience*).

**Charter of Athens** see *CIAM*

**School of Chicago** A group of American architects such as *William Le Baron Jenney* and *Louis Sullivan,* who took part in the rebuilding of Chicago in the late 19th century and built skyscrapers that became signposts for the new.

**CIAM** (Congrès Internationaux d'Architecture Moderne). International forum of the avant-garde for modernist architects founded in 1927 under the leadership of *Le Corbusier* and Siegfried Gidion. The congresses, which were highly ideological and formalistic, took a different theme each time. So, the outcome of CIAM II, in 1929, led by Ernst May, was a report titled "The minimal-living unit." In 1930 in Brussels there followed "Rational building methods," when Gropius was one of the speakers. CIAM IV (1933) was devoted to the functional city. From this emerged the "Charter of Athens," which bore the stamp of Le Corbusier's concepts. The Charter of Athens presupposes the division of the modern city into zones corresponding to their main functions: living, work, leisure and transport. Against a background of increasing criticism of the International Style and the advent of *Brutalism,* the 10th and last CIAM took place in Dubrovnik in 1956.

**classicism** Return of the classical formal repertoire of the architecture of *Antiquity* in Europe and North America in the late 18th and early 19th centuries (see *Schinkel*).

**climatization** A technical system for optimizing the balance of incoming and outgoing air in buildings. Especially important in museums, whose treasures require a constant climate, as well as buildings holding a lot of people, as for instance public halls and skyscrapers.

**clinker** *Brick* that has been baked at a very high temperature, so that the pores sinter, that is to say acquire a glassy waterproof surface.

**concrete** A resistant, relatively light and cheap substance, made of sand, gravel, and *cement*, which sets hard as stone, and can be cast in a desired shape using *formwork*. It was brought to perfection in France in 1879 by Hennebique in the form of reinforced concrete. This system enhances the load-bearing properties of concrete by the addition of an iron or steel skeleton, so that enormous roof areas can be spanned. The adaptability of concrete to a variety of usages has made it one of the most important building materials of the 20th century (see *Perret, Le Corbusier*).

**colonnade** Hall or walk with pillars. A roofed area with rows of pillars and *entablature*.

**column** Cylindrical support characterized by its swelling form (entasis). A column has a base, clearly differentiated from the structure underneath, and a *capital* which tops the column, and connects it to the *entablature*.

**conservation** Efforts, beginning in the 19th century, to preserve works of art from previous epochs (preservation), or to repair them (restoration).

**Constructivism** A theory of art held by *Tatlin* and *El Lissitsky* in the early days of the Soviet Union, according to which architecture must be reduced to its necessary functional (see *function*) elements, so that it is dominated by pure construction.

**cornice** A horizontal molded projection which crowns a building.

**Cubism** (Latin: "cubus" – cube) A style adopted by Picasso, Braque and Delaunay from 1907 onwards, whereby natural forms are reduced to their geometric basic construction. The corresponding movement in architecture was that of the Prague Cubists.

**curtain wall** A non load-bearing *façade* or wall of glass, granite or

plastic hung in front of a load-bearing construction.

**Deconstructivism** This movement became known through the exhibition "Deconstructivist Architecture" organized by Philip Johnson and Mark Wigley in 1988 at the Museum of Modern Art. Deconstructivist buildings differ from Modernist or Post-Modern buildings through their intersecting, splintered, and sharply inclined forms. They express a general sense of destabilization which has been widespread in the West (and not just in the West) in the 1980s and 90s. The viewer's first sensation on seeing many of these buildings is astonishment, aroused by their apparent technical impossibility, their astonishing use of materials and their unusual formal language. The chief representatives of Deconstructivism, which has now become an international movement are *Gehry, Libeskind, Hadid*, the COOP Himmelblau, Peter Eisenman, and Bernard Tschumi.

**De Stijl** A group of artists formed in Holland in 1917 under the influence of *Piet Mondrian*, and which included, among others, *Theo van Doesburg, Gerrit Thomas Rietveld*, and *Jacobus Johannes Pieter Oud*. Their aim was to produce applied arts and architecture in an *abstract* language of forms freed from the decoration of traditional architecture.

**Deutscher Werkbund** An association, founded in 1907, of craftsmen, industrialists, and architects to promote the production of art on a national scale, and extend its economic relevance and industrialization.

**Diocletian window** Also known as Thermal window. A semi-circular window, subdivided by two vertical supports. First appears in Ancient Rome.

**dome** A type of roof having the shape of part of a sphere, which has been in use since Ancient Rome. Has frequently appeared in the West since the *Renaissance* in palaces and sacral buildings, but it is also found in quite ordinary buildings in Islamic architecture.

**Doric** One of the three most important *orders of columns* of

Ancient Greece, which has a squat shaft with no base and broad *flutes*, and is crowned by a spreading *capital* and a frieze with triglyphs (surface in the *entablature* decorated with grooves).

**dry stone walls** Traditional walls where the stones are piled on top of each other and not bound together with any agent such as mortar.

**eclecticism** A mixture of several historical *styles* in a building. It predominates in *Historicism* but is also to be found in *Post-Modernism*.

**entablature** That part of an order which is above the column, including the architrave, the *frieze*, and the *cornice*.

**epoch** Historical period in which a particular *style* and its characteristic *ornamentation* develop.

**Expressionism** Art movement in the early 20th century, chiefly in western and eastern Europe, covering painting (*Die Brücke*, the *Fauves*) and architecture (the *Amsterdam School*). The distinguishing features of Expressionism in architecture are forms with a lot of movement and color and frequently with detailed ornamentation. *Brick* and *clinker* are the building materials most frequently used.

**façade** (Latin: "facies" – the external form) The "face" of a house, usually the front wall or the side that is most intended to be seen. The appearance and articulation of a façade often reveal the characteristics of an *epoch* or of a particular *style*.

**Fauves** (French: the wild men) A group of artists headed by Henri Matisse, roughly contemporaneous with the Dresden *Brücke* Artists, who created an art characterized by vivid movement and studies from nature.

**faience** Brightly colored pottery deriving its name from the Italian city of Faenza, which was the center of its production in the *Renaissance*.

**flat roof** See *roof*.

**flattened arch** See *arch*.

**fluting** Vertical grooves on the shaft of a *column*.

**formwork** Temporary, generally prefabricated hollow structure into which liquid *concrete* is

poured. After the concrete has hardened, the formwork is then removed. Bare concrete often shows the traces of the formwork, sometimes this includes the marks of the grain when it was made of wooden planks.

**frieze** An area, normally just under the roof or ceiling which has been used since *Antiquity* for decoration, either in an *abstract* or figurative way.

**function, functionalism** Basic to the design of ground plans and façades in modern architecture from *Sullivan* ("form follows function") right up till *Post-Modernism*. This concept, which implies that the function of a building should dominate its design, making it as economic as possible, was chiefly to be found in industrial building, but also occurred in residential building, where it implied doing away with elements considered to be superfluous, such as decoration, and with rooms that were mainly for show. It was chiefly through the Bauhaus that functionalism became the dominant principle in the organization of architecture in the 20th century. More recent movements such as *Post-Modernism* and *Deconstructivism* are characterized by their critical attitude to a one-sided emphasis on the functional in architecture.

**Futurism** Modern art movement in pre-First World War Italy, inspired by enthusiasm for the future. (In architecture see, for example, the designs of *Sant'Elias*).

**gable** A triangular surface in the *roof* between two sloping elements. In major building works such as castles, there are often remarkable sculptures in the gables. Split gables (or pediments) are to be found especially in *Renaissance*, *baroque* and *Post-Modern* buildings. These do not join at the top but have an interrupted form, giving a dramatic note to the culmination of the building.

**glass architecture** Glass has entered architecture more and more since *John Paxton*'s Crystal Palace. *Bruno Taut*'s glass pavilion at the *Werkbund* exhibition in Cologne united glass architecture with *Expressionism*. Glass, often with temperature and sun protection, is also an important material for the construction of *curtain walls* in the work of *Ludwig Mies van der Rohe*, but also in the works of 90s architects such as *Jean Nouvel*.

**Gothic** A style that includes all branches of medieval art, first identified around 1140, and originating in the Île de France region around Paris. The main identifying features of the Gothic are the soaring grouped pillars and the pointed arch. The Gothic took many forms in the different European countries. Whereas in Italy the Renaissance began in around 1400–1420, a late Gothic tradition continued in Germany well into the 16th century. As early as the 18th century the first *neo-Gothic* buildings began to appear in England, Germany and elsewhere.

**grid** Even rectangular network according to which towns may be laid out. Also used in relation to the pattern of fenestration, usually of skyscrapers.

**Heimatschutzarchitektur** (heritage protection architecture) German movement, starting from English models, which took root around 1900. Its aim was to promote architecture adapted to regional traditions and landscape. It was discredited by the Nazis' use of the idea for political ends.

**hewn stone** Worked form of *natural stone*. See also **stone**.

**high-tech architecture** Generic term in use since the 80s to describe emphatically technical-looking buildings. Main representatives are *Norman Foster* and *Richard Rogers*, who together with *Renzo Piano* designed the best-known high-tech building, the Centre Pompidou in Paris.

**historicism** Generic term for types of architecture that relate back to earlier styles (*classicism, the neo-Renaissance, neo-baroque, neo-Romanesque, neoclassicism*). Especially predominant between 1860 and 1910.

**housing schemes** Systematic large-scale building of new homes, which began at the end of the 19th century, in reaction

against the tenements of the outgoing era. The Netherlands were first, then Germany. The aim was to relieve the housing shortage and to improve the living conditions of those sections of the population with a low income (see *Kramer, Klerk, Taut, Wagner*).

**ideal city** This idea has kept coming to life again since *Antiquity*. It implies constructing a city along ideal social, economic, and political lines.

**Impressionism** Movement in painting emanating from France in the second half of the 19th century, which, in rebellion against *academic* art, starts out from pure color, showing scenes that are close to nature and flooded with light.

**incrustation** Already present in *Antiquity*, this form of covering for *façades* consist of variously colored bits of stone.

**infill** The material (e.g., brick or glass) used to fill the part of the wall between a system of supports in wood, iron or concrete.

**International Style** Description coined by Henry-Russell Hitchcock and *Philip Johnson* following the creation of the Weissenhofsiedlung in Stuttgart in 1927, for the modern architecture being celebrated at an exhibition in the Museum of Modern Art in New York in 1932.

**iron architecture** Since the 19th century iron and steel have been widely used for the load-bearing elements of a building. This structure could then either be filled or serve as the framework for a *curtain wall*. Paxton's Crystal Palace is an example of iron architecture, as are other buildings by engineers, the most famous of which is the Eiffel Tower in Paris, built by *Gustave Eiffel*.

**Jugendstil** See *Art Nouveau*.

**lintel** The horizontal upper part of a doorway.

**loggia** Open portico or hall with pillars.

**megastructure** (from the Greek for "large") Massive enlargement and extension in the technical age of the previously small-scale historically developed structures of cities. Describes many of the utopian town-planning ideals formulated since the 60s, which

have found expression in *high-tech* skyscrapers.

**Moorish architecture** Architecture of the Islamic countries.

**mosaic** *Abstract* or figurative images built into floors or walls, made out of flat glazed chips (tesserae) which fascinate with the luminous quality of their color. Mosaics of various kinds have been created from *Antiquity* up till the present, very often in sacral buildings.

**natural stone** "Real" *stone* as opposed to man-made substances such as *brick* or *concrete*. Can also be used to define stone that is not worked, as opposed to *hewn stone*.

**neo-baroque** *Historicist* style whose forms are derived from the *baroque*, first used by *Charles Garnier* in his rebuilding of the Paris Opera (1861-75).

**neo-Gothic** *Historicist* style, whose formal repertoire is borrowed from the *Gothic*. In Germany around 1820 it came to be considered the national style, since it was believed for a long time that it did not originate in France, but in Germany.

**neo-classicism** Reappearance of *classicism* in Europe around 1900, e.g., in the work of Peter Behrens.

**neo-Plasticism** Style originating in *Piet Mondrian*'s painting in which the *Cubist* experience of space is translated into a flat picture. Carried over into architecture by the *De Stijl* group in Holland.

**neo-Renaissance** *Historicist* reappearance of the forms of the Italian *Renaissance* in the work of *Gottfried Semper* but also in *Schinkel* and Klenze.

**neo-Romanesque** Reappearance of the Romanesque style with its massive volumes and round arches, in *historicist* architecture, e.g., that of Henry Hobson Richardson or Bruno Schmitz.

**Neues Bauen** ("new building") Description of facets of modern architecture in Germany after the First World War, especially at the Bauhaus, which was part of the developing *International Style*.

**noble orders** Buildings or parts of buildings that were originally reserved for rulers and significant personages, such as *triumphal*

*arches, pyramids, domes.* Other forms, as for instance *orders of columns*, constitute in themselves a noble order.

**orders of columns** An architectural system developed in Antiquity including various types of column having different regional and historical origins. The chief orders are the *Doric*, Ionic, Corinthian and Composite, which can be distinguished by the different handling of the shaft, the *capital* and the *entablature*.

**organic building** One aspect of the *Neues Bauen* movement, which put the needs of the inhabitants first in planning a building, often in conjunction with flowing forms. Attempts to build organically are already to be found in the early work of *Frank Lloyd Wright, Eero Saarinen* (TWA Terminal), and *H. Scharoun*.

**ornament** (Latin: "ornare" – to decorate) Special architectural forms, the purpose of which is to decorate a building or parts thereof. Different epochs developed their own specific forms of ornament, which became characteristic of their style (see *epoch*).

**Palladian** Architectural style developed by the late Renaissance architect *Andrea Palladio*, derived from the *classical* forms of *Antiquity*. Widespread in the 18th century, first of all in England, then later also in America and Germany, in the context of the *classicist* movement.

**pedestal** Base for, among other things, sculptures and *columns*.

**pergola** A covered walk in a garden, usually formed by a double row of posts or pillars with joists above and covered with climbing plants.

**pilaster** Representation in relief of a *column*, against the surface of a wall, which may be the visible part of an internal pier, and serves as vertical articulation of the wall.

**pillar** Vertical supporting element in architecture; several pillars can be combined to form a *colonnade*. A pillar embedded in a wall is called a *pilaster*.

**pilotis** French term for a series of pillars or stilts that carry a building. Buildings on pilotis were favored by *Le Corbusier* (Villa Savoye; Unité d'Habitation). Pilotis make it possible to leave the ground floor open. There can also be structural reasons for them, as, for instance, to protect against earthquake damage (see *Schindler* and his Lovell Beach House).

**pointed arch** See *arch*.

**polygon** A many-sided shape which occasionally forms the ground plan of a building, sometimes also in the layout of *ideal cities*.

**Pop Art** Derived from "popular art," the term describes a movement in the 60s which declared objects in daily use such as soup cans or the VW Beetle to be subjects for art, and thereby exalted them in a surprising way and made them seem strange. Among the leading figures of Pop Art were Andy Warhol, Robert Rauschenberg and Roy Lichtenstein.

**portico** Entrance where the roof is held up by pillars, looking like temple architecture from *Antiquity*.

**Post-Modernism** Movement that began in the late 60s with the work of *Robert Venturi* and *Charles Moore* in opposition to classical Modernism, its strict *functionalism* and its ban on the *orders of columns* and on traditional forms of ornamentation. It brought these banned forms to playful new life, especially in America (but also in Italy, for instance in the work of *A. Rossi*).

**Pre-Raphaelites** A group of English artists of the mid-19th century, linked to *William Morris* and *John Ruskin*. They rejected the *academic* painting of their time, and took as their model the painting of the Italian Renaissance before Raphael (1483–1520).

**proportions** The relationships of scale prevailing among the individual parts of a building of a particular volume.

**pyramid** Geometrical form with a square base which then narrows to a point at the top , whose four sides are inclined triangles. The pyramids of early history were the tombs of Egyptian kings; the glass entrance pyramid for the Louvre by *Ieoh Ming Pei* has become a late 20th-century icon.

**rationalism** (Latin: "ratio" – reason) In general, the trend in 20th century architecture and town-planning to go for rational solutions. Closely related to *functionalism* and the goals of *Neues Bauen*. In modern Italian architecture "Razionalismo" is also used to describe a style (see *Terragni*).

**rafters** Load-bearing elements (usually of wood) in a roof.

**reinforced concrete** See *concrete*.

**Renaissance** (Italian: "rinascimento" – rebirth) Reappearance of the treasury of forms deriving from the art of *Antiquity* in Italian art in the 15th and 16th century, which reached its architectural zenith in the buildings of *Andrea Palladio*.

**projection** Used in the sense of a volume projecting from the topmost part of a façade, the term derives from the construction of French chateaux in the 16th and 17th centuries. Middle and side projections are also possible.

**Romanesque** Period in the European art of the Middle Ages, beginning around 1000, which in many areas flows on into the Gothic. The massive forms of the Romanesque, with its round arches and square *capitals* relate it to the architecture of Ancient Rome.

**roof** Can take many forms. A pitched or saddle roof consists of two roof surfaces leaning against each other, forming a triangular gable surface at the narrow ends.  In a hip roof, all the sides of the roof lean towards each other and end in a narrow arris. In contrast to the steep forms of roof the *Neues Bauen* promoted the propagation of flat roofs, confining buildings to a purely rectilinear form.

**round arch** *See* arch.

**rustication** (from "rustic", derived from Latin "rus" – countryside) Masonry cut in massive blocks and separated from each other by deep joints, or an imitation of it in roughcast plaster, to give rich texture to an exterior wall and usually reserved for the lower part of it.

**saddle roof** see *roof*.

**Secession** (from the Latin for "parting") Name given to groups of artists who left the *academic* art scene around 1900. The most important was the Vienna Secession, a group of *Jugendstil* artists (see *Olbrich* and *Hoffmann*).

**skeleton** The load-bearing elements of a building, often in the form of a regular grid and made of steel, reinforced *concrete* or wood.

**skyscraper** The manifestation of a trend which started in America around 1880 to make the most economic use possible of a piece of land in a big city (*Chicago School*), which was largely independent of the development of a modern architectural language. In the 20s and again in the 90s there was lively competition to construct the world's tallest building.

**Socialist Realism** Type of art established under Stalin in the Soviet Union which rejected the utopian visions of abstract Constructivism in favor of a figurative rendition of the party line.

**span** The spread or extent between supports. Wide roof spans, achieved by architectural engineering, are especially necessary in the building of sports arenas (see *Nervi, Tange, Otto*). Construction materials such as *iron* and *concrete* have made possible wider spans than could be effected using traditional building materials such as wood or stone.

**set-back volumes** Volumes that are stepped to produce a livelier looking façade. Set-backs were essential early on in the history of the *skyscraper* in the USA, in order to let enough light and air into the street.

**steel skeleton construction** See *skeleton*.

**standardization** One of the chief aims of modern architecture is to achieve conformity among building elements and materials, so that they will be compatible with each other and be utilizable in the greatest number of contexts at the least expense.

**stone** Traditional building material. Natural stone or finished, hewn stone may be used.

**stereometry** A method of measuring geometric solids.

**style** Characteristic repertoire of forms of a particular *epoch*, which differentiate it in form and content from other epochs (for instance Antiquity, Romanesque, Renaissance, classicism, historicism, Expressionism, Modernism, International Style (or Neues Bauen), Post-Modernism, Deconstructivism).

**stucco** Any kind of plaster or cement used to make architectural moldings or coat exterior walls. It has been in existence since antiquity and various architectural styles have utilized it. *Historicist ornamentation* using stucco was rejected by modernist architects (see *Adolf Loos*).

**suprematism** (Latin: supremus – "the highest"). The description chosen by *Malevich* for his art, because of its pure, extreme *abstraction*.

**symmetry** Construction of a building or a garden so that one half is the mirror-image of the other. Especially prevalent in the *Renaissance*, *baroque* and *classicist* periods.

**tectonic** The fitting together of independent parts to make a complete building.

**tempietto** From the Italian: "little temple."

**temple** Non-Christian religious building. The temples of *antiquity* and their surrounding halls of *columns* have served as models for later architecture.

**triumphal arch** An architectural form that has existed since *antiquity*, consisting of one or more large arches which often have a great deal of figurative decoration. Originally erected in honor of Roman rulers, they are also found in the *Renaissance*, *baroque* and *classicist* periods.

**vegetal** Plant-like. Used in particular to refer to the decorative forms of *Art Nouveau*.

**wedding-cake style** A general description of the heavily ornamented architecture of Stalinism.

**wooden buildings** Traditional since *antiquity*, wooden buildings have seen a renaissance in the 1990s on ecological and economic grounds.

# INDEX OF NAMES

Page numbers in bold indicate illustrations

**Aalto, Hugo Alvar Henrik** (1898–1976) Finnish architect, influenced by neoclassicism and the International Style, who developed his own organic style of architecture. *72, 74*

**Alen, William van** (1883–1954) American architect, whose Chrysler Building in New York came to be regarded as the epitome of dynamic skyscraper architecture in the 20s. *46, **47**, 87*

**Ando, Tadao** (1941–) Japanese architect, whose strictly proportioned buildings, primarily in concrete and glass, emerge from an intense involvement with the architectural history of Japan and Europe. *98, **99***

**Behnisch, Günter** (1922–) German architect, who created the Munich Olympic stadium with Frei Otto in 1972. His more recent buildings are characterized by their Deconstructivist formal language. Chief works: general assembly chamber for the German Bundestag, Bonn (1992), Akademie der Künste, Berlin (1998–2000). ***81**, 92, 94*

**Behrens, Peter** (1868–1940) German painter, architect and designer. One of the founders of the Deutscher Werkbund (1907), he became a leading figure and teacher in the modern movement in Germany. His style includes elements of Jugendstil and Neo-classicism, moving after 1918 towards Expressionism and Neues Bauen. Chief works: house on the Mathildenhöhe (1901), AEG Turbine Hall, Berlin (1909), German Embassy, St. Petersburg (1911–12), headquarters of the Hoechst dyestuffs company (1920–24). *13, 17, 19, 22, **23**, 38, 39, 59, 96*

**Berg, Max** (1870–1947) German architect, who worked as the city architect for Breslau. *21, 74*

**Berlage, Hendrik Petrus** (1856–1934) Most important innovator of Dutch architecture. Overcoming the stylistic ossification of historicism with his Amsterdam stock exchange (1896–1903), he became very influential for German architects at the turn of the century. ***17**, 25*

**Bofill, Levi Ricardo** (1939–) Spanish architect, who, with his studio Buro Taller de Arquitectura (founded 1963), became one of the leading representatives of Post-Modernism in the 70s and 80s. *86, 95*

**Botta, Mario** (1943–) Swiss architect, the most important representative of the Tessin school, who, despite being very rationalist, also shows a notable sensitivity to the topographical aspects of the sites. Chief works: Casa Rotonda, Stabio (1965–67), house in Vacallo (1986–89). ***97**, 98*

**Calatrava Valls, Santiago** (1951–) Spanish architect, who has had his studio in Zürich since 1981. His architectural engineering skills produce a filigree quality in his work, which includes bridges and transport interchanges, designed with an expressive elegance. Chief works: Exhibition Building, Tenerife (1992-95), Alameda Bus Station, Valencia (1991–95). *103, **104**, 105*

**Coenen, Jo** (1949–) One of the leading contemporary Dutch architects, who developed his own plastic architectural language from the traditions of classical Modernism. His work is characterized by a surprising and diverse use of materials and by his exciting grouping of individual volumes. ***106***

**D'Aronco, Raimondo** (1857–1932) Italian Art Nouveau architect, whose buildings, as for instance his pavilion at the 1902 world exhibition in Turin, exhibit a positively baroque abundance of decoration, and multiplicity of ornamental details. *11*

**Dinkeloo, John Gerard** (1918–1981) American architect who worked first in SOM, then with Eero Saarinen. In partnership with Kevin Roche from 1966, he realized the Ford Foundation building in New York (1963–68). ***77***

**Doesburg, Theo van** (1883–1931) Dutch painter, architect, and architectural theorist, founding member and leading thinker of the influential Dutch De Stijl group of artists (1917). *26, **31**, 32-33, 59*

**Eames, Charles** (1907–1978) The American architect, film director and designer and his wife Ray (1916–1988) were among the most innovative artists of the 20s. They are most famous for their house in St. Monica (1949), built out of industrially prefabricated parts, and especially for their many designs for chairs, still classic today. *58, 60*

**Eiffel, Gustave** (1832–1923) French engineer, whose tower in Paris, constructed with Maurice Koechlin (1889) is still one of the icons of modern architecture. *8, 9, 110*

**Endell, August** (1871–1925) German Jugendstil architect and designer, whose characteristic buildings are decorated with organic ornamentation. Copublisher of the journal *Die Jugend*. Chief work: Photoatalier Elvira, Munich (1897). *11*

**Foster, Sir Norman Robert** (1935–) British architect, leading creator of high-tech architecture, where the appearance and use of materials breaks deliberately with the classic formal language of architecture. Chief works: Willis, Faber & Dumas Insurance, Ipswich (1970–75), Hong Kong and Shanghai Bank, Hong Kong (1979–86), rebuilding of Berlin Reichstag (1996–99), Daewoo main offices, Seoul (1997–2000). *61, **80, 81**, 102*

**Gallé, Emile** (1846–1904) French craftsman whose works in glass and glazed clay with their organic forms and delicately colorful appearance are among the masterpieces of Art Nouveau. *12*

**Garnier, Charles** (1815–1898) French architect, whose new Paris Opera (1861–75) set off the triumph of the neo-baroque throughout Europe. *8*

**Gaudí i Cornet, Antoni** (1852–1926) Spanish architect, outstanding exponent of Modernismo, the Spanish version of Art Nouveau, the majority of whose intensely imaginative buildings are to be found in Barcelona. Chief works: Casa Batlló (1904–06), Casa Milà (1906–10), Sagrada Familia (commenced 1883). *12, 13, 14*

**Gehry, Frank O.** (1929–) American architect, most important practitioner of Deconstructivism. Chief works: Gehry House, Santa Monica (1978), California Aerospace Museum, Santa Monica (1984), Guggenheim Museum, Bilbao (1997). *91, 92, **93**, 94, 99, **101**, 104, 105, 111*

**Gilbert, Cass** (1859–1934) American architect who became famous when he constructed the Woolworth Building in New York (1913), until 1930 the tallest building in the world *42, **43***

**Gočár, Josef** (1880–1945) Czech architect, chief representative of Prague Cubism. Chief work: "Black Madonna" department store, Prague (1911–12). ***28***

**Graves, Michael** (1934–) American architect, at first an adherent of the International Style, who in the 70s adopted the Post-Modernist language of forms and colors. Graves belongs with Richard Meier and Peter Eisenman to the New York Five. Chief works: Public Services Building, Portland, Oregon (1980–82), Humana Building, Louisville, Kentucky (1982–86). *87, 88*

**Gregotti, Vittorio** (1927–) Italian architect, influenced since the 60s by the clear forms of Rationalism. Chief work: University of Calabria at Consenza (1973). *97, 98*

**Grimshaw, Nicolas** (1939–) English architect, who achieved international recognition with the English pavilion for the world exhibition in Seville. *104, **110***

**Gropius, Walter** (1883–1969) German architect, outstanding figure in modern architecture, who founded the Bauhaus in 1919 in Weimar and in 1933 emigrated to the USA. Important works: Fagus factory, Alfeld (1911) with Adolf Meyer, Bauhaus Dessau (1925–26), Harvard Graduate Center (1948–50). *19, **20**, 23, 24, 32, **33**, 36–39, 43, **57–59**, 61, 69, 84*

**Guimard, Hector** (1867–1942) Art Nouveau architect whose masterpiece is the designs for the entrances to the Paris Metro. *11*

**Hadid, Zaha** (1950–) Iraqi architect, based in England; her expressive designs and buildings such as the Vitra fire station in Weil am Rhein (1993) are among the chief works of Deconstructivism. ***104**, 105, 108*

**Herzog, Jacques** (1950–) and **Pierre de Meuron** (1950–) Swiss team of architects whose recent buildings, sober yet poetic, may become the indicators of the next development in contemporary architecture. Chief works: Stone House, Tavole, Liguria (1982–88), Goetz Collection, Munich-Oberföhring (1993), rebuilding and extension of the Swiss accident insurance building Basel (1995). *105–107*

**Höger, Fritz** (1877–1949) German architect, leading representative of the German Expressionist movement, which was influenced by the Amsterdam School. Chief work: Chilehaus, Hamburg (1921–24). *27*

**Hoff, Robert van 't** (1887–1979) English architect, who was strongly influenced by the work of Frank Lloyd Wright when studying in the USA. Back in Europe he joined the De Stijl movement, and between 1918 and 1919 evolved a scheme for housing developments. *26*

**Hoffmann, Josef** (1870–1956) Austrian Jugendstil architect and designer, whose Cubist language of forms (Purkersdorf Sanatorium, 1904) had a great influence on the following generation of architects in the Neues Bauen movement. *11, 14, 15, 17*

**Hollein, Hans** (1934–) Austrian architect and designer, remarkable for his imaginative Post-Modern creations. Chief work: municipal museum, Abteiberg, Mönchengladbach (1972–82). *89*

**Hood, Raymond** (1881–1934) Most important American designer of tall buildings in the 20s, who carried over the forms of European Modernism to skyscrapers, thereby overcoming the Neo-Gothic repertoire of forms then prevailing. Chief works: (with John Mead Howells) Chicago Tribune Building, Chicago (1925), McGraw Hill Building, New York (1929), Rockefeller Center, New York (from 1931). *44, 48, 49, 87*

**Horta, Victor** (1861–1947) Belgian architect, leading member of the Art Nouveau movement. Chief works: Hôtel Tassel, Brussels (1893), Maison du Peuple, Brussels (1896–99). *10, 11*

**Hübsch, Heinrich** (1795–1863) German architect, whose book *In welchem Style sollen wir bauen* (In what style should we build?) was a decisive contribution to discussion on moving on from classicism. *8*

**Isozaki, Arata** (1931–) One of the leading Japanese architects. Chief works: Fujimi Country Club House, Oita City (1974), Headquarters of Tsukuba, Japan (1980–83), Debis-Center, Berlin (1996–97). *86, 98*

**Jacobsen, Arne** (1902–1971) Danish architect, who developed his own individual variant of the International Style, to be seen in the town hall at Rødovre, near Copenhagen (1954–56). *62*

**Jahn, Helmut** (1940–) Born in Germany, Jahn has become one of the most high-flying builders

of skyscrapers of the present day. His designs are based upon the use of glass. Chief buildings: Messeturm, Frankfurt am Main (1984–88), Sony Center, Berlin (1996–2000).

**Jenney, William Le Baron** (1832–1907) American architect, member of the Chicago School, pioneer in the architecture of tall buildings. Chief works: Home Insurance Building, Chicago (1883–85), second Leiter Building, Chicago (1889–91). *42*

**Johnson, Philip Cortelyou** (1906–) American architect, who, as director of the architecture department of the Museum of Modern Art in New York, supported the International Style in the United States. He later took a Post-Modernist direction. Chief buildings: Glass House, New Canaan (1949), AT&T Building, New York (1978–82). *58, 60, 87*

**Kahn, Albert** (1869–1942) American architect, whose generally sober and functional concrete industrial buildings for Ford gave an impetus to the European development of Modernism. *19, 20, 23*

**Kahn, Louis Isidore** (1901–1974) American architect, chief representative of Brutalism. His designs show a sophisticated study of geometric ground plans and the introduction of light. *64, 69, 71, 98*

**Karavan, Dani** (1930–) Israeli artist, whose sculptures generally consist of architectonically created spaces with a reference to history. An example of this is the memorial for Walter Benjamin at Port-Bou (1994). *108–110*

**Klerk, Michel de** (1884–1923) Dutch architect, member of the Expressionist Amsterdam School. With other members he created the Schiffahrtshaus in Amsterdam (1912–16). Chief works: residential buildings at Spaardammerplantson, Amsterdam (1913–20), De Dageraad housing development, Amsterdam, with Pieter Kramer (from 1918). *25*

**Kramer, Pieter Lodewijk** (1881–1961) Dutch architect, member of the Amsterdam School, worked (from 1918) with other members on the cooperative housing project De Dageraad, Amsterdam. *24, 25*

**Krüger, Johannes** (1890–1975) and **Walter** (1888–1971) German architects. Chief works: Tannenberg Nationaldenkmal (1927, modified 1935), Johannes

Krüger: Landeszentralbank, Berlin (1953–55). *51*

**Le Corbusier** (real name: Charles-Édouard Jeanneret-Gris, 1887–1965) Swiss-born French architect, who became one of the most influential town planners and architects of the 20th century. He was innovative both in terms of his use of materials (concrete) and in his favored style of construction using pilotis. Among his most important works are: Villa Savoye, Poissy, near Paris (1929–31), Unité d'Habitation, Marseille (1947–52), Notre-Dame-du-Haut, Ronchamp (1950–55). *16, 21, 23, 36–39, 44, 60, 63, 64, 65, 66, 69, 70, 79, 96–98*

**Libeskind, Daniel** (1946–) Created the Deconstructivist Jewish Museum in Berlin (1991-99): a unique type of memorial architecture embedded in a complex web of topographical and historical connotations. *108, 109, 110*

**Lissitzky, El** (1890–1941) Russian Constructivist artist and architect, whose work exerted a great influence on De Stijl and the Bauhaus. *34–35*

**Loos, Adolf** (1870–1933) Austrian architect, whose determination to build in an ornament-free rectilinear style paved the way for the renewal of architecture. *15–17, 43*

**Lutyens, Sir Edwin** (1869–1944) The most important English architect of the first half of the 20th century, his roots lay in the Arts and Crafts movement. Chief works: Viceroy's House in New Delhi, India (completed 1930), monument to the war dead at Thiepval, France (1927–32). *22, 51, 65*

**Mackintosh, Charles Rennie** (1868–1928) Scottish architect and craftsman. His most important work, the Glasgow School of Art (1896–1909) is remarkable for its angular, geometric language of forms, and shows the influences both of the Arts and Crafts movement and Art Nouveau. *11, 13, 14*

**Malevich, Kasimir** (1878–1935) Russian painter, inventor of Suprematism, the logical outcome of which was "pure" abstraction, as in *White Square on a White Ground* (1918). *34*

**Meier, Richard** (1934–) One of the most successful contemporary American architects, and a member of the New York Five, whose buildings at the beginning of the 70s relate

to the tradition of the 20s "White Modernism." Main work: City House, The Hague (1986–95). *90, 111*

**Melnikow, Konstantin** (1890–1974) Russian Constructivist architect, who developed from classicist beginnings to become the foremost representative of modern Soviet architecture. *35, 36, 96*

**Mendelsohn, Erich** (1887–1953) German Expressionist architect, who had to emigrate in 1933. The leading representative of Neues Bauen in the area of commercial buildings, famous for, among others, the Schocken department store. Chief works: Einsteinturm, Potsdam (1920–24), Columbus-Haus, Berlin (1929–30), house for Chaim Weitzmann, Tel Aviv (1948–52). *20, 26, 27, 53*

**Mendini, Alessandro** (1931–) Italian designer and theorist of design, who developed products for, among others, Alessi, Philips, and Swatch, and since 1989 has been working with his brother as an architect. *111*

**Meuron, Pierre de** see Jacques Herzog

**Meyer, Adolf** (1881–1929) German architect, who worked first with Peter Behrens, later in partnership with W. Gropius, with whom he built the Fagus works in Alfeld. Chief works: Planetarium, Jena (1925), and the Palace of the League of Nations, Geneva (1929). *19, 20, 43*

**Mies van der Rohe, Ludwig** (1886–1969) German architect and designer, outstanding in the creation of modern architecture based on pared-down geometric forms in glass and steel. Chief works: Barcelona Pavilion (1929), Tugendhat House, Brünn (1930), apartment buildings on Lake Shore Drive, Chicago (1950–52), Neue Nationalgalerie, Berlin (1962–68). *14, 16, 17, 22–24, 33, 37–39, 44, 52, 57–59, 60–62, 73, 83, 84, 87, 98, 102, 105*

**Mondrian, Piet** (1872–1944) Dutch painter, whose pictures, in which everything is reduced to primary colors and basic geometric forms, influenced the style of the De Stijl group of artists. *26, 31, 32*

**Moore, Charles** (1925–1993) American architect, one of the founding fathers of Post-Modernism. Chief works: his own home at Orinda (1962), Piazza d'Italia, New Orleans (1974–78). *85, 86, 88, 95, 96*

**Morris, William** (1834–1896) English craftsman and artist, theorist and reformer, founder of the Arts and Crafts movement. Decisive influence on Art Nouveau and the Deutscher Werkbund.   *10, 18*

**Muthesius, Hermann** (1861–1927) German architect, who chiefly built country houses based on English models. Influenced by the Arts and Crafts movement, whose aims he attempted to establish in Germany through the Werkbund. Chief work: Mittelhof, Berlin (1914–15).   *19*

**Nervi, Pier Luigi** (1891–1979) Italian architect and engineer, whose exceptionally large roof spans are aesthetically outstanding. Chief works: airplane hangar at Orbetello (1939–41), UNESCO building, Paris (1953–57), *Palazzetto dello Sport, Rome* (1956–57), *Palazzo dello Sport, Rome* (1960).   *75, **76***

**Neutra, Richard** (1892–1970) Austrian-born American architect, whose residential buildings (e.g., Lovell Beach House, California, 1925–26) established the avant-garde European language of forms in USA as early as the 20s.   *44, **45***

**Niemeyer, Oscar** (1907–) Brazilian architect, practitioner in the International Style, who became famous as chief architect for Brasilia (from 1956).   ***65, 66***

**Nouvel, Jean** (1945–) French architect, one of the most significant on the contemporary scene, whose buildings contain elements of high-tech and more traditional architectural styles in steel and glass. From this combination he has developed his own new, imaginatively poetic language of forms. Chief works: Institut du Monde Arabe (IMA), Paris (1981–87), Galeries Lafayette, Berlin (1991–96).   *61, 101, **102, 103,** 108*

**Olbrich, Joseph Maria** (1867–1908) Austrian Jugendstil architect, whose chief works include the building for the Vienna Secession (1897–98) and the buildings on the Mathildenhöhe (Hochzeitsturm, 1907).   *12, **13,** 15*

**Otto, Frei** (1925–) German architect and engineer, whose suspended roofs for exhibition and sports buildings combine esthetic effect with revolutionary technology (Munich Olympic Stadium, 1972, with Günter Behnisch).   *75, **81***

**Oud, Jacobus Johannes Pieter** (1890–1963) Dutch architect and theorist, founding member of De Stijl. As the city architect of Rotterdam he carried out building projects of a high quality with limited financial means.   *32, 38, 39*

**Palladio, Andrea** (1508–1580) Most influential architect and theorist of the High Renaissance, whose buildings, based on antique forms, have been taken as models up till the present day (see *Post-Modernism*).   *84, 96*

**Paxton, Sir Joseph** (1801–1865) In his work as a gardener, he designed greenhouses which served as the pattern for his revolutionary exhibition buildings in steel and glass (Crystal Palace, London, 1851).   *7, 9, 102, 110*

**Pei, I(eoh) M(eng)** (1917–) Chinese-born American architect. Pei's architectural practice is one of the most successful in the US. Chief works: Louvre pyramid, Paris (1983–88), Annexe to the Deutsches Historisches Museum, Berlin (1998–2000).   *89–**91***

**Perret, Auguste** (1874–1954) French building contractor and architect, whose buildings, such as the house at 25 rue Franklin, Paris (1902–03), had a decisive role in the swift and widespread adoption of what was to become the building material of the future: concrete.   *9, 21, 22*

**Piacentini, Marcello** (1881–1960) Italian neoclassical architect who rose to become the chief state architect under Mussolini. Chief work: Rectory, Rome University (begun 1932).   *36, 37, 55*

**Piano, Renzo** (1937–) Italian architect, who together with Richard Rogers realized the futuristic Centre Pompidou in Paris (1971–77). His more recent works are characterized by the recognizably individual interpretation he gives to the forms of classical Modernism, as in the Fondation Beyerle at Riehen near Basel (1997), and his delicate use of materials (terracotta-covered façade for the Debis skyscraper in Berlin (1995–97).   *79, 89, 90*

**Poelzig, Hans** (1869–1936) A leading exponent of Expressionism in Germany (Grosses Schauspielhaus, Berlin (1919), design for the Schaupielhaus, Salzburg (1920–22)). His later work has functional, monumental traits (Offices for IG-Farben, Frankfurt am Main, 1928–31).   *20, 27, 39, 52, 59*

**Riemerschmid, Richard** (1868–1957) German architect and craftsman influenced by the Arts and Crafts movement, who was one of the leaders of the Jugendstil in Germany.   *11*

**Rietveld, Gerrit Thomas** (1888–1964) Dutch architect and designer and accomplished maker of furniture in wood. His red and blue chair (1917) and his Schröder house (Utrecht, 1924) translate the concepts of the De Stijl movement in an exemplary manner.   *26, **32-34,** 44*

**Roche, Kevin** (1922–) Irish American architect who worked with Eero Saarinen, and together with John Dinkeloo realized the Ford Foundation in New York (1963–68).   ***77***

**Rogers, Richard** (1933–) English architect, who is one of today's most important architects. With Renzo Piano he created one of the key works of high-tech architecture, the Centre Pompidou in Paris (1971–77), and the headquarters of Lloyd's in London, in a similar style (1979–86). For the Potsdamer Platz in Berlin he designed several commercial buildings in a style dominated by glass with façades of non-linear design (1996–99).   *79, 80, 89, 102*

**Rossi, Aldo** (1931–1997) Leading Italian architect, whose concepts of architecture, grounded in Neo-Rationalism, had a formative influence on the renaissance of European city building in the 80s and 90s (publication: *L'Architettura della Città* (1966)). Chief works: Gallaratese residential area, Milan (1969–73), Cemetery at Modena (1971–84), Teatro Carlo Felice, Genoa (1982–90), Quartier Schützenstrasse, Berlin (1994–97).   *67, 94, **95,** 97, 99, 100, 105*

**Ruskin, John** (1819–1900) Influential English writer on the theory of art and historicism. In his publications he promoted the idea of Neo-Gothic architecture based on early English and Italian models. His idealization of the Middle Ages also influenced William Morris's campaign for artistic renewal (Arts and Crafts movement).   *10*

**Saarinen, Eero** (1910–1961) Finnish-born American architect, whose work includes prestige buildings in the International Style such as the General Motors technical center in Warren, Michigan (1948–56), and expressive organic buildings such as the TWA terminal at John F. Kennedy Airport, New York (1956–62).   ***61,** 70, **73**–75,

82*

**Saarinen, Eliel** (1873–1950) Finnish-born American architect, who created the main station in Helsinki (1910–14) in Art Nouveau style. In 1922 he took part in the competition for the Chicago Tribune skyscraper.   *43, **44,** 61*

**Sagebiel, Ernst** (1892–1970) German architect, who constructed monumental administration and service buildings for the Nazis, such as the Reichsluftfahrministerium (air ministry) and the Tempelhof airport (1935–39), both in Berlin.   *53*

**Sant'Elia, Antonio** (1888–1916) Italian futurist architect, whose visionary designs for city and industrial buildings exerted a great influence on the next generation of Italian architects.   *29*

**Scharoun, Hans** (1893–1972) German architect, whose housing developments (Siemensstadt, Berlin, 1930) and apartment buildings (Charlottenburg, Berlin, 1930) ensured him a place as one of the leaders of Neues Bauen. His highly original ground plans show his adherence to the principle of organic building. Chief works: Ledigenwohnheim (home for single people) exhibited at the Werkbundausstellung, Breslau (1929), Schminke House, Löbau (1930–32), Philharmonie, Berlin (1960–63).   *20, **37**–39, 59, 73, **74***

**Schinkel, Karl Friedrich** (1781–1841) German architect, the most important exponent of Prussian classicism (Neue Wache, Berlin, 1818–1821, Altes Museum, Berlin, 1822–1828), but who also chose a Neo-Gothic style for some of his buildings (Friedrichswerdersche Kirche, Berlin 1821–1830). Influenced by English industrialization, he was ready to use modern techniques, such as ornamental cast iron (Kreuzberg monument, Berlin, 1818–1821) and worked to rationalize and simplify the shapes of his buildings (Bauakademie, Berlin, 1836).   *24, 59, 63, 90*

**Schütte-Lihotzky, Margarete** (1897–) German architect, who in 1926 began working with Ernst May in the Frankfurt city architect's office. While designing public housing, she developed the Frankfurt kitchen, predecessor of today's fitted kitchens. Chief work: Briansk School, Ukraine (1933–35).   *38*

**Semper, Gottfried** (1803–1879) German architect and art theorist, who built in a sober style akin to that of the Italian practical forms and spare articulation which reference to various historical styles. Chief works: Hoftheater (opera house) in Dresden, (1838–41 – rebuilt after a fire, 1871–78), Polytechnikum, Zürich (1855–57), Burgtheater, Vienna (1875–83). *8*

**Sert, Josep Lluís** (1902–1983) Spanish architect working in the International Style, whose Spanish Pavilion at the Paris World Exhibition of 1937 was the antithesis of the classicist monumentalism of the German and Soviet pavilions. *54*

**SITE** (Sculpture in the Environment) Multidisciplinary group of American architects, founded 1970, who aroused interest with their dramatically staged supermarkets for the BEST chain. *82, 91, 103*

**Siza Vieira, Alvaro** (1933–) Portuguese architect, influenced by classical Modernism, who has developed his own contemporary language of forms, which is remarkable for its aesthetic effect, and its artistic organization of space. Chief works: faculty of architecture at Porto (1986–95), rebuilding of the Chiado, Lisbon (from 1988), Centro Galego de Arte Contemporánea, Santiago de Compostela (1988–94). *67, 107*

**Skidmore, Owings & Merill (SOM)** American architectural partnership composed of Louis Skidmore (1897–1962), Nathaniel Owings (1903–1984) and John O. Merill (1896–1975), who enjoyed worldwide success with their tall offices buildings. Chief work: Lever House, New York (1952). *61*

**Smithson, Alison** (1923–) and **Smithson, Peter** (1928–) British architects, influenced by Mies van der Rohe, leading exponents of Brutalism. Chief works: Hunstanton School, Norfolk (1954), *Economist* Building, London (1963–67). *62, 69, 78*

**Speer, Albert** (1905–1981) German architect, who rose to the position of chief architect of National Socialism under Hitler, through his construction of neo-historicist monumental buildings of exaggerated size. As General Inspector of Buildings, he planned the transformation of Berlin on a gigantic scale into the capital Germania, an ambition thwarted by the course of the Second World War. Chief works: Neue Reichskanzlei (Chancellery), Berlin (1938–39), arena for the Nazi rally in Nuremberg (1934–37). *52, 53, 54, 55, 57, 86*

**Stirling, James Frazer** (1926–1992) British architect, who first adopted Brutalism (Institute of Engineering, University of Leicester, 1959–63), then became the leading representative of a playful kind of Post-Modernism, as for instance in the Neue Württembergische Staatsgalerie, Stuttgart (with Michael Wilford, 1977–84), and the Clore Wing of the Tate Gallery, London (1980–85). *86, 90, 91, 96, 108*

**Sullivan, Louis Henry** (1856–1924) American architect, leading representative of the School of Chicago. The façades of his buildings were articulated in a strict grid, as for example the Guaranty Building, Buffalo (1894), and the Carson, Pirie & Scott Store, Chicago (1897–1904), They were also specifically designed to serve functional needs. This enabled him to overcome historicism, and he was the precursor of the function-orientated architecture of the 20th century. *15, 16, 42, 44*

**Tange, Kenzo** (1913–) Japanese architect, whose use of bare concrete leads to outstandingly aesthetic results (Olympic Arena, Tokyo, 1964). Most of his constructions also exhibit a strongly plastic articulation (Yamanashi Radio Center, Kofu, 1961–67). *64, 75, 81, 83*

**Tatlin, Vladimir** (1885–1953) Russian painter and architect, leading representative of Constructivism. His main work is the design for the Monument to the Third International (1919–20), which was never built. *34, 35*

**Taut, Bruno** (1880–1938) German architect who, after an early Expressionist phase (Glaspavillon, Werkbundausstellung, Cologne, 1914), devoted himself to the construction of large housing schemes (Hufeisensiedlung, Berlin-Britz, 1925–30). His criticisms introduced a revision of Modernism as early as 1929. Chief works: Carl Legien Siedlung (housing scheme) Berlin (1930–32), School at Senftenberg (1930–32), Faculty of Literature for the University of Ankara (1937–40). *19, 26, 37, 39, 43, 102*

**Terragni, Giuseppe** (1904–1941) Leading Italian rationalist, whose buildings, constructed strictly in the International Style, show the close relationship of Italian architecture of that period with the fascist regime. Examples are the Novocomum apartment block (1927–28) and the Casa del Fascio (1932–36), both in Como. *36, 37, 94*

**Tessenow, Heinrich** (1876–1950) German architect, who was one of the most influential teachers at the Hochschule in Berlin. The calm neoclassicism of his Festspielhaus (festival hall) in Dresden Hellerau (1910) became a model for many architects. An example of his sensitive aesthetic sense is the transformation of Schinkel's Neue Wache into a war memorial (Berlin, 1930–31). *22, 24, 52, 55*

**Utzon, Jørn** (1918–) Danish architect, whose best known building is the Sydney Opera House (1956–74), with its exciting sail-like roof, which has become emblematic of the city. *74, 75*

**Van der Mey, Johann Melchior** (1878-1949) Dutch architect, a member of the Expressionist Amsterdam School, leading architect of the Schiffahrtshaus, Amsterdam (1912–16). *24, 25*

**Velde, Henry van de** (1863–1957) Belgian architect, artist-craftsman, and reformer, whose work shaped the German Jugendstil. His most important architectonic works include the interior decor for the Folkwang Museum, Hagen (1901–02), and the Kunstgewerbeschule (school of decorative arts) in Weimar (1906). Within the Deutscher Werkbund he favored the production of handcrafted objects (1914), but was overruled by Hermann Muthesius, who supported industrialized means of production. *12, 13, 19, 33*

**Venturi, Robert** (1925–) American architect, town-planner and theorist, whose writings place him among the founding fathers of Post-Modern architecture. They include *Complexity and Contradiction in Architecture* (1966) and *Learning from Las Vegas* (1972). His Chestnut Hill House, Pennsylvania (1962), is an early example of his many-sided and playful use of traditional architectural forms which had been rejected by the International Style. *71, 84*

**Vitruvius** (1st century BC) Roman architect and engineer, whose ten books *De Architectura* (about 31 BC) are the basis for the interaction with Roman Antiquity of contemporary architecture, from the time of the Renaissance to the present day. *37, 84*

**Wagner, Martin** (1885–1957) German architect and town-planner, who, as city architect for Berlin between 1926 and 1933, was responsible for the realization of large housing projects by Bruno Taut, Hans Scharoun, and Walter Gropius. Chief work: Strandbad (lakeside bathing area), Wannsee (1928–30), with Richard Ermisch. *37*

**Wagner, Otto** (1841–1918) Austrian architect, who prepared the way for Modernism with his writings *Moderne Architektur* (1896) and *Grossstadtarchitektur* (1911). Some of his buildings can bo regarded as manifestos: the Postsparkassenamt (Post Office Savings Bank), Vienna (1904–06), the church at Steinhof (1903–06) and the second Villa Wagner (1910–12). Widely influential through the publications of the "Wagner Schule" (1897–1916). *14, 27, 44*

**Webb, Philip** (1831–1915) English architect, who translated the ideals of William Morris's Arts and Crafts movement into buildings, e.g., the Red House, Bexley Heath, Kent (1859–1860). *10*

**Wilford, Michael** Partner and coworker in the architectural practice of James Stirling, q.v. *86, 90, 108*

**Wright, Frank Lloyd** (1867–1959) The most important American architect of the 20th century, whose early "Prairie Houses" (e.g., the Robie House, Chicago, 1908) exerted a great influence on European architects. His buildings integrated organically with nature, as for instance Falling Water, which is constructed over a waterfall in Bear Run, Pennsylvania (1936), and are characterized by spectacularly cantilevered terraces and cornices which emphasize the horizontal. In the context of town planning he developed the "Usonia" garden city project (1935–38). He also realized dynamic office buildings (e.g., Johnson Wax Company, Racine, Wisconsin, 1936–39). The final achievement of his long and productive career was the Guggenheim Museum, New York (1956–57). *16 17, 26, 31, 41, 44, 45, 62, 63, 74, 89, 90, 96*

## ILLUSTRATIONS

The publishers thank the institutions, archives and photographers for granting them the right to reproduce works belonging to them, and for their friendly support in the production of this book. In spite of intensive research it has proved impossible to find the copyright owners of certain pictures. Photographers with justified claims in this respect are requested to contact the publishers.

Alvar Aalton Museo, Jyväskylä: 72 bottom right (Maija I Iolma), 72 top left and top right (M. Kapanen)

Collection Consuelo Accetti, Milan: 29

Akademie der Künste, Berlin, Stiftung Archiv, Sammlung Baukunst: 37 (Arthur Köster)

© Tadao Ando: 99 middle, 99 bottom

Arcaid, Kingston upon Thames: 8 (© William Bryant), 64 (© Stephane Couturier), 83 middle left (© William Tingey), 84 (© Richard Bryant), 93 (© Natalie Tepper), 96 bottom left, 99 top (© Richard Bryant), 110 (© John Edward Linden)

Architectural Association Photo Library, London: 9 (Morrison), 22 (© Erno Goldfinger), 45 top (© Hazel Cook), 45 bottom (© J. Stirling), 57 (© Cecil Handisyde), 58 bottom (© Dennis Wheatley), 62 top (©John T. Hansell), 70 (© Gardner/Halls), 76 top (© Dennis Crompton), 82 (© SITE), 86 (© Alan Chandler)

Archive of the author: 51 top

Archiv für Kunst und Geschichte, Berlin: 6 (AKG), 7 (AKG), 11 (Erich Lessing), 12 (Lothar Peter), 15 middle (AKG), 16 top (Tony Vaccaro), 17 bottom (Markus Hilbich), 18 (AKG), 23 top (Dieter E. Hoppe), 23 bottom (AKG), 26 bottom (Markus Hilbich), 27 (Markus Hilbich), 33 bottom (Erik Bohr), 39 top (Markus Hilbich),

47 (Keith Collie), 56 (AKG), 59 middle (AKG), 08 bottom left (AP), 68 bottom right (AKG), 72 middle left (Gert Schütz), 78 (AKG), 81 (Markus Hilbich), 87 (Keith Collie), 88 (AKG), 89 bottom (Markus Hilbich), 100 (Irmgard Wagner), 104 bottom (Markus Hilbich), 109 top (Dieter E. Hoppe)

© Ch. Bastin & J. Evrard: 10, 14 bottom, 106

Bauhaus-Archiv, Museum für Gestaltung, Berlin: 33 top and middle (Fred Kraus)

Bildarchiv Preussischer Kulturbesitz: 50

Mario Botta, Lugano: 97

British Architectural Library Photographs Collection: 16 middle, 28 bottom, 55, 62 bottom, 69, 71 top, 77, 83 top, 96 top left, 101

© Friedrich Busam/Architektur-photo: 102

Central State Machruschin Museum for Theatre History, Moscow: 34 top

Keith Collie: 28 top, 35, 79, 95 bottom, 103 right

Commonwealth War Grave Commission: 51 bottom

Deutsches Technikmuseum, Berlin; 23 left

© Esto Photographics Inc., Ezra Stoller: 16 middle, 59 bottom, 61

© Klaus Frahm/CONTUR: 25, 36, 76 bottom, 92, 96 bottom right

Christian Gänshirt, Berlin: 107

Klaus-Peter Gast, Berlin: 71 middle and bottom

Graphische Sammlung Albertina, Vienna: 15 top and bottom

© Jochen Heller/ARCHITEKTON: 104 top

© Karin Hessmann/CONTUR: 94

© Markus Hilbich: 20 both, 21 top, 74 both, 89 top, 95 top, 96 top right

Architektur-Bilderservice Kandula/Lachmuth; 48, 75, 80, 91

Landesbildstelle, Berlin: 53, 59 top

Daniel Libeskind, Berlin: 109 bottom

Bildarchiv Foto Marburg: 19 top, 21 bottom, 38

Philipp Meuser: 63 bottom

Museum of the City of New York: 43 (John H. Heffren), 44 bottom (The Wurts Collection), 49 (The Byron Collection)

© Norman McGrath: 58 top, 85

Netherlands Architecture Institute, Sammlung Van Eesteren, Fluck en Van Lohuizen Foundation, The Hague; inventarnummer III.ISI/Tafel 54: 31

Anna Neumann, Berlin: 111 bottom

Frank den Oudsten, Amsterdam: 17 top, 26 top, 32

Karl Ernst Osthaus Museum, Hagen, Foto Achim Kukulies, Düsseldorf: 13 bottom

Wolfgang Pehnt, Cologne: 14 top

Uwe Rau, Berlin: 67 top

© Ralph Richter/Architektur-photo: 13 top, 111 top

Bernhard Schurian, Berlin; 108 both

© Margherita Spiluttini, Vienna: both

Staatlich Museen zu Berlin - Preussischer Kulturbesitz, Kunstbibliothek: 26 middle (Petersen)

Staatliche Museen zu Berlin - Preussischer Kulturbesitz, Nationalgalerie: 30 (Jörg P. Anders)

Bildarchiv Steffens, Mainz: 54, (SLIDE/Pontanier), 65 both (© Rudolf Bauer), 66 bottom (Bildagentur Buenos Dias, Peter Koller)

Wolfgang Steinborn, Darmstadt: 63 top, 73

Transglobe Agency, Hamburg: 60, 103 left

Tretyakov Gallery, Moscow: 34 bottom

© Gerhard Wolfren: 83 middle right and bottom, 98

Zentrales Staatl. Bachruschin Museum für Theatergeshichte, Moscow: 34 top

Cover Illustrations

left: Bauhaus Dessau by Walter Gropius. Photo © Klaus Frahm/CONTUR
right: Guggenheim Museum Bilbao by Frank O. Gehry. Photo © Karin Hessman/CONTUR
background: detail of a design for a business center in Turin by Renzo Piano. Drawing from *Detail - Zeitschrift für Architektur + Baudetail*, Munich 1996−3